The Old French Fabliaux

The Old French Fabliaux

Essays on Comedy and Context

Edited by KRISTIN L. BURR,
JOHN F. MORAN *and*
NORRIS J. LACY

McFarland & Company, Inc., Publishers
Jefferson, North Carolina, and London

LIBRARY OF CONGRESS CATALOGUING-IN-PUBLICATION DATA

The old French fabliaux : essays on comedy and context /
   edited by Kristin L. Burr, John F. Moran and Norris J. Lacy.
       p.   cm.
   Includes bibliographical references and index.

   ISBN-13: 978-0-7864-3290-5
   softcover : 50# alkaline paper ∞

   1. Fabliaux — History and criticism.   2. French poetry — To
1500 — History and criticism.   3. Humorous poetry, French —
History and criticism.   I. Burr, Kristin L.   II. Moran, John F.,
1966–   III. Lacy, Noris J.
PQ207.O43   2008
841'.109 — dc22   2007032731

British Library cataloguing data are available

©2007 Kristin L. Burr, John F. Moran and Norris J. Lacy.
All rights reserved

*No part of this book may be reproduced or transmitted in any form
or by any means, electronic or mechanical, including photocopying
or recording, or by any information storage and retrieval system,
without permission in writing from the publisher.*

Cover art ©2008 Clipart.com; Front cover by TG Design

Manufactured in the United States of America

*McFarland & Company, Inc., Publishers
 Box 611, Jefferson, North Carolina 28640
    www.mcfarlandpub.com*

Table of Contents

Introduction	1
Hamming It Up: Porcine Humor in the Old French Fabliaux KRISTIN L. BURR	7
Fabliaux as Fair Exchange: *Boivin de Provins* and *La Bourse pleine de sens* ELIZABETH W. POE	19
"So This *Vilain* Walks into a Bar...": The Fabliau as Stand-up Comedy JOHN F. MORAN	30
Customary Law in the Old French Fabliau F.R.P. AKEHURST	42
Rhetorical Reasoning, Authority, and the Impossible Interlocutor in *Le Vilain qui conquist paradis par plait* ELIZABETH KINNE	55
L'Esquiriel, or What's in a Tail? CAROLINE JEWERS	69
Trickery, Trubertage, and the Limits of Laughter NORRIS J. LACY	82
"No, No, Nonete!": Reciting Jean de Condé's Virgin-less and Miracle-less Virgin Miracle ADRIAN P. TUDOR	93
Rhyme or Reason: *Le Prestre comporté* and *Le Prestre et le chevalier* ANNE COBBY	107

Contents

The Non-Conformist Fabliau Genre and Its Transgressions: A Bakhtinian Analysis of Two Old French Fabliaux JEAN E. JOST	120
The "Fin Humour" of *Guillaume au faucon* JOAN TASKER GRIMBERT	134
Modern Dirty Jokes and the Old French Fabliaux LOGAN E. WHALEN	147
Esprit gaulois for the English: The Humor of the Anglo-Norman Fabliau KEITH BUSBY	160
Marie de France in the Manuscripts: Lai, Fable, Fabliau RUPERT T. PICKENS	174
About the Contributors	187
Index	191

Introduction

As the story goes, a husband who suspects his wife of an extramarital dalliance hatches a plot to catch her in the act. She cleverly arranges to have him roundly beaten by their servants. Moreover, she has manipulated the situation in such a way that the cuckolded husband, thinking that his servants have mistaken him for his wife's suitor, is convinced of her innocence and thus delights in his own pain, even as his wife receives her lover elsewhere in the house.[1]

In another narrative, a grieving widow declares on her husband's grave that she wishes to die. A passing squire, overhearing her, informs her that he himself had killed his beloved by means of sexual intercourse. He then accepts the widow's invitation to put her out of her misery the same way, but strangely enough, his actions instead relieve her suffering.

Yet another: a peasant whose job is to haul manure takes a detour through the spice merchants' street. Overcome by the unaccustomed odor, he recovers only when a perceptive bystander holds a shovel of manure under his nose, thus restoring him to his "natural" state.

And one more: three fairies grant to a man the power to make female pudenda speak; a countess later wagers with him that his power will fail with her. He is frustrated by a silent vagina until the anus informs him that its neighbor has been stuffed with cotton.

These anecdotes, reduced to their barest bones, are but four of the more than one hundred medieval French stories, most of them relatively brief, that are considered by common consent to be fabliaux.[2] Even short summaries, such as those provided above, hint at the substantive themes underlying the fabliaux: they explore issues of gender and class identity, among other topics. As serious as the subjects they treat may be, however, these stories are far more notable for another feature. Simply put, they are funny.

Introduction

The tales' lighter aspects are at the heart of the most traditional definition of the genre: fabliaux are "des contes à rire en vers." This formulation, which is Joseph Bédier's (30), is extremely concise, admirably straightforward, and — unfortunately — not very helpful. First of all, we must ask whether *any* humorous tale in verse is automatically a fabliau, and the answer is clearly no. Next, we must wonder why there are not, or at least *could not* be, prose fabliaux, since a great many prose texts of the Middle Ages — and later — exhibit the same kind of comedic structure and elicit the same kind of laughter as do many of the texts identified as fabliaux.

In addition — and this is doubtless the most substantial objection to Bédier's definition — the fabliau texts themselves[3] and modern critical practice alike identify as fabliaux a number of texts that do *not* appear to have as their central purpose the creation of humorous effect. Some are overtly moralistic in nature, whereas others appear to be simple anecdotes or observations of manners or class. Still others deal with violent themes (including torture and murder) that may prevent some readers from appreciating any comic elements they contain. The largest groups of fabliaux treat erotic themes — seductions or attempted seductions or occasionally rapes — or justified revenge for an affront, and sometimes these two themes intersect in ways that may or may not be amusing.

That the tales do not unanimously share the same goals offers little surprise, given the wide range of narratives classified as fabliaux. Indeed, delimiting the fabliau corpus is as notoriously difficult as seeking to fix a definition of the genre itself. The number varies with the scholar but ranges from fewer than seventy to 160, depending on the definition according to which a text is measured.[4] The shortest work taken sometimes as a fabliau is a mere eighteen lines long; the longest, discussed in this volume, is *Trubert* at some 3000 lines. The fact is that any definition except the strictest (that is, those that call themselves fabliaux) is arbitrary in its application, grouping under one generic umbrella a large number of texts of varying lengths, methods, and apparent purposes. Bédier's definition is ultimately of limited value and may even be misleading.

Nonetheless, it is true that in the vast majority of cases, the fabliaux are intended to amuse, to entertain, to provoke laughter; perhaps three-fourths of the tales appear to be primarily comic in nature (even though

Introduction

a good number of them carry explicit — and sometimes illogical — concluding morals). These are the texts that will interest us here. However, humor — or at least the analysis of it — is a serious business. That statement is to be taken in two senses. First, such analysis is an academic enterprise that requires the same methodological rigor that underlies the study of any other subject. More important, however, is the fact that most studies of literary humor situate themselves at a considerable distance from the humorous or sometimes even carnivalesque spirit that characterizes most fabliaux. The result is scholarship, most often sound and useful, that is too frequently devoid of the fun that, we believe, ought to attend discussions of comedic creations like the Old French fabliaux.

E.B. White once remarked that "Humor can be dissected, as a frog can, but the thing dies in the process and the innards are discouraging to any but the pure scientific mind." And Robert Benchley said, "Defining and analyzing humor is a pastime of humorless people." We do not have to look far to find these views echoed widely and frequently. For example, syndicated columnist Molly Ivins, on 18 January 2005, observed that "Being earnest about humor is deadly." And just a week later (24 January 2005), comedian Stephen Colbert (on the National Public Radio interview program "Fresh Air") commented that "nothing sucks the juice out of a joke faster than analyzing it."

One would like to think that these contentions are — or potentially are — false, but there is comparatively little evidence to overturn them. Nor does there have to be, in principle. Critics do not need to be (and rarely are) humorists: their job is to analyze and explain rather than entertain. Nevertheless, it is a pity that works like the fabliaux, whose primary purpose is to offer entertainment, so often spawn critical studies in which little or none of their humor is apparent. Only one previous book on fabliaux carries a title that explicitly announces the intention to examine fabliaux humor; that is the volume edited by Thomas Cooke and Benjamin L. Honeycutt.[5] Most of their chapters treat aspects of technique, narration, and setting, and as with the majority of fabliau studies, these chapters are valuable as scholarly enterprises, but the point of view often is situated well outside the actual humorous sphere of the fabliaux themselves.

The contributors to this volume would like to remedy the paucity of studies that capture the humor of the fabliaux. More so than some other

Introduction

books or collections of articles on the fabliaux, ours proposes to offer serious analyses of the tales without losing sight of their comedic content and appeal, without "sucking the juice" out of fabliau humor. We wish to accomplish in a modest way what Horace said was the purpose of literature itself: to please while remaining instructive.

The fabliaux lend themselves readily to such a project. Certain subjects, although not fundamentally humorous, are often exploited for comic purposes. Most notable are the erotic themes mentioned earlier, including seductions (often accomplished through deceit), failed seduction attempts (most often by priests), triangle relationships, and the like. Some of the sexual humor is crudely similar to adolescent humor of any era, whereas other fabliaux employ subtle wordplay and intricate chains of events to reach what Cooke calls their "comic climax." In other words, they are not entirely unlike modern jokes in their range (a fact highlighted in several of the essays in this volume). Some are merely vulgar and simplistic, though vulgarity is not by any means incompatible with humor and may even be, in some instances, the very basis for that humor; others are clever and complex narratives. A number of them involve physical violence, including murder, though — again, as in the joke — the nature and purpose of the narratives, their unrealistic premises, generally prevent us from responding to the violence as we might in another context.[6] In most cases the violence serves merely as a component of the "joke" or as a means of setting up the humorous conclusion. An example is *Estormi* (Noomen, I, 1–28), which belongs to the tale type known as "the corpse many times killed": a character is to dispose of a body, but in fact there are several bodies, and he is led to believe that they are the same one and that it has returned repeatedly from where he deposited it.

Whether the content is sexual or not, fabliaux that provoke smiles or laughter display an impressive array of forms of humor. At times, physical comedy — and even slapstick — reigns. At other times, wordplay, from puns to invented language, dominates. In some cases, the situation in which characters find themselves is humorous in and of itself. In still others, irony is the composer's preferred method of poking fun at a character or a situation. Most of the time, however, a tale derives its humor from a combination of the above forms, with each type of humor heightening the comedic aspects already present.

Introduction

Ultimately, the types of fabliaux are so numerous and varied as to make further cataloguing of them pointless. They vary from the scatological to the sexual to the merely clever rejoinder or trick, and from what we termed "adolescent humor" to subtle and refined humor (though the latter variety admittedly comprises a small minority). Although we can discuss only a small number of texts belonging to the fabliau corpus, the range of approaches taken in these essays reflects the diverse and often intertwined forms of humor found in the genre. We hope that the choice of fabliaux discussed in this volume, and in particular our approach to them, will offer helpful — and enjoyable — discussions of types of fabliaux but will at the same time manage to maintain and communicate, in more than a purely descriptive and impersonal sense, the fun and the humor of individual works.

Except where otherwise noted, all of the essays in this volume cite fabliaux from the edition by Noomen and Van den Boogaard listed below.

Notes

1. The four fabliaux mentioned very briefly here are *La Bourgoise d'Orliens, De Cele qui se fist foutre sur la fosse de son mari, Le Vilain Asnier,* and *Le Chevalier qui fist parler les cons*. All are edited in the ten-volume edition by Noomen and Van den Boogaard; the specific references for the four texts in question are III, 337–74; III, 375–403; VIII, 207–14; and III, 45–173.

2. The "standard" fabliau corpus dates from the thirteenth century (or the very last years of the twelfth) through the first forty or so years of the fourteenth.

3. Medieval terminology (and consciousness) related to genres is exceedingly vague and unreliable: generic distinctions were clearly considered far less crucial to medieval authors than to modern critics. Some texts will be designated "fabliau" in some manuscripts but not in others, and the word "fabliau" often seems to refer to the fictional nature of the anecdote, even as some of them insist at the same time on their veracity.

4. The smaller number is the count of those texts that identify themselves as fabliaux (in formulas such as "Now I wish to tell you a fabliau about..."). Noomen's now-standard edition offers 127 fabliaux. Earlier discussions of the fabliaux offered other numbers, the most frequently quoted being 147 (Nykrog) and 160 (Bédier).

5. Ostensibly, there is a second one that highlights humor; that is the book by Ménard, but his title is a reference less to the humorous content of the fabliaux than to Bédier's traditional definition of the genre. In fact, Ménard devotes but a single chapter to actual questions of humor, the remainder of the book being given over to a presentation of the categories and sub-categories of fabliau subjects and methods. A number of articles and single book chapters treat fabliau humor more specifically. See, for instance, chapter 8 of Lacy.

Introduction

6. We say "generally" both because responses to fictional violence are personal and variable and particularly because there are a few fabliaux in which the violence is so extreme as to provoke repugnance in a good many readers. For instance, *La Dame escolliee* involves the brutal physical torture of a woman.

Works Cited

Bédier, Joseph. *Les Fabliaux: Etudes de littérature populaire et d'histoire littéraire du Moyen Age.* Paris, 1894; 6th ed., Paris: Champion, 1964.

Cooke, Thomas D. *The Old French and Chaucerian Fabliaux: A Study of their Comic Climax.* Columbia: University of Missouri Press, 1978.

_____, and Benjamin L. Honeycutt, eds. *The Humor of the Fabliaux.* Columbia: University of Missouri Press, 1974.

Lacy, Norris J. *Reading Fabliaux.* 1993; Birmingham, AL: Summa, 1999.

Ménard, Philippe. *Les Fabliaux: Contes à rire du Moyen Age.* Paris: Presses Universitaires de France, 1983.

Noomen, Willem, and Nico van den Boogaard, eds. *Nouveau Recueil complet des fabliaux.* 10 vols. Assen: Van Gorcum, 1983–98. [Abbreviated NRCF or cited simply as Noomen. Both editors were responsible for the first five volumes; Noomen edited VI-X alone.]

White, E.B. "Some Remarks on Humor." In *Essays of E.B. White.* New York: Perennial Classics, 1977, 1999.

Hamming It Up: Porcine Humor in the Old French Fabliaux

Kristin L. Burr

One does not have to look at the fabliau corpus very closely to realize that food is everywhere. Entire plots turn on what characters eat, hope to eat, or do not eat. Moreover, when a good meal is provided, sexual encounters are almost sure to follow. As scholars such as Larry Crist and Marie-Thérèse Lorcin have noted, fabliaux regularly make explicit links between sexuality and the act of eating. Women lay tables of succulent dishes and fine wine when welcoming their lovers, a far cry from the less enticing food they generally provide to their husbands. A hearty appetite for food can serve as a metaphor for sexual voracity, and not infrequently, the body itself becomes food, particularly in the case of men. Tales regale us with descriptions of penises mistaken for sausages and, less frequently, parsnips (although the reverse does not seem to hold true — parsnips and sausages do not masquerade as penises). One memorable portrait in *Le Fevre de Creil* (Noomen, V, 71–82) uses food comparisons to evoke both the size and color of a man's genitalia: so large that not even a broad bean could block its eye, it is as red as an onion (vss. 33–38).

Yet food does more than merely whet characters' sexual appetites in a number of fabliaux, as *Barat et Haimet*, *Aloul*, and *Le Sacristain II* demonstrate.[1] To be sure, all three do contain sexual overtones. In both *Aloul* and *Le Sacristain II*, physical desire overtly plays a central role. The wife of the jealous Aloul finds pleasure with a lustful priest, and the sacristan meets his death when he attempts to bed the lovely Idoine — an occurrence that Idoine's husband, Guillaume, refuses to allow. Although no amorous encounters appear in *Barat et Haimet*, it, too, associates food with sexuality, particularly in the scene in which Barat, disguised as a woman, touches "her" genitals with a piece of meat.[2] Still, food is less intimately connected to lasciviousness in these tales than in others; even in *Aloul* and *Le Sacristain II* little or no emphasis is placed on eating as a prelude to seduction. Instead, the three fabliaux highlight a decidedly unromantic comestible: bacon.[3] Initially, one might attribute the presence of the product to a composer's desire for realism, reflecting the food's place in the medieval diet. It also underscores the materiality of the fabliau universe, as Charles Muscatine has observed (73). A closer look at each tale, however, reveals that bacon is not merely a slab of meat meant to add a touch of authenticity: it becomes a critical element of the plot, for characters are closely allied with — and often transformed into — pork. Bacon's significance is thus more profound than it first appears, and its role in each fabliau proves to be integral on multiple levels. It adds to the comedy of the tale, is essential for character development and narrative coherence, and offers sly comments on characters' morals. The success of these fabliaux rides on their ability to tackle the age-old question of who brings home the bacon.

While the best-known romances are likely to have produced smiles of amusement rather than outright laughter, as Philippe Ménard has discussed (*Le Rire*), many fabliaux must have elicited some hearty guffaws. In *Aloul*, *Barat et Haimet*, and *Le Sacristain II*, these laughs stem from the bacon, which plays a comic role in a very physical sense. There is simply something funny in the image of a priest mistaken for bacon crashing down from the ceiling upon the unsuspecting cowherd who seeks only to cut off a sausage for himself (*Aloul*, vss. 818–25) or a tavern servant trying to cut through the boot of a dead monk believed to be bacon and then remarking that the meat seems to be wearing shoes (*Le Sacristain II*, vss. 624–27). (The same sacristan whose footwear keeps his body intact will later perform the classic fabliau bacon-move of falling down upon another character, vss. 720–26.) The constant changing of hands of the bacon in *Barat et Haimet* is no less entertaining. Hidden by Travers, the hapless thief who goes straight after deciding that he can never equal Barat and Haimet in skill, the bacon is stolen by Barat and Haimet only to be retaken by Travers, stolen once more by the pair of thieves, and recovered again by Travers.

Even cooking the meat cannot guarantee that Travers and his wife will have the pleasure of eating it: the sleepy Travers, who has dozed off a bit, notices Haimet stealing bits by spearing them from the roof. He finally invites his former partners to share his bounty, probably figuring that it is better to have some of the food than to risk its loss altogether.

The likelihood of these scenarios occurring is quite slim. Only in stories are people believed to be salted pork discovered in dung heaps or suspended from ceilings. Yet despite the fictional nature of the situations, the meat itself plays a realistic role for the simple reason that pigs are big. The sheer bulk of the piece of pork is central to the plot and makes the physical comedy possible. The scenes are funny not because they actually happen, but because theoretically they could, thanks to the size of the meat. They are therefore easier for the audience to imagine, which adds to the episodes' appeal — the effect of a partridge tumbling down upon a hungry man or characters jockeying for a rabbit, for instance, is far less satisfying (not to mention that confusing a priest with a partridge would be difficult for even the least savvy character). While these scenes *could* take place, however, they strain the limits of credulity, and readers or listeners would easily classify them as fiction rather than reality. Bacon straddles the border between the possible and the implausible, and the tension between the two heightens the humor.

The comedy of these episodes derives equally from the sheer absurdity of characters' reactions to and interaction with the bacon. Travers, Haimet, and Barat are willing to go to great lengths to obtain and then retain the meat. They spend an entire night passing the pork among themselves, during which ruses often help the bacon change hands. Cases of mistaken identity are rampant: living up to his name, Barat first employs the "forgotten ham trick." Pretending to be Travers, he tells the man's wife that the pork's location has slipped his mind. Later, having stolen the meat, Barat gives it to the person he believes to be his brother (actually Travers). Travers next innocently passes the bacon to his wife — or so he thinks, since the "woman" is none other than Barat, who offers a convincing imitation of femininity by removing his white shirt and wrapping it around his head (vss. 334–37). To make his act even more persuasive, he talks to himself as if he were Marie, and he readily accepts Travers's suggestion that to safeguard the bacon, "she" should then thrice touch her cunt (*con*) with the meat (a custom without documented efficacy in terms of protection; vss. 348–49). In fact, Barat ups the stakes by proposing to use both vagina and derrière — but only in private (vss. 353–57).[4] Finally, Travers plays the role of the brothers' executed father, hanging himself from an oak with his breeches undone so as to create a more impressive appearance (vss. 400–04). The ease with which one character persuades another that he is someone else — and generally of another sex or world — does not speak well for the mental acuity of any of them. As the bacon is stolen and re-stolen, we are implicitly asked to consider who will ultimately triumph. Each scene with the meat thus sets the stage for later action.

The relationship between bacon and monks in *Aloul* and *Le Sacristain II* paints an even less flattering picture of characters' intelligence. At least five people confuse a murdered sacristan with a slab of bacon in the latter fabliau. Guillaume's efforts to rid himself and his wife of the body consistently meet with frustration. Deposited in an outhouse, the corpse makes its way back to Guillaume's home thanks to a prior scared of being blamed for the death; Guillaume next attempts to bury the sacristan in a dungheap, whereupon he discovers bacon hidden by a thief. Naturally, he can only conclude that the bag must hold a monk, too (and a particularly black one, at that). When he returns home after exchanging the monk for the sack of bacon, his wife makes the same mistake, inquiring: "Est ce le sougretain?" ["Is that the sacristan?" vs. 569]. Whereas Guillaume and Idoine see monk where there is bacon, others see bacon where there is monk. The bacon thief transports the bag he assumes contains his booty to the tavern, where the servant's endeavors to carve the meat lead to her exclamation that the bacon appears to be shod. Finally, the man to whom the bacon originally belonged enters the picture when the thief opts to hang the monk back where he found the bacon (vss. 644–49). When the bacon/monk falls as Tibout tries to cut off a slice, the latter can only call for his assistant, Martin, to help him rehang it.

A similar situation occurs in *Aloul*, where a lecherous priest who has seduced Aloul's wife hides in a barn among the bacons in order to avoid punishment. A hungry herdsman quickly identifies this particular specimen as the most desirable, knowing that the fattest piece is unfailingly the best (vss. 797–800). Finding a rump that is both soft and hard, knobby knees, and the parson's prick does not make him suspicious about his discovery;

to the contrary, he assimilates each body part to a portion of the meat — rennet, pork knuckles, and sausage (vss. 802–17).[5] Plummeting to the floor when the herdsman begins to cut off the mysterious sausage, the priest causes no little harm to the man. Nonetheless, the herdsman does not doubt that a bacon has nearly killed him.

In each instance, the characters are not naive enough to believe that a man is a bacon (or vice versa) once they have actually seen him — these tales take place at night or in dim rooms for good reason. Nonetheless, the very fact that the mistake is made initially is ridiculous. How could one not recognize either human or animal traits by touch alone? Rather than aim for pure realism in these cases, the fabliaux composers use the scenes for character development. They use references to bacon to paint a portrait of key figures, suggesting that the bewildered characters are either less than sharp-witted or are so blinded by the circumstances that they can see only what they expect to find, even if their conclusions are not necessarily reasonable. Whether the actors are lacking in intelligence or are merely gullible, the instances are comic — and, as is the case with the physical comedy, the laughable aspects are made possible by pork.

Indeed, in these fabliaux, the bacon serves as more than a mere prop: it becomes a character itself. As Levy notes, the meat has the role of the straight man in *Barat et Haimet* (44); it plays the same part in *Aloul* and *Le Sacristain II*. Although it never has any lines and cannot move on its own, the pork makes the action possible, disappearing from and reentering the stage as if it were alive (which it was at one point). In tales such as *Barat et Haimet*, we wait for the meat to appear and reappear, guessing what will likely happen next. Moreover, the bacon amplifies a theme already present in the tales: food in general. Well before any pork changes hands in *Barat et Haimet*, Haimet offers eggs stolen out from under a magpie in her nest to his brother and Travers with the suggestion that they cook them (vss. 42–43). The fate awaiting thieves, too, is presented in terms of eating: in explaining that the brothers' father, no more honest than his offspring, is hanged, the narrator informs us that "C'est as larrons li derrains mes!" [It's the last dish served to robbers; vs. 11]. The ham adds further nuances to the motif, for it is important in its ability to mirror the luck of Travers, Haimet, and Barat in the rest of the tale. Constantly moved up and down, it calls to mind the revolution of fortune's wheel, just as Travers's luck shifts throughout the fabliau. The bacon provides coherence to the plot and gives form to the tale.

The role played by the bacon in *Le Sacristain II* is also foreshadowed by an earlier emphasis placed on food. When the unfortunate Guillaume and Idoine first devise their plan to take money from the sacristan without compromising Idoine's honor, Guillaume uses the initial sum offered by the cleric to buy bread and meat. He and his wife then sit down for a meal typical of those served by women to their paramours before an amorous liaison — a meal that the sacristan expects himself as part of his seduction of Idoine, since he expressly gives her money to purchase food before their assignation (vss. 210–16, 267–68).

Aloul, too, emphasizes the importance of eating. Aloul's stinginess and jealousy inspire his wife to partake of the unusual herb offered to her by the priest, who notes that the plant's physical appearance distinguishes it, explaining that "Corte est et grosse la racine" ["The root is short and thick"; vs. 79]. (This herb, of course, provides exceptional health benefits for women and is not harvested in the usual way, but requires that the picker be lying on her back.) After realizing that he has been cuckolded, Aloul offers his herdsmen extra food for catching the priest — not a surprise, considering that herdsmen are never happy unless they are eating, as the narrator informs us (vss. 782–83). This information is especially important, as it justifies the trip to the barn during which the priest/bacon falls upon one of the men. In each instance, the meat enhances a theme deeply embedded in the fabliau, providing a narrative thread that gives structure to the tale even as it adds the element of humor.

Why, though, does the privileged food have to be pork? In terms of size (important, as already noted, for the physical comedy), composers could easily have chosen a sheep — and do, in other fabliaux, including *Estula* (Noomen, IV, 346–61) and *Le Bouchier d'Abeville* (Noomen, III, 237–335). The selection of bacon must hold special significance. That the meat can become a character has, I believe, to do with the social role of pigs. Claudine Fabre-Vassas, an anthropologist who closely examines the role of the pig in a book entitled *La Bête singulière: Les Juifs, les chrétiens, le cochon*, suggests that pigs are on the human/animal border (11). Domesticated and raised almost as though they are a member of the family, they are then slaughtered. They thus have a complicated relationship with humans. In these fabliaux, we might just as easily say that the dynamic works in both ways: characters such as the lustful sacristan are no less on the border between the human and the bestial.

Still, many animals raised for their meat could be said to illustrate the complex bond between man and beast. None of them, however, could add to the humor of these fabliaux in the way that pigs do. If pigs do not feature prominently in bestiaries as some other creatures do, they nonetheless evoked particular traits. The expression "to eat like a pig," still widely used today, is hardly of recent date. By the fifteenth century, according to Mireille Vincent-Cassy, the pig was regularly used to represent the deadly sin of greed (121) because of its eating habits; the association had begun centuries earlier. One might also say that the pig can facilitate avarice: Fabre-Vassas observes that owning a pig in the Middle Ages was a status symbol, evoking abundance and wealth (13). In the world of the fabliaux, where characters often try to outwit others, it is not unexpected to learn that what one person has, another wants. Covetousness and greed quickly converge.

Greed serves as a strong motivator for Haimet and Barat. The narrator offers no sign that their decision to abscond with Travers's bacon results from either hunger or necessity. To the contrary, their main inspiration is to deprive Travers of some of his wealth (not surprising, since they are professional thieves and can be expected to steal anything of value). Noticing the meat hanging from the ceiling, Barat tells his brother: "Bien voi qu'an grant paine se met / Travers d'avoir amonceler; / Mais il se fait por nous celer / En sa chambre ou en sa despanse" ["I see clearly that Travers takes great pains to accumulate wealth, but he has worked to hide it from us in his room or in his storeroom"; vss. 152–55]. The pair soon decides to eat the bacon simply because Travers is attempting to prevent them from doing so: whoever has the meat has the sign not only of abundance — especially because it is unnecessary in that they are not starving — but also of superior criminal skills. The pork is thus linked to the issue of one-upsmanship.[6] Since Travers abandons his life of crime not for moral reasons but because he believes that he can never equal his partners, Barat and Haimet cannot accept that Travers has outwitted them or somehow become more successful than they are.

The link between pork and greed is even more significant in *Aloul* and *Le Sacristain II*. The priest and the sacristan are greedy not only for a fine meal, but also for women. The pig is a perfect choice to highlight their desire to satisfy multiple bodily appetites: while the male animal was associated with greed, the female was tied to rampant sexual desire.[7] That is not to say that *Aloul* or *Le Sacristain II* feminizes the male religious figures in any way; the salacious priest or monk is a stock character in many tales. Furthermore, the bestial nature of the priest in *Aloul* manifests itself in several animals. It is appropriate that this man who neglects his duty to guide his flock takes refuge among the sheep and that the dog at the entrance to Aloul's bedroom takes a strong dislike to him (vss. 208–18).[8] At the same time, audiences could very well have smiled at the merging of man and pig, which emphasizes the sinful acts of these supposed men of God. As Levy notes, instances of humans acting like animals may teach lessons, but they also infuse the tales with humor (77).

Yet both *Aloul* and *Le Sacristain II* go far beyond simply pointing out the inappropriate behavior of the punished priest and sacristan. Each man becomes the exact opposite of what he is supposed to represent. A wounded herdsman in *Aloul* exclaims to his master that "je ne sai quels antecris / M'a si feru seur cel degré" ["I don't know what Antichrist attacked me on the stairway"; vss. 552–53]. Later, when Berenger seeks help from his colleagues after being felled by the priest-bacon, he calls God's hate upon the butcher who hung the meat (vss. 834–35). In essence, he curses the priest, who has hung himself in place of the bacon and has also caused the fall. *Le Sacristain II*, too, alludes to the evil side of the sacristan. His "dirty" nature takes concrete shape in the bond created between the man and excrement; Guillaume hides the body in an outhouse and then in the dungheap.[9] Equally telling, upon discovering that the object that has fallen is not a bacon, Martin crosses himself. He subsequently announces to Tibout: "N'est pas bacons, ainz est malfez / Qui sanble moine coronez" ["It's not a bacon, but a devil/demon that looks like a tonsured monk"; vss. 737–38]. In short, a diabolical creature, the bacon, and the monk come together. Martin's words are humorous — in large part because he is not far off the mark. His comments serve as an accurate assessment of the sacristan's character and forge a bond among the man's greed, lasciviousness, and unpriestly behavior.

Drawing parallels between the sacristan, priest, and pork may also imply a deeper level of judgment on their comportment. If the men are associated with demons and the Antichrist through the words of other characters, it is equally possible that they are linked to Jews through animal imagery.[10] Fabre-Vassas argues persuasively that the pig was used to create a sense of religious identity from the Middle Ages on (14). Jewish law forbade the consumption of pork. In part, this regulation stemmed from the Jewish view that the animal was a taxonomical aberration, according to Mary Douglas; pigs are cloven-hoofed but do not ruminate, placing them between two categories. Douglas also traces the prohibition's roots to a story in Maccabees: the Maccabean brothers refuse to eat pork as decreed by Greek invaders and pay with their lives. Later Jews following the Maccabean brothers' example were thus affirming their Jewish identity (Fabre-Vassas 12).

Christians saw the matter differently and drew unflattering conclusions from the interdiction. A myth developed proposing that Jews refused pork because they themselves were closely related to pigs — in fact, their children could be transformed into the animals, and they could not therefore consume the flesh of their own people. This belief gave rise to another, suggesting that since Jews could not eat pork, they sought the flesh of Christian children as a substitute (Fabre-Vassas 11). Jewish rites such as circumcision were also reinterpreted to present evidence that with such blood-spilling rituals, Jews treated humans like pigs and revealed their own porcine nature (Fabre-Vassas 14).

Eating pork thus confirmed one's Christian faith.[11] Given the ties between Jews and pigs, could *Aloul* and *Le Sacristain II* be adding an additional level of commentary on the priests? They would thus be doubly antithetical to all that they were supposed to represent. Not only would they become demonic, but also they would be seen as having left Christianity altogether. Furthermore, transforming the priests into pork relegates the men to a position inferior even to thieves and herdsmen who, despite their lower-class status, remain Christian (and, as such, make every effort to procure a meal of pork).

While this essay has insisted on the ways in which pig imagery can transform the depiction of men, it is also important to remember that these fabliaux accord a large role not to a pig, but to bacon. In Levy's detailed study of the manifestations of the animal world in the fabliaux, he does not distinguish between the two — but doing so is useful. After all, the bacon is a pig that came to a bad end (at least from the animal's point of view). Greedy characters, too, may meet an unpleasant fate. Most notably, the sacristan dies. The degree of triumph often displayed in the fabliaux is missing in even the happier endings. Barat and Haimet do not get all of the meat that they seek, nor does Travers; there is, as Ménard states, no real victor in the tale (*Fabliaux* 192). The priest in *Aloul* does finally make his escape, but only after two near-castrations and in particularly poor shape. None of this provokes laughter in the way that the bacon scenes do. Still, it does contribute to the humor of the tale. An audience making the connection between men, animals, devils, and Jews could very well appreciate those associations and the fate that befalls those whose greed can at times literally turn them into bacon.

To understand the message that the three fabliaux ultimately send about food, a brief look at the final comments they offer is in order. *Barat et Haimet* alone provides a moral, informing us that thieves make poor companions (vs. 508). *Aloul* remarks, undoubtedly with some irony, that the exhausted priest had been greatly tormented, as evidenced by the poor state of his clothes (vss. 978–84). Since the man owes his escape and intact body to two women with whom he has slept, the tale may also hint at women's sexual appetite. *Le Sacristain II* laments the losses of Tibout, who sacrifices his colt and never recovers his bacon. Given the crucial role played by bacon in each fabliau, however, it seems as though the pork must be taken into account in considering the lessons offered. These fabliaux demonstrate that bacon can aid in character development, shape a work's structure, amplify other themes, and hint at moral judgments. All the while, it is versatile, creating situations that are humorous on multiple levels — which is especially important when length is of the essence. Or maybe the composers are simply trying to lead us to one unavoidable truth: you can't keep a good ham down.

Notes

1. The texts are, respectively, Noomen, II, 27–75; III, 1–44; and VII, 1–190. *Le Sacristain II* is perhaps better known as *Du Segretain Moine*; I have chosen to use Noomen's title. More specifically, as the title indicates, I refer to the second of the three versions Noomen presents as *Le Sacristain*.

2. See Gordon (especially 115 and 136) and Mole for more on the fabliau's sexual themes.

3. The precise meaning of the term "bacon" is somewhat ambiguous; Jean Dufournet explains that in certain regions, the word designated an entire butchered pig rather than a section of the animal (356). Regardless, fabliaux featuring bacon refer to a very large piece of pork.

4. As Levy observes, the word "*con*" is found within "bacon" (49, n. 35), lending further sexual overtones to the scene.

5. See Levy for a detailed analysis of this scene (48). It is important to recall, however, that the priest is a pig but not a pig in the scene. The herdsman's expectation of finding bacon, combined with the priest's impressive plumpness, colors his perception — and ours — of the "animal" he has found.

6. In this respect, too, pork amplifies a theme introduced earlier in the fabliau. When Haimet steals the eggs from the magpie's nest, he suggests that his feat proves that he is the best thief. Barat does Haimet one better: after convincing his brother that the real feat consists of replacing the eggs, Barat steals Haimet's breeches while Haimet is back in the tree. More difficult to steal and conceal owing to its size, the bacon offers even more of a challenge than the eggs, implying that whoever possesses the meat is the preeminent thief.

7. Fabliaux such as *Le Meunier d'Arleux* (Noomen, IX, 215–36), *Estormi* (Noomen, I, 1–28), and *Porcelet* (Noomen, VI, 185–91) make the most of this imagery, likening women to pork. In such cases, the animal is most often a plump or greedy piglet to which the woman's body (particularly her thighs) or sexual appetite is compared.

8. Similarly, Levy links the pastor's loss of his sheep in *Le Bouchier d'Abeville* to his lack of attention to his spiritual flock (40).

9. After gorging themselves greedily, pigs were known to roll about in manure, according to Vincent-Cassy (127). The sacristan's pork-like qualities are thus doubled.

10. Gordon identifies additional religious contexts in which pigs were significant. She proposes that the animal "distinguished Christians from Saracens in the minds of many" and notes that one collection of *exempla* drew parallels between sinners and pigs (134).

11. These connotations persisted for centuries and often took on concrete form. Fabre-Vassas's study of pig merchants in the nineteenth- and early twentieth-century France explicitly connects Jews and pigs. She explains that the animal trade was especially left to Jews and that the pork merchant was associated with sexuality and avidity (33). Pig castrators, on the other hand, had to be Christian and practiced a respectable trade (51).

Works Cited

Crist, Larry. "Gastrographie et pornographie dans les fabliaux." In Norris J. Lacy and Gloria Torrini-Roblin, eds. *Essays on Medieval French Literature and Language in Honor of John L. Grigsby*. Birmingham, AL: Summa, 1989. 251–60.

Dufournet, Jean, ed. and trans. *Fabliaux du Moyen Age*. Paris: Flammarion, 1998.

Fabre-Vassas, Claudine. *La Bête singulière: Les Juifs, les chrétiens et le cochon*. Paris: Editions Gallimard, 1994.

Gordon, Sarah. *Culinary Comedy in Medieval French Literature*. West Lafayette, IN: Purdue University Press, 2006.

The Old French Fabliaux

Levy, Brian. *The Comic Text: Patterns and Images in the Old French Fabliaux.* Amsterdam: Rodopi, 2000.

Lorcin, Marie-Thérèse. "Manger et boire dans les fabliaux, rites sociaux et hiérarchie des plaisirs." In *Manger et boire au Moyen Age: Actes du Colloque de Nice (15–17 octobre 1982).* Nice: Publications de la faculté des lettres et sciences humaines de Nice, 1984. 227–37.

Ménard, Philippe. *Les Fabliaux: Contes à rire du Moyen Age.* Paris: Presses Universitaires de France, 1983.

_____. *Le Rire et le sourire dans le roman courtois en France au moyen âge.* Geneva: Droz, 1969.

Mole, Gary D. "Du bacon et de la femme: Pour une relecture de *Barat et Haimet* de Jean Bodel." *Neophilologus*, 86 (January 2002), 17–31.

Muscatine, Charles. *The Old French Fabliaux.* New Haven: Yale University Press, 1986.

Vincent-Cassy, Mireille. "Les Animaux et les péchés capitaux: de la symbolique à l'emblématique." In *Le Monde animal et ses représentations au Moyen Age (XIe-XVe siècles): Actes du XVe Congrès de la Société des Historiens Médiévistes de l'Enseignement Supérieur Public.* Toulouse: Service des Publications de l'Université Toulouse-Le Mirail, 1989. 121–32.

Fabliaux as Fair Exchange: Boivin de Provins *and* La Bourse pleine de sens

Elizabeth W. Poe

When a husband is away, his wife will play. And if that husband happens to be a merchant, he is away a lot, and his wife has an abundance of playtime. This is arguably the most common scenario among the Old French fabliaux (Ménard 78–79). In this typical set-up, we the audience neither know nor care what the absentee husband is up to — we assume him to be a bore anyway and a stupid one at that; it is the stay-at-home wife whose outlandish intrigues hold our attention. The plot revolves around her.[1] What interests me here, however, are those admittedly exceptional fabliaux that bring the shadowy figure of the merchant to center stage, that show us where he goes and what he does, and that play themselves out at his place of business rather than at his residence. I have identified two examples, *Boivin de Provins* (Noomen, II, 77–105), which is set at the fair of Provins, and *La Bourse pleine de sens* (Noomen, II, 107–49), which unfolds at the fair of Troyes.[2]

In the first of the two fabliaux, the protagonist, Boivin [Drink-Wine], posing as an inept farmer-merchant, sits down in front of the brothel near the fair and pretends to be counting out the money he has just made from the sale of two oxen. He acts as though he cannot keep track of all his earnings, but in fact he has exactly twelve deniers that he keeps passing back and forth from his left hand to his right, again and again and again. Knowing that the madam of the brothel is named Mabile, Boivin laments loudly that he has lost touch with his dear niece Mabile, who left town long ago. If only he could find her, she would be a rich woman because she is his sole heir. At this point the madam comes up to Boivin, who introduces himself to her as Fouchier de la Brouce [Stuffer of the Purse?],[3] and remarks on how much she reminds him of his niece. Mabile falls for the ruse, thinking that she is devising one of her own, as she claims to be the very person that he is looking for. She invites him to join her and the pimps for a copious and spirited meal and, in lieu of dessert, offers him the services of one of her girls, Ysane, who is prepared, in accordance with her instructions, to cut the client's moneybag loose from his belt in the course of their nocturnal activity. Anticipating this stunt, Boivin detaches the purse himself and sticks it under his shirt next to his skin. The whole time that Ysane is screwing him literally, she is trying to do so figuratively as well, groping his genitals in a fruitless search for his purse. As he is putting his pants back on, Boivin pretends to discover that his purse is missing and accuses Ysane of having stolen it. Mabile orders Ysane to surrender the purse, which, as we know, she does not have. When Ysane insists that she never could find it, Mabile, disbelieving, starts beating her, and the two engage in a heated wrestling match. This *combat singulier* degenerates into a *mêlée* as Mabile and Ysane are joined by the other inhabitants of the brothel. Merchants from the fair run up to watch the free-for-all. Meanwhile, Boivin slips away to tell his story to the local magistrate, who makes him repeat it to his family and friends, all of whom find it very amusing. Boivin stays in Provins for three days with the magistrate, who gives him ten sous for this fabliau.

In *La Bourse pleine de sens*, a rich merchant, Renier, has a wife and a mistress. The wife tries time and again to make her husband repent and be a faithful spouse, but he refuses to forgo his extra-marital interest. One day as he is leaving for the fair at Troyes, he asks his wife if he can bring her anything. She says that her only desire is for him to come back with a purse full of sense. At the market he sells the products that he has taken with him, packs his carts with the things that he has bought, and entrusts them to his employees and their escorts. He then selects a pretty dress[4] for his mistress, which suddenly reminds him of his wife's request. He has no idea where to begin to look for the sense that she wants him to acquire. It is clearly a rare commodity that is not to be found among the cloths or even among the exotic spices. He encounters a wise old man who instructs him to return, as though empty-handed, and to tell his mistress that he has lost everything and that he is now a poor man. If she kicks him out, as she surely will, then he should go home and try the same lie on his wife. Things transpire exactly as the wise man predicted. The girlfriend does not want to have any more to do with him once she thinks that he is penniless, while the wife immediately offers to sell her entire inheritance to help her wanton husband dig his way out of his fiscal hole. As word of the merchant's ruin spreads, his creditors begin to gather at his doorstep. But at this very moment the convoy of his loaded carts arrives, whereupon the merchant tells the assembled crowd what really happened and, as a token of appreciation, awards his wife the dress. Upon hearing this story (and receiving the dress), the wife announces with relief that her husband has finally found the purse full of sense.

There are several similarities between these two fabliaux. In both, the merchant stays in control of things throughout the episode, and in both he comes out ahead. Boivin hangs onto the twelve deniers he had at the start and collects another ten sous at the end from the local official. If we add the free wine, free food, free lodging, and free sex, then the profit, even if most of it was immediately consumed, is not negligible. Renier, for his part, retains the affection of his wife, though he does not deserve it. He keeps everything that he has gained at the market, and is all the richer for his knowledge that his mistress valued him only for the presents that he bestowed on her. Being rid of her is basically money in his pocket, since she has expensive tastes, in contrast to his wife, who does not seem to care about material goods. In both of these fabliaux the merchant achieves his goal by means of a deception concerning his financial situation. Boivin, who is poor, pretends to be rich. Renier, who is rich, pretends to be poor. Both men are preoccupied with the contents of their purse.[5] In the first instance the would-be merchant pretends that his is fuller than it is; in the second the real merchant earnestly seeks to fill his.

Both Boivin and Renier are storytellers: Boivin, a professional; Renier, an amateur. Indeed, Boivin's only motivation in the complex ruse that he devises is to generate an anecdote. He wants nothing more than to stir things up a little, draw attention to himself, and, ultimately, create a fabliau that he can peddle for profit. For him the story is an end in itself.

Renier, however, uses his story as a means to an end: to test the fidelity of his mistress and thus to obtain the sense that his wife would like for him to possess. It bears noting that Renier does not invent the story that he recounts about how he lost all his possessions. That one was provided for him by the wise old man at the fair. The only story that Renier is capable of telling is not a story at all. It is the truth.

The first fabliau teaches us that there are certain things that money can buy but sometimes does not have to. The second shows that there are certain things that money cannot buy, period. If only implicitly, both of these fabliaux illustrate the same point: whores will be whores.

Perhaps the most conspicuous connection between the two fabliaux is that both contain a woman of loose ways who goes by the name of Mabile. Thus far, I have been unable to determine whether this was a standard designation for a prostitute, on the order of Robin for a shepherd or Marion for a shepherdess, or whether there really was a notorious hussy by that name who plied her trade in the vicinity of the Champagne fairs. In any event, there is no other Mabile among the surviving fabliaux.

I am not the first to see the link between these two texts. At least one medieval compiler thought that they belong together.[6] In MS *A* (Paris BnF fr. 837), which is by far the most comprehensive of the fabliau collections, they occur in succession: *Boivin de Provins* runs from fols 66c to 68c, *La Bourse pleine de sens* from 68c to 70c.[7] Although each of these fabliaux also had an independent transmission (*Boivin* shows up in one other manuscript [*P* = Paris BnF 24432][8] and *La Bourse* in three [*C*= Deutsche Staatsbibliothek, Hamilton 257, *E* = Paris BnF 1593, and *O* = Pavia Bibliotecca de l'Università, Aldini 21]), it would appear that they sometimes traveled as a pair.

Moreover, I cannot help being struck by the abruptness with which we are introduced to Boivin in the first of these two fabliaux (cf. Zink 7): "Mout bons lechierres fu Boivins! / Porpenssa soi que a Prouvins / A la foire voudra aler, / Et si fera de lui parler!" [A clever trickster was Boivin. He thought to himself that he would like to go to Provins to the fair and make people talk about him; vss. 1–4].

As Noomen has observed (*NRCF*, II, 369; *Le Jongleur* 245; "Auteur" 345–46), the author seems to take for granted that we already know who Boivin is and what kinds of pranks he pulls. He speculates that, despite the fact that this is the only extant fabliau to feature this character, there may have been other Boivin stories and that the compiler of MS *A* may have drawn this one from a larger collection. With reference to *La Bourse pleine de sens*, Noomen (*NRCF*, II, 387) notes that, having eliminated the twenty-verse moralizing epilogue found in the other three manuscripts, the compiler of the *A*-version of *La Bourse pleine de sens* concludes curtly: "From this you can hear and understand, that one can never get joy from a whore today, tomorrow, or the next day. So there you have the end of my fabliau" (vss. 407–10). The fact that, in MS *A*, *Boivin* has no proper beginning and *La Bourse* no proper end lends weight to the theory that these two fabliaux may have been extracted as a unit from a larger context.

Even more intriguing is the possibility that these two fabliaux belonged to a little repertoire of stories about real characters familiar to the frequenters of the thirteenth-century fairs of Champagne. This hypothesis finds support not only in the recurrent figure of the prostitute Mabile but also in the staggering number of personal names contained in the two stories. In a genre in which characters are normally identified by type — peasant, priest, wife, mistress, knight, clerk — the onomastic specificity of *Boivin* and *La Bourse* is quite remarkable. In the first instance, named characters include Boivin, Mabile, the oxen Rouget and Sorin, Giraut, Gautier, Tiece, Siersant, Ysane, and Fouchier de la Brouce. In the second, the author is identified as Jehan le Galois, the protagonist as Renier, his wife as Felise, his mistress as Mabile, his palfrey as Rousel, the livery boy as Giefroi, the warden at the fair as Alexandre, the escorts as Simon, Aleaume, Gautier, and Guillaume. It sounds like a Who's Who of thirteenth-century Champagne market-goers.

A single passage from *Boivin de Provins* will suffice to demonstrate the extent to which some of the minor figures in that fabliau are portrayed as having distinct personalities.[9]

> "J'oi de Rouget trente et nuef saus;
> Douze deniers en ot Giraus,
> Qui mes deus bués m'aida a vendre.
> A males forches puist il pendre
> Por ce qu'il retint mes deniers!
> Douze en retint li pautoniers,
> Et si li ai je fet maint bien!
> Or est ainsi: ce ne vaut rien.
> Il me vendra mes bués requerre,

> Quant il voudra arer sa terre
> Et il devra semer son orge.
> Mal dehez ait toute ma gorge
> S'il a ja mes de mi nul preu!
> Je li cuit mout bien metre en leu!
> Honiz soit il et toute s'aire!
> Or parlerai de mon afaire.
> J'oi de Sorin dis et nuef saus;
> De ceus ne fui je mie faus,
> Quar mon compere, dans Gautiers,
> Ne m'en donast pas tant deniers
> Com j'ai eü de tout le mendre.
> Por ce fet bon au marchié vendre!
> Il vousist ja creance avoir,
> Et j'ai assamblé mon avoir:
> Dis et nuef sous et trente et nuef,
> Itant furent vendu mi buef.
> ...
> Et neporquant me dist Girous
> Que j'oi des bués cinquante sous.
> Qui les conta si les reçut ...
> Mes je ne sai s'il m'en deçut
> Ne s'il m'en a neant emblé!" [vss. 35–60, 69–73]

["For Rouget I got thirty-nine sous; Giraut got twelve deniers of that for helping me sell my two oxen. May he hang like a thief on the gallows for keeping my deniers! Twelve of them that rascal kept, in spite of the many favors I've done for him. But it's a done deal now, so it doesn't matter. He'll come asking to borrow my oxen when it's time to plow his field and sow his barley. May God strike me dumb if he ever profits from me again! I'll get even with him. Shame on him and his whole clan! Now back to my own business here. For Sorin I got nineteen sous. I didn't get a bad deal at all from that transaction, for my friend Gautier wouldn't have given me as much for that one, by far the inferior of the two. That's why it's good to sell at the market. Why, that Gautier wanted to buy from me on credit, but, look here, I have gotten hard cash instead. Nineteen sous plus thirty-nine, that's how much my oxen sold for.... But that's not right either. Giraut told me that I got fifty sous for the cattle. He's the same one who counted the coins and received them.... But I don't know whether he cheated me and stole some of them from me!"]

I have to think that Giraut, the finagling middle-man, and Gautier, with his cash-flow problem, were based on real people.

Fabliaux as Fair Exchange (Poe)

I would even venture to suggest that these two stories were intended to be performed at the fairs where they are set (Noomen, "Performance" 129–30). The following scene from *La Bourse pleine de sens* has unmistakable dramatic qualities:

> Devant li garde et voit venir
> Un mestre c'on claime Alixandre.
> "Sire, fet il, savez a vendre
> Nulieu pleine bourse de sen?
> Se le savez, conseilliez m'en!"
> Tantost li mestre li enseigne
> Un mercier de terre lointaigne:
> "Je cuit, fet il, que cil en a."
> Adont sire Renier i va;
> Son estre conta au mercier.
> Et cil li a dit sanz targier
> Qu'il n'en a point, mes i l'envoise
> A un espicier de Savoie,
> Qui de vieillece estoit chanuz.
> Sire Renier i est venuz:
> Sens li demande qui li faut.
> Et cil jure, se Deus le saut,
> Onques a nul jor de sa vie
> N'en vit denree ne demie.
> Lors s'en part iriez et pensis;
> Et par mautalent s'est asis
> Sus les changes desus un fust,
> Et jure, s'a pou ne li fust,
> N'en queïst plus n'avant n'ariere.
> Lors li vint devant a la chiere
> Un vieil marchaant de Galice.
> "Volez vos, fet il, ricolice,
> Ennis, gengivre ou quenele?
> De quoi demandez vos novele
> A cel marcheant de Savoie?
> — Sire, nenil, se Dieus me voie!
> Je n'ai cure de ricolice,
> Ne de gengibre, ne d'espice,
> Eins quier pleine bourse de sens [vss. 124–57].

[(Renier) looks in front of him and sees a warden named Alexander coming toward him. "Sir," he says, "Do you know any place where I can buy a purse full of sense? If you do, tell me where." Then the warden points out a tradesman from a distant land. "I think," he says, "that he has some." Then Renier goes over there. He explains his predicament to that merchant, who tells him without hesitation that he doesn't have any sense for sale but sends him to a spice dealer from Savoy. Renier goes up to him and asks him for the sense that he needs. And the spice dealer swears, so help him God, that never on any day of his life has he seen even a smidgen of such a thing. Then Renier withdraws, upset and pensive. In his frustration he sits down on a stump at the change table and swears that he is about to give up. At that moment an old merchant from Galicia comes up and faces him. "Do you want," he said, "licorice, anise, ginger, or cinnamon?" "No sir, I don't care for licorice, ginger, or any other spices. All I am looking for is a purse full of sense."]

We follow Renier as he wends his way through the streets of Troyes, addressing a series of merchants, each of whom sends him on to another. We picture him as he sits, sulking, on a stump near the change table. We can almost smell the exotic spices as they are enumerated, perhaps with a flourish.

Boivin de Provins, too, presupposes its own performance. Over half of its lines (202 of 380) are in the form of direct speech. The costume of the protagonist is described in detail (vss. 6–13). The props, consisting of a staff, a purse, and twelve deniers, are listed (vss. 15–19) (Bianciotto 30–31). The positioning of characters is carefully plotted: "Illuec s'assist desus un fust / Qui estoit delez sa meson; / Delez lui mist son aguillon, / Un poi torna son dos vers l'uis" [There he sat down on a stump that was beside her house; he set his staff down beside him and turned his back a little towards the door; vss. 24–27]. Further on, we read, "e puis se s'en retorne. / Vers Ysane sa chiere torne, / Et s'en vindrent li uns vers l'autre: / Andui se vont couchier el piautre" [Then he turns back. He faces Ysane, and they come toward each other. The two of them go off to bed together on the straw mattress; vss. 265–68].

Gestures are cued. Mabile beats her breast three times (vs. 252); the pimps pluck capons and geese (vss. 184–85); Boivin/Fouchier reaches under his cape as if to bring out money to pay for his meal (vss. 222–23); before going to bed with Ysane, he cuts his purse loose and hides it under his clothes, against his breast (vss. 262–64); as he is putting his pants back on, he pretends to notice that his purse is missing (vss. 282–83). Emerging from the brothel, he reveals to the assembled crowd that his purse has been cut from its strings (vss. 302–03). Even facial expressions are scripted. Fouchier clenches his teeth (vs. 137); Mabile sticks out her tongue and twists her cheek (vs. 153);[10] the pimps scowl (vs. 154); Boivin scowls (vs. 180); the whores look askance (vs. 209); Mabile winks at Ysane.

With its wealth of stage directions, *Boivin de Provins* could easily have been presented as a mime, with a professional jongleur assuming the role of the peasant-merchant and with the walk-on characters playing themselves. There would have been no need for the amateurs to learn their parts in advance, for they knew that, built into the lines pronounced by the narrator, was adequate guidance for an impromptu sketch.

The fairs of Champagne would have lent themselves to the exchange of fabliaux. The merchants, money-changers, wardens, escorts, tavern keepers, and, yes, the prostitutes, must have become friends (or rivals) over the years. Everybody knew everybody. The fairs allowed these people to meet at regular intervals to add new fabliaux to their repertoire and to recall old stand-bys. If relatively few of the fabliaux set at the fairs have survived, it may be in part because their frequent allusions to local characters limited their appeal and thus their circulation. On the other hand, if the fabliau as a genre gained any currency in its own day beyond its native Picardy, the merchants at the fairs of Champagne may deserve much of the credit.

Notes

1. Ménard (16, 139, and esp. 97) provides a corrective to Bédier (374), who views the original purpose of the fabliau as a glorification of the merchant.

2. The fairs of Champagne in the late twelfth and early thirteenth centuries have been generally recognized as "the center of the international commercial activity of the western world" (Postan, Rich, and Miller 132). It was there that the Italians acquired cloth from the North for subsequent distribution throughout the Mediterranean lands. In addition to cloth, one could also trade grain, livestock, leather goods, precious metals, and spices (Postan, Rich, and Miller 127). The fairs of Champagne were well organized, thanks, in large measure, to the Counts of the region, who established an annual rotation among four towns: Bar-sur-Aube in January, Lagny in February, Provins in May, Troyes in June, Provins again in September, and Troyes in October. Wardens patrolled the fairgrounds, and escorts ensured safe conduct along the roads leading to and from the giant market places (Bautier 103–17).

3. Bloch (98) finds Fouchier to be reminiscent of *fauchier* [swindler], *foutier* [for-

nicator], and *fou-chier* [trickster]. Independently of Bloch, Corbellari (291) interprets Fouchier as *foutier* 'fouteur.' Noomen (*Le Jongleur* 254–55, n. 125) takes Fouchier to be 'fouiller la terre avec le groin, en parlant des sangliers ou des cochons' and locates a hamlet called la Brosse about seven kilometers northwest of Provins. Like me, Bianciotto (37) takes Brouce as a metathesis of *bourse* [purse]. The P-version preserves the form bource. I wonder further whether Fouchier could be the agent-noun based on the infinitive *foucir* [to stuff].

    4. Apparently misunderstanding OF *pers* [fine dyed cloth], Bloch (73) refers to the dress as "tattered" in spite of the fact that Jehan le Galois, author of the fabliau, reaffirms on three occasions (vss. 87, 177, 366) how valuable *pers* is.

    5. Several scholars view this purse as a metonym for testicles. For Bloch (73–74), the purse full of sense is a scrotum full of semen. This interpretation requires the introduction of an unattested word **sem* to the OF lexicon. Corbellari (291) believes that Boivin suffers from "angoisse de la castration." Bianciotto (37), however, is not convinced that Boivin's purse necessarily has an erotic connotation.

    6. Nykrog (25–27) cites the sequence of texts from MS *A* in which these two fabliaux occur but, his purposes being different from mine, he draws no particular conclusions from their juxtaposition. I hope that my study of these two fabliaux, which I associated initially because of their similar settings, will provide useful corroboration of Busby's thesis ("Fabliaux" 160; *Codex*, I, 463) about the essential coherence of collections like fr. 837, which have often been dismissed as "miscellanies."

    7. Noomen (*le Jongleur* 10), echoing Van den Boogaard (60), entertains the possibility that fr. 837 represents the repertoire of a guild of jongleurs and that codices of this type were used principally to teach apprentices what they were supposed to learn. Van den Boogaard (60) asserts that fr. 837 is a coherent whole. Busby ("Fabliaux" 141; *Codex*, I, 440–41) points out that the fabliaux in this codex are "scattered throughout, usually in pairs or groups of three, four, or five, followed by something more openly edifying." Busby's observation certainly holds true for this little fabliau cluster, for the text immediately preceding *Boivin* is *Courtois d'Arras* and the one immediately following *la Bourse* is Hélinand de Froidmont's *Vers de la mort*.

    8. After examining the differences between the *A*- and *P*-versions of *Boivin*, Rychner (I, 83) concludes that the latter was intended for a less cultivated public than the one for which the fabliau was originally composed.

    9. This monologue has been cited for its dramatic qualities (Nykrog 17; Noomen, "Performance" 136). In comparing the two surviving manuscript versions of *Boivin*, Rychner (I, 69–70) points out that in MS *A* the numbers tally, while in MS *P* they do not.

    10. Ménard (177) describes this gesture as "un signe de malveillance, de ricanement, d'hostilité." Noomen (NRCF, II, 374; Le Jongleur 256, n. 151) remarks that the gesture is still common in various parts of southern Europe.

Works Cited

Bautier, Robert-Henri. *Sur l'histoire économique de la France médiévale: La Route, le fleuve, la foire*. London: Variorum, 1991.

Bédier, Joseph. *Les Fabliaux: Etudes de littérature populaire et d'histoire littéraire du Moyen Age*. 1893; Paris: Champion, 1964.

Bianciotto, Gabriel. "Y a-t-il un 'sens' à une dégradation? A propos de *Boivin de Provins.*" *Reinardus*, 10 (1997), 17–43.
Bloch, R. Howard. *The Scandal of the Fabliaux*. Chicago: University of Chicago Press, 1986.
Busby, Keith. *Codex and Context: Reading Old French Verse Narrative in Manuscript*. 2 vols. Amsterdam: Rodopi, 2002.
_____. "Fabliaux and the New Codicology." In Kathryn Karczewska and Tom Conley, eds. *The World and its Rival: Essays on Literary Imagination in Honor of Per Nykrog*. Amsterdam: Rodopi, 1999. 137–60.
Corbellari, Alain. "*Boivin de Provins* ou le triomphe du monologue." *Vox Romanica*, 49/50 (1990/91), 284–96.
Ménard, Philippe. *Les Fabliaux: Contes à rire du Moyen Age*. Paris: Presses Universitaires de France, 1983.
Noomen, Willem. "Auteur, narrateur, récitant de fabliaux: le témoignage des prologues et des épilogues." *Cahiers de Civilisation Médiévale*, 35 (1992), 313–50.
_____. *Le Jongleur par lui-même*. Louvain: Peeters, 2003.
_____. "Performance et mouvance: A propos de l'oralité des fabliaux." *Reinardus*, 3 (1990), 127–42.
Nykrog, Per. *Les Fabliaux: Etude d'histoire littéraire et de stylistique médiévale*. 1957; Geneva: Droz, 1973.
Postan, M.M., E.E. Rich, and Edward Miller. *The Cambridge Economic History of Europe. Volume III: Economic Organization and Policies in the Middle Ages*. Cambridge: Cambridge University Press, 1963.
Rychner, Jean. *Contribution à l'étude des fabliaux*. 2 vols. Neuchatel: Faculté des Lettres, 1960.
Van den Boogaard, Nico H. J. "Les Jongleurs et leur public." In Sorin Alexandrescu, Fernand Drijkoningen, and Willem Noomen, eds. *Autour de 1300: Etudes de philologie et de littérature médiévales*. Amsterdam: Rodopi, 1985. 59–70.
Zink, Michel. "Boivin: auteur et personnage." *Littératures*, 6 (1982), 7–13.

"*So This* Vilain *Walks into a Bar ...*": *The Fabliau as Stand-up Comedy*

John F. Moran

In a large field stand several tents, two or three topped with flags fluttering in the late-afternoon breeze. Hundreds of people mill about in the grass and on the dirt, some walking among the noisy merchants' stalls, considering the different items offered for sale; some purchasing an early dinner, perhaps a sausage and a cup of ale; and still others making their way through the crowd to a small wooden stage that has been erected off to one side of the field. On that small stage stands a lone, lively performer surrounded by an audience of some fifty to sixty laughing people. This skilled performer is no mere storyteller, no mere jokester, but rather a seasoned narrator of humorous anecdotes and bawdy tales, comic texts upon which the teller comments and invites those assembled to comment as well.

Where are we? When are we? Who is the person on the stage? This could easily be a thirteenth-century European fair, perhaps a large trade fair such as those held in northern French cities like Provins and Troyes. The performance in question has all the hallmarks of the work of a medieval jongleur, a traveling minstrel making a living from regaling an audience not only with lofty, moving tales of romance and chivalry, but also, as would be the case in the above example, with comic stories such those recounted in many fabliaux. However, this is not the case. We are not in medieval France but in modern America, and the ale and sausages being consumed are Bud Lite and Lucky Dogs. This description was inspired by an afternoon event held nearly eight centuries after the heyday of our hypothetical medieval jongleur — a late twentieth-century performance by stand-up comedian Phyllis Diller at Boomtown Casino, a riverboat casino docked on the southern shore of Lake Pontchartrain, near New Orleans, Louisiana.

The resemblance between the setting for our hypothetical jongleur and that for our very real comedienne is perhaps coincidental, but the parallels between the performances of these two professionals reveal a shared intent that runs much deeper than simply a chance likeness. While the positing of a jongleur as the distant, medieval mirror of a modern-day stand-up comedian might at first seem to lead to an incongruous pairing, those familiar with the Old French fabliaux cannot help but be struck by the aspects of content and execution that the activities of these two entertainers have in common. The diversity of the material presented, the importance of the actual delivery of that material within a specific performance by a specific performer, the presence of an audience, the fundamental role of that audience in determining the success of the entire venture, indeed, the notion of the audience as a defining element of the event, all of these striking similarities indicate that the fabliaux and modern stand-up comedy share more than just laughter; they are very much the same performative comic beast.

First a brief word on what this essay is not. No attempt is made here to place medieval and modern comic performance on the same theoretical footing. Such an undertaking would present two obstacles to our analysis. First of all, there is little theory that addresses stand-up comedy as distinct from comedy or the comic in general. Unlike the extensive body of scholarship that treats these topics from diverse theoretical and epistemological perspectives, the vast majority of material that discusses stand-up comedy specifically tends to take the form of how-to manuals, books that provide the up-and-coming comedian with pointers for creating effective jokes, dealing with comedy clubs, and surviving life on the road. When these texts do momentarily delve into the realm of theory or the historical development of the genre, much of the commentary offered tends to be either too obvious to shed any new light on the subject — Robert Stebbins informs us that stand-up comedy could only have taken root in societies that had developed verbal communication (6) — or so opaque as to defy interpretation — John Limon comes to the dauntingly indecipherable conclusion that "from two points (comedian and crowd) of the stand-up circle diametrically opposed, stand-up is the resurrection of your father as your child" (27). Furthermore, theory that addresses comedy poses its own problems for analysis. Thomas Cooke, referring to such theory as a "critical labyrinth," explains, "The universal and daily phenomenon of the humorous inspires a maze of explanations that leads everywhere, and hence, nowhere" (20).

Neither the fabliaux nor stand-up comedy will be forced into a particular theoretical framework here, nor will any one specific theoretical approach to the comic be stretched and refashioned in such a way as to fit both the entire fabliau corpus and the wide range of modern stand-up comedy. The focus in this essay will not be on any possible shared theoretical underpinnings of the humor of these performed comic texts, but rather on their shared comic spirit and its creation and manipulation within the context of performance. Indeed, it is precisely that unruly comic spirit coupled with the gregarious nature of the fabliaux — not to mention the considerable diversity of the corpus — that not only made, and makes, them widely appealing, but also identifies them as the obvious distant forerunners to modern stand-up comedy. By understanding and approaching the fabliaux as instances of medieval stand-up comedy (and jongleurs as, at least in part, medieval comedians), we can better appreciate their place within the development of performed comic narrative as well as underline and further explore the importance of the performative element of these texts.

While issues involving the theory of comedy can be left aside for the purposes of this study, issues of genre cannot. Indeed, a discussion of genre highlights one of the similarities between the fabliaux and stand-up comedy. The label "fabliau" (as well as the label "stand-up comedy") has been applied to an impressive range of texts and performances over the years. It is thus no surprise that questions of genre have always been of considerable concern to fabliau scholars, and these questions are of even greater importance if the fabliaux are to be held up as predecessors to another, centuries-distant genre. Given the current critical disagreement as to just what is and what is not a fabliau, how can the genre as a whole be designated as the precursor to the equally diverse, equally difficult to define genre of stand-up comedy? The fabliaux have long been defined as short, funny stories; however, not all of what many would consider fabliaux are obviously humorous. In fact, reactions to some fabliaux among modern readers range from outbursts of hearty laughter, to chuckles, to smiles, to no physical manifestations of amusement whatsoever. *Le Couvoiteus et l'envieus* (Noomen, VI, 273–87), for example, rather than providing an audience with comic release, borders on a dour moral tale, and many audience members would probably cringe in distaste at certain violent moments of *Les Treces* (Noomen, VI, 207–58). Positing "capable of provoking laughter" as the crucial attribute for a text's inclusion in the fabliau corpus is problematic at best.

In *Reading Fabliaux*, Norris Lacy provides an enlightening discussion on the problems underlying notions of genre, particularly in relation to the Old French fabliaux. An absolute, fixed notion of what constitutes membership in a given genre is both difficult to establish and counterproductive. As Lacy explains:

> Whereas we tend to think of genres as containing entities, into which works somehow either "fit" or do not fit, perhaps we should define literature, in terms of its various forms, as a continuum, with works distributed across its entire length but clustered more or less heavily at certain sections. Instead of "genre," the appropriate notion, at least for medieval literature, may be that of a "nexus," a group of texts that resemble each other rather closely without excluding others [33].

What is particularly satisfying about this approach to understanding the fabliaux is that it describes equally well modern stand-up comedy. Stand-up, like the fabliaux, has at its core (its "nexus") comedy, and indeed, we can pick examples from the performances of modern stand-up artists that no one would have trouble identifying as stand-up comedy: a Jerry Seinfeld performance, for example, or an Eddy Izzard show; however, like the fabliau genre, the stand-up genre has not only an ill-defined core but also fuzzy edges. Sandra Bernhard, for example, regularly combines in her routines comic anecdotes and songs with scathing social commentary that is meant less to provoke laughter than to inform and move to action. Even Ellen DeGeneres, one of today's most widely recognized stand-up comedians, sprinkles her stand-up performances with moral messages for her audience. Thus, in terms of genre, the fabliaux and stand-up comedy routines seem to share a comedic nexus as well as permeable borders with satire, moral tales, and other text types.

The Old French Fabliaux

Turning now to the physical settings and the nature of the performances of the fabliaux and stand-up comedy, one might ask if the performance spaces at medieval *foires* and festivals were the medieval precursors to modern-day comedy clubs. Similarities certainly exist, but care must be taken not to slip into anachronism when looking at these performances through modern eyes. It would be equally risky to imagine a wealthy bourgeois or nobleman who happened to host traveling jongleurs on a regular basis as a thirteenth-century Johnny Carson. However, when the discussion is focused specifically on textual evidence found in the fabliaux themselves concerning performance and performers, there emerge clear parallels between these medieval texts and modern stand-up comedy. The actual performance spaces from centuries ago have obviously changed, yet the need for an audience has not. The success of both a fabliau and a stand-up comedy routine depends in very large part on the physical presence of an audience and the creation of certain expectations within members of that audience. With regard to the role of the physical setting in the creation of these expectations in an audience, the patrons in a modern comedy club today know without a doubt the type of performance they will witness. The same can most likely be said of audience members who gathered some seven hundred and fifty years ago to hear a jongleur well known for his comic skills. However, beyond the contributions of the physical setting to the creation of atmosphere and expectation in both genres discussed here, one finds clear indications of the great amount of care taken by both jongleurs and modern comedians to include their audience in the proceedings and to convey a particular attitude toward their subject matter. These performers achieve their goals through what can be thought of as the establishment of structural settings in the texts themselves, that is, actual framing devices employed in the delivery that serve both to prepare the audience to laugh and to ensure that the audience is "in on" the joke.

Many a fabliau narrator signals his intentions to the audience by introducing his text explicitly as a fabliau. For example, the narrator of *Cele qui fu foutue et desfoutue* (Noomen, IV, 151–87) announces his narrative intent explicitly to his audience: "Voudré je un fabliau ja fere" [I would like to do (perform) a fabliau; vs. 3]. Of course, such obvious statements of performative intent are not the only option available to the creative jongleur. A similar set of audience expectations can be tapped into with other introductory sequences that signal the ribaldry to come. The narrator of *Le Prestre comporté* (Noomen, IX, 1–66) begins his tale thus: "D'un priestre vous di et recort / Ki avoit tourné son acort / En luxure et en lecherie" [I shall tell you of a priest who had given himself over to lust and lechery; vss. 1–3]. If a jongleur announced his intention to talk about a lecherous priest, those among his listeners who had even a passing acquaintance with the fabliau genre would have had a fairly good idea of what to expect. Similarly, there could have been little doubt in a medieval audience member's mind as to the type of story to follow if he or she had heard the following opening line from *Boivin de Provins* (Noomen, II, 77–105): "Mout bons lechierres fu Boivins!" [What a lecher was Boivin! vs. 1].

Modern stand-up comedians rely on remarkably similar narrative devices to establish like expectations among their listeners. A comedian may signal his intent explicitly through conventionalized introductions of the type "Did you hear the one about the drag queen in the woods?" or "So let me tell you about my mother-in-law." Some performers may rely on other formulaic phrases to set up the narration and prepare the audience, such as "My husband is so stupid...." All these phrases are red flags to modern audience members, signaling the imminent telling of a comic narrative or joke.

Note that the success or failure of a joke or anecdote initiated by the last example ("My husband is so stupid...") depends crucially on the participation of the audience; if there is no answer ("How stupid is he?"), the joke will fall flat. Even if the audience is not actively participating in a performance, both fabliaux and stand-up comedy routines require of those present at least tacit involvement in the process, and certain structural elements of the texts under discussion here ensure that involvement. One common method by which audience members can be drawn into the proceedings is for the narrator to make explicit his reliance on a pre-existing text or a "true" story he has heard told. For example, to cite more fully from the beginning of *Cele qui fu foutue et desfoutue*: "Voudré je un fabliau ja fere, / Dom la matiere oï retrere / A Vercelai devant les changes. / Cil ne sert mi de losenges / Qui la m'a racontee et dite" [I would like to do (perform) a fabliau, the story of which I heard related in Vézelay before the exchange tables. He who recounted it to me did not mislead with empty words; vss. 3–7]. Such explicit statements of source material, both oral and written, abound in the fabliau corpus: from *La Housse partie* (Noomen, III, 175–209) — "Ce nous raconte li escris" [This the writing tells us; v. 103], from *Le Sot Chevalier* (Noomen, V, 313–35) — "Si com li fabliaus nos tesmoigne" [As the fabliau shows us; v. 252], and from *Les Braies le priestres* (Noomen, X, 11–21), whose narrator appears to be referring to an entire category of existing stories — "Recorder ai oÿ maint conte / Que priestres ont fait as pluisors honte, / Et ont a leur femme jeü" [I have heard told many a tale about priests that shame many men and lie with their wives; vss. 1–3]. The narrator of *Charlot le Juif* (Noomen, IX, 237–50) claims to be recounting an event he actually witnessed: "Je meïmes, qui i estoie, / Ne vi piesa si bele faire" [I myself, who was there, hadn't seen such a nice affair in a long time; vss. 54–55].

Such declarations are very similar to the type of modern comic introduction seen briefly before: "Did you hear the one about the drag queen in the woods?" Such a question not only indicates a performer's comic intent, but also specifies that the narrator is relating a pre-existing joke, story, or narrative, and that he is not responsible for the content of what is about to be related, only its transmission. The effect of such declarations, whether medieval or modern, is the creation of a specific attitude, one of complicity. For the humor to work, the narrator has to have the audience on his side. By telling the audience that the story they are about to hear has been culled from another source, whether it be another person's story, a story from a written source, or something the narrator has seen (but not been a party to), the audience's gaze is redirected. Instead of looking *at* the performer (and laughing *at* him, an often uncomfortable or undesired situation for both parties, in particular for the performer), the audience is looking *with* him (and laughing *with* him) at something else. This complicity, established in the opening verses of a fabliau or the opening lines of a comic monologue or joke, must be maintained throughout the performance, and both fabliau narrators and stand-up comedians take pains to maintain this necessary relationship throughout the entire telling of their texts.

I borrow the term "telling" here from Thomas Cooke as he uses it in his book *The Old French and Chaucerian Fabliaux: A Study of Their Comic Climax*. Cooke differentiates between the showing of a narrative (the relating of action, dialogue, and characterizations) and the telling of a narrative (the overt commentary provided by the narrator during the course of the story, examples of which have already been examined). While the showing and the telling of the story are inextricably bound together, it is the elements constituting the telling that serve to maintain audience complicity. In the fabliaux, the elements of telling are various in form — the references to preexisting stories seen above, omnipresent formulaic phrases such as "ce m'est avis" [it's my belief] or "ce me semble" [it seems to me], prologues and epilogues, overt narrator commentary on characters or actions, proverbs relating to the events in the story, and so on — but they all signal a temporary, and explicit, reemergence of the narrator from behind his narration. Indeed, since all we have of the fabliaux are written texts, it is interesting to note the frequency with which such interruptions occur. The fabliaux are preserved in a writing that is clearly aware of its performative nature.

These narrative asides in which the performer addresses us directly are the verbal equivalents of a wink or a nudge, and there is no reason to assume that the skilled jongleurs did not enliven their performance with corresponding physical gestures, much as comedians do today. These intrusions allow the narrator to reaffirm his connection with his audience and to remind them that, while he is leading them through the performance, they are nonetheless traveling this narrative road together, and thereby laughing together at the ingenuity and/or misfortune of some other, non-group member. The narrator of *Boivin de Provins* spends an uninterrupted ninety-five verses establishing the setting and the characters for his tale and describing the plans of Mabile, a madam, to steal the money of the clever Boivin. When the narrator interrupts his story to tell us, "Mes autrement ira le geus / Qu'ele ne cuide, ce me samble" [But things will go differently from what she thinks, I believe; vss. 96–97], he is killing two signifying birds with one textual stone. First of all, he is temporarily stepping out of the story, distancing himself from it and giving the audience his own privileged insight to the action and the characters, thereby further developing his rapport with the audience by sharing his own perspective. Second, he is in effect giving the crowd information about what to expect without revealing exactly what is going to happen, thereby further stoking the fires of anticipation for the fabliau equivalent of the punch line.

The Old French Fabliaux

Another example from the many found in the fabliau corpus comes from *Le Sohait des vez* (Noomen, VI, 259–72), in which the narrator does similar performative duty: having presented his audience with a lengthy description of both a woman's elaborate welcome-home meal for her husband (whom she hasn't seen, or, more important, been to bed with, for three months) and her plans for some post-repast marital relations, the narrator addresses his listeners directly: "Ne cuidiez pas la dame siece / Qant son seignor endormi trove!" [Don't think the lady was happy when she found her husband asleep! vss. 52–53]. This narrator's humorous aside, underlining by means of the rhetorical play of litotes just how unhappy the wife is at the discovery of her slumbering husband, allows him to step out of his role as story teller and commune with the audience. In much the same manner as the narrator of *Boivin de Provins*, this narrator is both momentarily distancing himself from the story proper to gaze with us at the action as it unfolds and providing us with commentary that highlights actions (or in this case, reactions) to come.

Modern comedians step outside the story in this way equally if not more frequently than medieval jongleurs. For example, during one of his opening monologues, Jay Leno interrupted a comic narrative about Michael Jackson by asking the studio audience, "What's with this guy?" Just like a fabliau narrator, Leno momentarily emerges here from behind his story both to align the audience with his perspective, thus cultivating complicit solidarity, and to make clear that a punch line—in this case preceded by a comic narrative—is to follow.

A popular form of modern stand-up comedy, observational comedy, relies heavily on just such asides directed to the audience. The entire premise of observational comedy is the placing of a comic spin on everyday objects, situations, and behaviors. The very everydayness of what is presented, however, needs to be confirmed with the audience. Comedians such as Jerry Seinfeld and Ellen DeGeneres pepper their routines with phrases such as "When you think about it..." and "Have you ever noticed how...?" While not expecting an actual answer from the audience, comedians use these elements of "the telling" to bring us in on the joke, to direct our mutual gaze outward, saying in essence, "Here are elements of *our* world, *yours* and *mine*, that we can laugh at—and we're going to laugh at them, *together*."

"So This Vilain *Walks into a Bar..."* (Moran)

The essential role of the audience in the process of both these types of performance occasionally passes beyond that of tacitly complicit observer to verbally active participant. This is the case in fabliaux that end with a direct entreaty to the listeners to become speakers. At the close of *Le Bouchier d'Abeville* (Noomen, III, 237–335), the tale of a much-sold sheepskin, the narrator, instead of revealing who most deserves the sheepskin in question, proclaims to his audience:

> Et vos, qui molt ce bien savez,
> Huitasce d'Amiens vos demande,
> Par amors vos prie et commande
> Que vos faciez cest jugement
> Bien et a droit et leaument [vss. 538–42].

[And you, who know well what is just in this matter, Eustache of Amiens asks you, willingly requests of you, that you pass judgment, honestly and well.]

A number of other fabliaux end in the same fashion: at the end of *Les Trois Meschines* (Noomen, IV, 217–26), the audience is asked to decide which girl out of three must pay for an expensive powder that has been blown away by an intestinal gas mishap; the narrator of *Les Trois Dames qui troverent l'anel* (Noomen, II, 215–40), upon the completion of his story, asks the audience to determine which "dame" has best duped her husband; the narrator of *Le Jugement des cons* (Noomen, IV, 23–33) appeals to the audience to judge which young maiden has answered best the question, "Who is older, you or your vagina?"

Such direct appeals for audience participation are even more frequent in modern-day stand-up comedy, where it is not uncommon to turn up the lights at the end of a show for questions, though comedians do not need to wait until the close of the show to engage in this activity. In a recent performance in New Orleans, Jeffery Roberson, as Varla Jean Merman, often posed direct questions to the audience. These were not rhetorical questions, but questions for which s/he wanted actual answers: "How many people here tonight live in the French Quarter?", "Where are the straight people in the audience tonight? Go on, don't be afraid to show yourselves. Where are you?" and so on. The answers given to such direct questioning provided Varla with fodder for further, largely ad-lib, comic repartee. And of course, there is no reason to believe that talented jongleurs of centuries past did not use the judgments offered by audience members in the cases presented above as an entrée into further jokes and anecdotes.

Looking at the fabliaux through the window of modern stand-up comedy does not necessarily tell us anything new about the content itself of these texts. However, such an approach does provide us with a different, additional, path toward understanding each fabliau not just as a text on parchment, but as an event both in the sense that the fabliaux occupy a moment in the history of this type of performance and in the sense that each fabliau, at each performance, was an event in and of itself. Jean Bodel was no Phyllis Diller, and Phyllis Diller is certainly no Jean Bodel, but seeing the two of them as engaged, at least in part, in the same comic enterprise provides an enlightening continuity in the history of performed comedy. Furthermore, moving to the forefront the performative nature of these texts is essential to understanding them within their cultural context. Reading a fabliau with no consideration or appreciation of how it was brought to life as a performance involving both a jongleur and, crucially, a complicit audience would be akin to reading the transcript of a Margaret Cho stand-up routine alone in one's library study; the text is funny, and one can appreciate its structures and themes. Nevertheless, something essential is missing from the experience: the telling of the text. Without the telling, without the performance, these texts, both fabliau and modern comedy routines, cannot be fully understood for the culturally significant events that they are.

Finding the parallels between modern stand-up comedy and medieval fabliaux can thus supply us with additional tools to bring to bear on our analyses of the fabliaux and their role in medieval literary and social culture. Finally, and perhaps most important, it is certainly satisfying to see that such an approach can also provide the uninitiated modern reader with a familiar springboard from which to plunge into the distant world of the fabliaux and develop an appreciation of the lively originality and communal nature of these performative texts. And that is no laughing matter.

Works Cited

Cooke, Thomas. *The Old French and Chaucerian Fabliaux: A Study of Their Comic Climax*. Columbia: University of Missouri Press, 1978.

Lacy, Norris. *Reading Fabliaux*. 1993; Birmingham, AL: Summa, 1999.

Leno, Jay, host. *The Tonight Show with Jay Leno*. NBC. 18 Apr. 2005.
Limon, John. *Stand-up Comedy in Theory, or, Abjection in America*. Durham: Duke University Press, 2000.
Roberson, Jeffrey, perf. *Varla Jean Merman's Girl with the Pearl Necklace: An Act of Love*. Dir. Michael Schiralli. Le Chat Noir, New Orleans. 7 Jan. 2005.
Stebbins, Robert A. *The Laugh Makers: Stand-up Comedy as Art, Business, and Life-Style*. Montreal: McGill-Queen's University Press, 1990.

Customary Law in the Old French Fabliau

F.R.P. AKEHURST

The law is important in Old French literature. It enters the canon with the treason trial in the *Chanson de Roland*, the earliest of the epics. Trial scenes, like that found in Marie de France's *Lanval*, or in the *Roman de Renart*, appear in virtually all major authors and genres, including many works for the theatre, right up to and beyond *Maître Pathelin* and *La Condamnation de Banquet*. People are accused of murder, fraud, treason, breach of contract, adultery, and other misdeeds. Sometimes they escape punishment by eluding their captors (Tristan), or by swearing equivocal oaths (Iseut, Guenevere), and sometimes they are condemned and executed (Ganelon, Banquet). Legal language, especially feudal law terms, is ubiquitous and the authors seem to expect that their audience will understand this language without explanation.

Was I the only student in my law school torts class who, on reading that false imprisonment could include removing a bather's clothing left on the bank thus forcing the person to remain in the water against their will, thought of the squire in *Le Chevalier qui fist parler les cons* (Noomen, III, 45–173, vss. 104–241), who stole the clothing of some fairies who were skinny-dipping? I wondered if the fabliaux contained more examples of torts and other legal matters that could have helped medieval students, and myself, to remember their lessons. Were the fabliaux mere mnemonics, a kind of medieval Nutshell?[1]

Many fabliaux contain legal elements, but many others do not. By my count, there are about fifty that do, or just under forty per cent of the

127 tales in the *NRCF*. If the fabliaux not contained in this collection were taken into account, the number and/or percentage might be higher. I will not take such stories into consideration here.

In considering the legal elements in the fabliaux, I have tried to answer several questions:

1. What legal elements are there in the fabliaux?
2. Is any of the legal material of interest to the modern lawyer?
3. Would a medieval lawyer quibble about any of it?
4. Does the presence of a legal element imply a legally savvy audience?
5. What, if anything, does the legal material add to the humor?

Legal elements in these stories include words and notions or rules. Firstly, words familiar to a medieval lawyer appear without explanation in some of the stories. Some examples of essentially legal language include the use of the words *compagnon* (or *compagnie*) for some sort of a partnership (as defined by Beaumanoir in his Chapter 2) in *Le Prestre et les deus ribaus* (Noomen, V, 145–62, vs. 21), and the word *recorder*, meaning to recall from memory a prior proceeding in a court, as in *Le Chevalier a la robe vermeille* (Noomen, III, 241–308, vs. 23). In the same story, a party in a suit comes home quickly from court because his suit has been "contremandé" [continued; vs. 80 (cf. Beaumanoir §§57, 59)]. There are other examples of the use of legal vocabulary in the fabliaux.

In some of the tales, however, the author goes beyond the mere use of words, and the legal rule or procedure itself becomes an element of the story. For example, in *Le Vescie a prestre* (Noomen, X, 285–303) a priest makes a will, and two *frères prêcheurs* who have been omitted try to persuade him to change it. He leaves them his bladder. The description of the will, although it does not contain the actual terms of the document, suggest much care and thought on the part of the dying man, who disposes of all his possessions, and this legal document is integral to the story. In *La Housse partie* (Noomen, III, 175–209) the parents and relatives of a young woman insist on an agreement whereby a rich man gives everything he owns, using much formulaic language, to his son before he marries her. This is not quite a prenuptial agreement, since it does not govern the financial arrangements of the married couple themselves. At the other end of a marriage, there is a sort of separation agreement in *Le Pescheor de Pont seur Saine* (Noomen, IV, 107–29), where a wife who thinks that her husband has lost his penis decides then and there to leave him: "Certes, or departiron nos!" ["Indeed, now we will part company!" vs. 134]. She is driving off the cattle, and taking the best of the beans, when he offers to give her, as it is right, half the cash he has on him: "J'ai bien vint et deus sous sur moi; / Vien avant, s'en pren la moitie" ["I have twenty-two sous on me; come and take half of them"; vss. 162–63]. Of course, in fumbling through his pockets, she finds proof that he has not lost his member, and they are reconciled. In a story full of ambiguous words, *Le Damoiselle qui sonjoit* (Noomen, IV, 45–55), a young woman arrests her ravisher by holding on to him: "Giete les poinz, si l'a saisi. / 'Estez, fait el, vos iestes pris'" [She put out her hands, and grasped him. "Stop," she said, "you are taken"; vss. 22–23]. At the same time, she accuses him of breaking into her property: "Qui vos fist lo parc peçoier / sanz congié, quant je me dormoie?" ["Who made you break into the park, without permission, when I was asleep?"; vss. 26–27] in which lawyers may recognize the words of art of the English Common Law: Clausum fregit [He broke the close]. There is also question of an arrest of an intruder in *Le Prestre comporté* (Noomen, IX, 1–66, vss. 647–50).

The transfer of property (a cow) is made in due form in *Brunain, la vache au prestre* (Noomen, V, 39–48).

> Sa vache prent par le lien,
> Presenter le vait au doien.
> Le prestres ert sages et cointes.
> "Biaus sire, fet il a mains jointes,
> Por l'amor Dieu Blerain vos doing."
> Le lien li a mis en poing,
> Si jure que plus n'a d'avoir [vss. 23–28].

[He takes his cow by the rope, and goes and presents her to the dean. The priest was wise and well-mannered. "Fair sir," he (the peasant) said, with his hands folded together, "I give you Blerain for the love of God." He puts the rope in the priest's hand, and swears he has no more possessive rights in her.]

On two occasions, there is talk of an animal that has committed a crime. In the first, *Le Vallet aus douze fames* (Noomen, IV, 131–50), a wolf that has been ravaging the country has been captured, and various ways of dealing with it are suggested, including maiming it, skinning it, using it as a target, hanging it, and burning it. The hero of the tale, who has married an insatiable woman, suggests another method of giving the wolf a long punishment: "Fetes li tost espouser feme, / Si l'avrez dont si bien honi / C'onques ne fu si mal bailli!" ["Make him marry a wife, and you will have shamed him so that he never had it so bad"; vss. 132–34]. In the second, on the other hand, a sheep that has killed a priest appears to escape punishment in *Le Chapelain* (Noomen, VI, 77–99). An English rule concerning inheritances is invoked in *La Male Honte* (Noomen, V, 83–134), where the narrator explains about escheats to the crown: "Qu'en Engleterre ert us et drois / Que, quant li hom mouroit sanz oir / Le rois avoit tout son avoir" [In England it was custom and law that when a man died without an heir, the king got all his wealth; vss. 6–8]. Honte justifies his sending his possessions to the king in a line later in the poem: "Car ce est raisons et droiture" ["that is (according to) reason and by right"; vs. 21]. It should be noted that Honte's executor, qualified as "preudom et loiaus" [a worthy and honest man; vs. 88], is a most conscientious executor, even at risk of his own life, and this, along with the King's misunderstanding about language, is what really drives the plot.

In the misogynistic mode, *Du con qui fu fet a la besche* (Noomen, IV, 13–21) tells of the creation of the eponymous organ by the Devil, after God forgot to create one for woman. The author declares it is desirable for a man to beat his wife, in order to improve her.

> Qui acoustume fame a batre
> Deus foiz le jor, ou trois ou quatre
> Au premier jor de la semaine,
> Dis foiz ou douze la quinsaine,
> Ou ele jeünast ou non,
> Ele n'en vaudroit se mieus non [vss. 13–18].

[If someone accustomed his wife to being beaten, twice a day, or three or four times, on the first day of the week, ten or twelve times every two weeks, whether she was fasting or not, it would only make her better.]

Similar advice is found in Beaumanoir, where the beating must be reasonable and deserved: "il loit bien a l'homme a batre sa fame sans mort et sans mehaing, quant ele mesfet...," [For a man may beat his wife (although without loss of life or limb), when she offends against him;

The Old French Fabliaux

Beaumanoir §1631]. However misogynistic this fabliau, it is not in disagreement with the law.

Several fabliaux go beyond mere beating of a wife, however. As Beaumanoir mentions several times, a husband who catches his wife *in flagrante delicto* with her lover after he has warned them can immediately kill her, and her lover as well, without legal consequences. Knowledge of this rule, even omitting the warning, appears to be widespread, so that on the various occasions that a wife hears her husband coming while she is with her lover, the fear of this punishment is a powerful spur to her behavior. Such is the case, for example, in *La Dame qui se venja du chevalier* (Noomen, VII, 331–50). A lover hidden in a lady's bed when her husband comes home expects to face death. She sends her husband to change his leggings, whereupon:

> Li haus hons s'en va la atant,
> Et la dame remest jesant
> Delés le chevalier el lit,
> Qui petit prise son delit:
> Et mout puet cel delit haïr,
> Que meintenant cuide morir! [vss. 112–17].

> [At this the nobleman went away, and the lady remained lying in the bed beside the knight, who prizes his delight very little: and well he might hate this delight, for he is expecting to die right away!]

When she jokingly tells her husband she has a lover, he offers to kill him, and she sends him to get his sword. But she reveals that what has been between her legs that week more often than her husband was only the threshold of the door, and the lover is saved. The lady and her husband and the lover all think it quite plausible, and indeed probable, that the husband will kill the lover.

The fear of death when discovered in adultery is more plainly stated in *Le Pliçon* (Noomen, X, 23–32). Here a woman manages to save her lover when her husband comes home by asking what her husband would have done to the lover if they had been found *in flagrante*: "Et cil respont: 'A ceste espee / Lui eusse se tieste copee, / Et vous morte par compaingnie!'" [And he answers: "I would have cut off his head with this sword, and killed you along with him!" vss. 71–73]. Neither husband nor wife considers this a joke.

Customary Law in the Old French Fabliau (Akehurst)

An element of law and perhaps of life is the notion of notoriety. In its thirteenth-century meaning, a *fait notoire* is one that is well enough known to people in general that it needs no proof (Beaumanoir §§1155, 1169). Notoriety is also allied to the notion of reputation, and they are both denoted by the Latin term *Fama* (see Fenster and Smail). This notion plays a part in two fabliaux. In the first, *Auberee* (Noomen, I, 161–312), a young woman is afraid that she will get a bad reputation: "Qu'el porroit acuillir tel los / Par ses voisins et tel renon; / Jamais n'avroit se honte non" [For she might gain such a reputation and such a bad name; she would never have anything but shame; vss. 398–400]. The bourgeoise who entertained a clerk in *Les Braies au cordelier* (Noomen, III, 211–36) needed to explain how her husband had on a clerk's breeches and to repair her reputation: "Quant fu grant eure et grant jorz / Por changier sa honte a hennor, / S'en vint a un Frere Menor" [When it was late and full daylight, in order to change her shame to honor, she went to see a Minor Friar; vss. 239–41]. Finally, in *La Borgoise d'Orliens* (Noomen, III, 337–74), a classic tale of "le mari cocu, battu et content" [the husband cuckolded, beaten, and happy], a woman who is deceiving her husband and indeed having him beaten by the servants yells out for her disguised husband's benefit as she plays the part of the outraged wife, egging on the servants who are beating him:

> "Or du ferir, bone mesnie!
> Fetes tant a ceste foïe
> Le clerjastre, le renoié,
> Qui de folie m'a proié,
> Que ja mes jor ne soit tant os
> De tolir dame son bon los" [vss. 235–40].

["Strike on, good servants! Give him (such a beating) that this time, the clerkling, the renegade, who has begged me to do something foolish, will never again be bold enough to take away a lady's good reputation."]

There are several fabliaux that include contracts. In addition to tales with contracts discussed elsewhere in this paper, *Un Chevalier et sa dame et un clerk* (Noomen, X, 115–42) includes among other elements a sort of contract. In a plot reminiscent of a portion of Philippe de Remy's *Jehan et Blonde*, a clerk is dying for love of a lady. When it seems that unless she gives in to his desire he really may die, which she thinks might be a homicide on her part, and thus a grave sin, graver than adultery, they make a contract: if he will get well, she will allow him to have sex with her. He does and she does, but sends him away immediately afterwards; and he obeys as a courtly lover must. The arrangement is called a *covenant* by the author at vs. 404 and a *covine* by the lady's maid, who is in love with the clerk, at vs. 434.

Another bargain is struck in *L'Anel qui faisoit les vis grans et roides* (Noomen, VIII, 311–17) when a bishop picks up and puts on a ring that causes penises to grow. No one understands why the bishop's penis is soon dragging on the ground; but the owner of the lost ring quickly hears about the problem. The bishop is ready to pay anything at all for relief, and accepts the owner's offer of paying his two rings and a hundred livres to be cured. As soon as the bishop slips off the ring he is of course no longer afflicted.

These bargains clearly operate in a society where bargains and contracts are considered to be enforceable, either as a moral obligation or a legal transaction. Another tale, *Le Prestre et le chevalier* (Noomen, IX, 67–124), includes a double promise: a knight and his squire without cash must spend the night with a grasping priest who lives with his mistress and his niece. The priest and the knight exchange promises: the knight that he will pay five sous for each item he uses, the priest that he will furnish each thing in his power the knight asks for. In addition, the priest demands that the payment will be made "trestout sans noise" ["without protest"; vss. 95, 222]. The priest makes separate claims for each dish, even the salt and the cover charge; whereupon the knight asks first for the services of the niece, then of the mistress at five sous apiece, reluctantly granted by the priest, and finally the services of the priest himself. Appalled, the priest rebargains for a large sum, which the knight insists on having at once, and he leaves in the morning richer than he came. After the solemn undertakings of the evening bargain, the priest is unwilling to refuse the knight what he asks for within the contract. The knight, as befits, perhaps, his superior station, is imperturbable; the squire, however, is afraid he will end up in prison for debt: "Mais durement se desconfortent / Entre l'escuier et le prestre: / Car en prison cuidoit bien estre / Li escuiers por le despense" [But the priest and the squire were both very upset: for the squire fully expected to be in prison for the expense; vss. 935–38].

No transaction is more unusual, probably, than the two bargains made by a young man with a lady and her maid to satisfy their sexual desires in *Le Foteor* (Noomen, VI, 51–75). The eponymous hero charges, he says, more for his servicing of ugly women than for that of attractive ones. The lady first bargains for a bout in bed for twenty sous (one livre), and the maid asks how much for herself. The outrageous price of ten livres (she must have been very ugly!) is then bargained down to a hundred sous (five livres). The bargain is made with the equivalent of a hand shake: "Tenez donc ça, sire, vos mains, / Si sera la paumee faite, / Car cist marchiez mout bien me haite, / Si avroiz l'argent en baillie" ["Hold out your hands, then, sir, and we will strike palms, for this bargain pleases me very much, and you will have your money in a safe place"; vss. 263–66]. When later the *fotere* tells the husband about his bargain with the wife, but stating falsely that he has not yet been paid or performed his part of the bargain, the husband is glad to pay him the twenty sous and call it quits. The women both seem satisfied with the servicing, and the husband will not challenge the (clearly illegal) bargain.

The fabliaux where there is the most legal content are those which include some sort of a trial, serious or frivolous. There are several fabliaux that contain courtroom scenes, in either seigneurial courts (where the seigneur might even be the king) or ecclesiastical ones (where the presiding judge might be a bishop) or material that resembles litigation. The procedure may be summary or even cursory, but it generally includes an exposition of the case and a judgment.

In some cases, the procedure is rapid but fair, as when the woman complains of her husband's black sex organs in *La Coille noire* (Noomen, V, 163–89). After seeing the said organs, she complains to the bishop, who immediately sends for the husband. The latter manages to obtain from the wife an admission that she has not cleaned herself in over a year; and the peasant explains thus the color of his organs. The bishop reconciles the pair amidst general hilarity. In a similar vein, in *Connebert* (Noomen, VII, 215–37) a priest who has been forced to castrate himself by a smith and his apprentice who catch him *in flagrante* complains to the court (presumably the bishop's) and the complaint is very rapidly dispatched:

> Si s'en ala clamer a cort;
> Mais il n'i ot ne lonc ne cort
> Qu'il ne deïst trestot a hait:
> "Si lor aïst Deus, bien a fait:
> Car fussent or si atorné
> Tuit li prestre de mere né
> Qui sacremant de mariage
> Tornent a honte et a putage!" [vss. 298–305].

[He went to court to complain; but everyone said to him right away, "God help them, he did well: for all the priests should be treated this way who turn the sacrament of marriage into shame and whoring."]

In *La Plantez* (Noomen, VII, 203–13) a tavern keeper whose customer was a Norman does no better in a seigneurial court: the two men fight over some spilled wine and do lots of damage. Haled before the king (in fact, Henry of Champagne), the Norman tells the whole truth, as his adversary admits. The king's men all laugh, and Henry dismisses the case, saying "Qui a perdu, si ait perdu" ["Whoever has lost has lost"; vs. 134].

In *Le Testament de l'asne* (Noomen, IX, 237–50), a priest who has buried his donkey in holy ground is denounced to the bishop, summoned, and appears in court to answer the charge. He asks for a "jor de conseil" [counsel day; vs. 109], which is a normal liminal request for a person who hears for the first time what the charge against him is (Beaumanoir §149). It allows the defendant to seek advice and perhaps an advocate. The hearing is then continued for fifteen days (two weeks). The priest knows he can pay for a fine or a default if necessary: his purse is his friend. When he returns to court he asks to confess to the bishop (to ensure that they will not be overheard), and they speak privately. The priest reveals that the donkey has left his savings, twenty livres, to the bishop, who thereupon pronounces the animal a good Christian. These summary procedures, especially in the bishop's court, amount to little more that being "called on the carpet" in front of a superior, although some of the steps in a formal suit are named and gone through.

In the secular court of the *bailli* in *Le Meunier d'Arleux* (Noomen, IX, 215–36) the miller and his apprentice Mousés plot to cause a young woman to stay overnight at the miller's house, where they will take advantage of her, with Mousés paying the miller a pig for the privilege. The intended victim informs the miller's wife, who changes places with her. The miller and Mousés each enjoy the wife five times. But when they discover the deception, Mousés wants his pig back, or else strict performance of the contract. He complains to the *bailli*, who summons the parties and they tell their stories. The *échevins*, who form a kind of jury, bring back a recommendation that the miller must give back the pig or provide the young woman, strict performance. The author finds this decision reasonable, and so does the *bailli*. The author further suggests that he who does evil will find he is repaid with evil. This trial is as formal as is to be found in the fabliaux, and it and *Le Testament de l'asne* contain quite a bit of legal procedure, named with the proper terminology.

In two trials, there is a surprising development at the moment of judgment. In *Le Meunier d'Arleux*, once the jury has decided that Mousés must get his pig back, the miller hands it over to the court, which announces it will pay Mousés thirty sous and eat the pig at a feast! But such an act is authorized by Beaumanoir who says, "Quant aucunes choses sont prises en mesfet, lesqueles sont perilleuses a garder por ce qu'eles ne perissent ou empirent ... en tous teus cas et en semblables doivent estre les choses prises vendues a ceus qui plus en vuelent donner...." [When property is seized for an offense, and the property is hard to keep so that it does not perish or spoil ... in all these and similar cases the seized property should be sold to the highest bidder; Beaumanoir §1563].

The other surprise ending (although perhaps not unforeseeable) is when two women on a pilgrimage in *Les Trois Dames qui troverent un vit* (Noomen, VIII, 269–81) find a penis and argue over who shall keep it. They choose as an arbitrator a local abbess, who, inspired by motives one can only guess at, quickly claims that the object in question is the bolt of the door of the abbey, and confiscates it.

No example of legal argument is more remarkable that that found in *Le Vilain qui conquist paradis par plait* (Noomen, V, 1–38). The soul of a *vilain* enters Paradise, only to be confronted by Saint Peter, Saint Thomas, and Saint Paul, each of whom tries to send him away as a *vilain*, unworthy of being there. But the soul points out that *they* are there, each having sinned mightily, and they are defeated. They appeal to God, who hears the soul's *plait*, namely that in life he was a good man and kept the commandments. God lets him in. The soul's arguments to the saints resemble those of a party trying to get a judge to recuse himself, and its arguments to God are like a person claiming to have performed on a contract, who now demands strict performance of the other party. Even God admits that the soul has done well in argument: "Bien ses avant metre ta verbe!" ["You make good use of your words"; vs. 172].

A fabliau that includes a good deal of legal material including an appeal is *Le Chapelain* (Noomen, VI, 77–99), whose beginning is missing, but can be easily reconstructed. Two fishermen, Gui and Bernart, who are partners, share profits: "Que compaignon andui estoient / Et lor gaainz par mi partoient" [For they were partners, and shared their earnings; vss. 60–61]. When they fish up the body of a murdered priest in a sack, they are convinced that the sack contains clothing which they will divide and profit from. While Gui goes to fetch his wife, Bernard opens the sack and finds the body. Gui accuses him of appropriating the clothes and putting the priest in the sack. Gui complains to the prevost, who summons Bernart. The prevost sees, however, that while the suit is brought as one of fraud, with one partner against the other, there is also the problem of the dead priest. There is a wager of battle, which is accepted by the prevost, and the author remarks that neither is guilty of the murder: "Mes nus d'aus deus n'en a lo tort: / si en face Deus demonstrance / par la soe digne puissance" [But neither of them is at fault. Let God make things plain by his proper power; vss. 265–67]. The adversaries are *vilains*, but they nevertheless proceed to a judicial combat. They fight for a while, but then there is a divine intervention, just as there is supposed to be in a judicial duel, when the guilty party wanders by the body, which immediately begins to bleed. It happens that the actual killer is a sheep [sic] and by experimentation (the dead man's wounds bleed in the presence of his murderer) the prevost identifies the animal. The sheep's owner disclaims responsibility, and threatens to appeal to the countess. The man at whose door she left the body, and who threw the body into the Seine, also claims innocence and threatens to appeal to the count. The prevost sees he will get nowhere with this litigious band of *débrouillards*, separates the combatants, buries the priest, and all is once again calm in Nogent.

This may be the most amusing of the fabliaux where the law is an important element. The event that gives the story its start, the death of a priest, caused by a (jealous?) sheep while the priest and the sheep's owner are having sex, seems hardly likely to evolve into a series of real or conjectured law suits which lead to no legal solution. The moral exposed by the author is generic (and hardly apposite): your sins will be discovered. Getting rid of the body, which forms the basis of other fabliaux, seems almost an interpolation here. But murder, partnership, concealing a body, fraud, and a full-fledged judicial duel keep the tale moving and in the end no one seems sorry for the victim. While a knowledge of the law may help to understand this tale, it is hardly a requirement, and the humor arises from the human situations more than from the legal proceedings as such.

In the end, then, there is relatively little that might be shocking to modern lawyers in the legal elements of the fabliaux. The punishment of animals, the laughter of court personnel including jurors might seem unusual, but not unprecedented; the way that people honor a contract, even one that cannot be proved and may be illegal or immoral seems of another age. But the way a prevost has trouble dealing with aggressive and obstreperous suspects seems strangely modern, as seen in recent (2005–06) trials of such figures as Zacharias Moussaoui and Saddam Hussein. Like the judge in *Pathelin*, the prevost in *Le Chapelain* can only do his best.

Likewise, a thirteenth-century French customary law practitioner would find little to cavil at in the legal rules and procedures that appear in these tales, which hardly seem to be aimed at an audience of lawyers, and where the law rarely plays much of a part in the plot. At most there may be found a few terms of art, but the language of the law is closer to ordinary language in the thirteenth century than at any time since, and many of the terms would have been transparent even to non-lawyers.

If the fabliaux are indeed comic tales, it is not the law that provides the comedy. However, the aspects of law that can be found in these tales can help to explain what the fabliau is about, and above all the legal elements contribute to the realism so often found in the stories, which also permits certain authors to attribute them to a bourgeois origin. While the nobility and the bourgeois could be expected to know something of customary law, and the clergy of canon law, the peasant probably knew very little except by direct experience. But not every fabliau contains legal elements, and their presence is thus not part of the definition of the genre.

Notes

1. The Nutshell series of books are convenient student and practice aids to many aspects of the law.

Works Cited

Beaumanoir, Philippe de. *Coutumes de Beauvaisis: Texte critique publié avec une introduction, un glossaire et une table analytique*, ed. Am[édée] Salmon. 2 vols. 1899–1900; Paris: Picard, 1970.

———. *The* Coutumes de Beauvaisis *of Philippe de Beaumanoir*, trans. F.R.P. Akehurst. Philadelphia: University of Pennsylvania Press, 1992.

Fenster, Thelma, and Daniel Lord Smail, eds. *Fama: The Politics of Talk and Reputation in Medieval Europe*. Ithaca: Cornell University Press, 2003.

Rhetorical Reasoning, Authority, and the Impossible Interlocutor *in* Le Vilain qui conquist paradis par plait

Elizabeth Kinne

Impossible settings, actions, events, conversations, and characters populate the pages of the fabliaux, inviting the audience to suspend disbelief temporarily and be taken in by the logic of the fabliau world. In many of these texts, humor arises from the absurd premise that a stock fabliau character, such as a knight or a *vilain*,[1] enters into dialogue with an impossible, or at least highly improbable, interlocutor. Whether genital organs endowed with the capacity for speech, or characters such as saints and God himself, whose speech one would expect to find in a medieval genre other than the fabliau, the pairing often makes for strange bedfellows. This incongruous combination renders both the interlocutors and their speech "impossible" in any other context than that of the fabliaux, and allows for an abstract exercise in comedy. A saint who speaks to inspire devotion in a miracle text might be commonplace, but a fabliau saint who is called upon to defend his place in heaven may at first seem quite impossible. However, such is the premise of *Le Vilain qui conquist paradis par plait* (Noomen, V, 1–38), one of a number of fabliaux that rely on the representation of an impossible interlocutor to solicit laughter. It also belongs to a category of fabliaux that stage medieval scholastic traditions such as the *jugement* [judgment] and *disputatio* [disputation] in a humorous light. This, along with its religious (or sacrilegious) content, implies a certain familiarity with the university system for its appreciation and, perhaps, composition.[2] By examining the formal and rhetorical mechanisms that compose this fabliau, this discussion seeks to demonstrate how what might have been initially scholastic concerns are transformed into a story that has a wider interest and is thus capable of soliciting a much wider appreciation. In *Le Vilain qui conquist paradis par plait* larger philosophical enterprises expressing very real and timely concerns are made possible through a humorous flight of fancy, the basis of which is an impossible dialogue with the medieval scholastic tradition and its truth seeking discourses.

A brief reading of *Le Vilain qui conquist paradis par plait* suggests that an irreverent hand was at work at its inception. A contemporary non-initiate to the fabliaux may be shocked to know that their generic *raison d'être* often consists of stretching the limits of propriety or simply ignoring them. It may also come as a surprise that a clerical authorship or audience was ever suggested for these texts. Knud Togeby, in responding to Joseph Bédier's and Per Nykrog's theories regarding bourgeois or aristocratic genesis for the fabliaux, suggested the possibility that, in the second half of the twelfth century, emerging students groups could have provided a milieu for both the creation and appreciation of these texts. He follows this by stating that "[students] viewed the world at the distance from each social group which is said to be a necessary condition of comic enjoyment" (11). Instead of engaging in tenuous observations about fabliaux audience and production, suffice it to say that this proposition merits both nuance and further exploration. Students of the time would have had the cultural baggage necessary to compose these tales that rely heavily on intertextuality, and some fabliaux do represent scholastic concerns in a humorous light. It might be a bit ingenuous to infer a group's inability to appreciate a fabliau that could have hit rather close to home, and indeed, contemporary humorists have gone to great lengths to prove the contrary. Familiarity might have been what made the fabliau at hand funny, and it is the best representative of its genre to be considered a scholastic fabliau, given its adherence to two scholastic forms, the *jugement* and *disputatio*.

The tale's humor remains intact to this day, even if the *disputatio* as a pedagogical method has fallen (some might say quite fortunately) into disuse. The *disputatio*, or disputation, is a didactic exercise based on Socratic question and answer method that evolved in the Parisian university setting during the thirteenth century, reaching its pinnacle under the influence of Thomas Aquinas's school of thought. Béatrice Périgot traces the rise of the disputation in the university system and its eventual incorporation into literature during the Middle Ages and the Renaissance. She affirms that an early form of the disputation is found in the structure of Peter Abelard's *Sic et Non*, which poses a question and then argues both sides of the matter. This style of debate evolved from the questions arrived at through gloss commentaries into very formal and tightly structured public exercises (16). It was meant to arrive at greater theological truths, or at least purported reconciliations in doctrine, in a public forum, not only teaching the art of rhetoric to those who listened to these public debates, but also serving as a guarantor of authority and mastery within university circles. Participation was often a requirement for successful completion of the university curriculum, a proto-comprehensive exam of a sort. These events could last for several days, as students and masters took turns presenting arguments. Their form was as follows: the master would propose a question and provide the basis for both responses, yes or no; an *opponens*, or opponent, would refute the master's thesis; a *respondens*, or respondent, would join the debate and find a preliminary solution to the problem or at times speak first and give a first response as well as provide a solution to contrary arguments; if a second *respondens* did not intervene, the *opponens* would respond in opposition to the *respondens*, providing proof to refute his arguments; last, the master would share his *determinatio* or solution, addressing the arguments provided by the first *opponens* (20). What is known with certainty is that the disputation and its rhetorical and dialectical forms were to have a great influence on later literary forms, and, in the case of our fabliau, an immediate one. If the schema of the disputation is applied to *Le Vilain qui conquist paradis par plait*, the text's affiliation with this form of logical argument becomes plain. The question is posed when an ambiguity arises regarding the fate of a peasant soul whose destiny has not been divinely determined: does the soul deserve to dwell in heaven or does he not?

As *Le Vilain qui conquist paradis par plait* begins, the narrator immediately gets to the heart of the matter, announcing in his prologue that he will relate a marvelous adventure (vs. 2) that he has found in writing. A truly fortunate peasant soul, met by neither angel nor demon upon his death, follows St. Michael, busy accompanying another dearly departed, directly to heaven. St. Peter, a first *respondens*, reprimands him for his lack of chaperone and declares that no one is received in heaven if not by his own orders, most certainly not vile peasants such as this one.[3] The peasant soul, the *opponens*, states his own criteria for a celestial stay, admonishing St. Peter for denying his faith on three occasions and concluding that he, an honest and loyal peasant, is more worthy of heaven than the saint. St. Peter walks away, dumbfounded and most likely concerned about his position as heaven's premiere civil servant. He then tells St. Thomas about the incident.

Determined to remedy the problem, St. Thomas, as a second *respondens*, confronts the soul. However, the *vilain* is ready with some hard empirical evidence against him and subsequently reminds the saint of his apostolic faux-pas of refusing to believe in the resurrection of Christ until he touched the wounds. Outraged, St. Thomas leaves and, licking his own wounds, confides in St. Paul. St. Paul, the third *respondens*, takes matters into his own hands, confronts the peasant, and tries to show him the door. The soul again brings forth his evidence and proceeds to illustrate St. Paul's tyrannical misdeeds, incriminating him in the stoning of St. Stephen and the deaths of other holy men. St. Paul, dumbstruck and understandably miffed, goes to find the *vilain*'s other saintly victims. They decide to leave the matter in God's hands and tell him their tale of woe. God, intrigued by their account, wants to hear out the peasant soul. After explaining the appropriate channels for entry into heaven, God listens as the soul tells of his exemplary conduct while on earth. He reminds God that before dying he had confessed and received extreme unction, thereby, according to the scriptures, meriting God's grace. Last, he reminds God that it was he himself who declared that whosoever entered heaven should never leave. God, unable to argue with this infallible logic and perhaps worried about how a reputation as a liar might undermine his heavenly dominion, provides a *determinatio* that concedes a place in paradise to the soul, and he then congratulates him on his mastery of the spoken word.

Many critical observations can be made about *Le Vilain qui conquist paradis par plait*'s relationship to the disputation and its subsequent interest in the predominant philosophical and dialectical modes of the time. Roy J. Pearcy has addressed the fabliaux' concern with logic and maintains that logic and epistemology are the bases of these texts. He traces the role of logic from Peter Abelard onward to the period of composition of the fabliaux and indicates the importance of the sophismata, a collection of logical fallacies, to the fabliaux, concluding that similar fallacies are used by fabliau dupers to deceive their victims and serve their own immoral or base ends; he attributes this influence to the possibility that fabliaux authors could have numbered among the students of Northern European universities (98–99). A form of sophistry, these fallacies represent "...a tear in the intellectual fabric of the age..." and through their incorporation "...[the fabliaux acquire] significant intellectual implication..." (100). Pearcy's statements explain much about this particular fabliau, but one could contend that there is a deeper concern in the *vilain*'s arguments. Although the peasant soul may intend to deceive God and his saints, his goal is not immoral. Interested in saving his own skin, he points out a weak link in the charter rules to do so. This existential dilemma is also a logical fallacy: how does one understand divine judgment and mercy in a world where theological questions are determined by argumentation and masterly authority? The fabliau may be referring to this "tear in the intellectual fabric of the age," but it also takes on the problematic creation of authority through speech. By refuting a judgment through the use of empirical evidence provided in scripture and therefore bearing the stamp of medieval *auctoritas*, the peasant soul is making reference to the discrepancy between the supposed physical world of actions and the abstract world of speech and, consequently, judgment. The *vilain*'s interest in legal language and rhetorical structures that establish truth but ignore being true to one's word might express some discontent with nascent scholastic doctrinal tools but also with the medieval conception of authority.

The problem of the authentication of fabliaux texts has been discussed by many scholars. Fabliau narrators often assert that what they are about to tell is the truth only to allow their story to reveal the contrary. Many fabliaux also attempt to establish the validity of the story by referring to its transmission in text, found elsewhere in another written source. This practice of citing "authentic" sources lends socio-cultural weight to what is to follow. Norris J. Lacy states regarding this textual tradition of *auctoritas* that: "...literary authority may reside partly in the narrative act and in the mimetic activity within texts, but it also resides elsewhere, in the authority of precedent texts, existent or imaginary" (104). In the case of our fabliau, the text that it refers to very much exists (the Bible), but its content is modified. Preference is given to the rhetorical act, at once lending authenticity to a recreation of conventional authority and questioning this very same authority from the outset.

The rhetorical act in the context of impossible dialogues brings the reader's attention to the disconnect between emitter and receiver. While medieval textual authority is often claimed through reception of previous texts and their subsequent transmission in a new context, our fabliau narrator chooses to get the story wrong and embellish the tradition with his own original creation. The narrator begins with an ambiguity when he states "Nos trovomes en escriture / Une mervellose aventure" [We find in writing a marvelous adventure; vss. 1–2]. The authenticating moment of the fabliau comes about in its allusion to an "escriture." In this instance, the term provides for a certain ambiguity and can be understood to be both writing and Scripture. The reader's interpretation of this word can greatly modify his or her perception of the text, a written source being radically different from a scriptural one, and the audience understands immediately that this story is definitely not biblical. However, the story does bring up the question of authority. The common medieval narrative practice of referring to a source text only to modify it greatly becomes comic premise in this tale and the means to draw attention to language and the metanarrative moment. The *vilain*'s conversation, much like the narrator's originality, takes precedent over tradition and demonstrates how both literature and the disputation can contest authority in the same way that they can construct it. As the tale develops, as is the case with most fabliaux, the interest will turn not to the validity of the written word, but rather the spoken word as imagined by the text. Like the narrator who uses tradition and authority as a means to an end in his or her own literary production, the *vilain* will interpret religious tradition poorly and derive his own original interpretation. This self-reflexive and self-referential movement in the fabliau makes it difficult to refute the observation that many of the fabliaux are quite simply language about language.[4] *Le Vilain qui conquist paradis par plait* uses language in a way typical of the fabliaux, varying literary commonplaces, registers, and styles to create humor. As the tale ranges from references to the courtly world to those from a judicial and scholastic tradition, the narrator's ability to manipulate the reader's expectations mirrors the ability of the peasant soul to manipulate his impossible interlocutors.

A courtly element of the intertextual nexus of the fabliau, the reference to a "mervellose aventure" (vs. 2), leads the reader to expect a fantastic romance in which reality merges with the marvelous. However, the fabliau brings the reader to an imagined setting that must have been very real in many a medieval mind, the pearly gates. The audience may have immediately known that parody was to be the name of the game, especially since the reference to a "marvelous adventure" lies entirely within the courtly register. At the same time, the protagonist of the tale is a peasant, not a knight as one would expect, who becomes the unlikely actor of an impossible adventure that does not normally befall those of his social class. However, this particular fabliau does not hinge on the "courtliness of the *vilain*" premise as so many others do, but rather on the premise of the "erudite *vilain*."

The peasant soul almost immediately makes clear his belief in the importance of the spoken word, and each accusation that he will make revolves around a linguistic transgression. His use of juridical terms connotes not only the author's familiarity with these forms, but also the peasant soul's interest in linguistic forms that are designed to seek truth. He is also more than ready to castigate those who, he feels, use them inappropriately or, at least, attempt to turn his own weapons against him. Clearly sensitive to questions of language and appropriate usage, he expresses his displeasure with what could be called medieval "legalese" early on in the fabliau when he accuses St. Thomas of being a poor jurist. "Tumas, Tumas, plus estes cois / des responsaus que nus legistes!" ["Thomas, Thomas, you are slower at answering than a jurist"; vss. 62–63]. The peasant soul accuses St. Thomas of doing exactly what he himself is doing, but of doing it poorly. He also implies that quick wit is more useful than a jurist's bag of rhetorical tricks when it comes to matters of redemption. The use of this erudite register does not correspond to his identity as a *vilain* and creates an incongruity within the text. The "erudite" *vilain* is an unlikely character in a genre in which many *vilains* are characterized by their stupidity. Who then are truly impossible interlocutors: God and his saints or rather the peasant soul?

The problem of the impossible interlocutor presents a double bind in this tale. The initial comical premise of making the saints and God speak provides an imaginative exercise for the reader, since in his or her daily experience, the only access one would have to their "speech" would have been through either biblical text or a literary genre other than the fabliaux. A peasant, or *vilain*, in keeping with the fabliaux' interest in "reality," would have been a much more probable interlocutor for a comic dialogue. However, given this particular fabliau's philosophical interest in the problematic establishment of authority and truth through discourse, one is obliged to conclude that a peasant interlocutor might have been as improbable as a saintly or divine one, no textual precedent according sincerity and truth to speech of the *vilain*. The speech of an erudite peasant is thus all the more impossible. The question then becomes: can the *vilain* speak?

The peasant soul, in fact, can speak and in order to do so usurps forms that in other literary examples are unavailable to his fictional peers, his interest in truth and justice not corresponding to the traditional picture that is painted of the *vilain*. On several occasions, the peasant soul brings up his concern with speaking the truth and being true to one's word. His position as an outsider whose voice is often considered to have little truth value puts him in a very precarious position for getting to the bottom of problems of theological exegesis but in an ideal position from which to deconstruct the establishment of truth through authoritative discourse. The humor of the fabliau and his ability to approach truth lies in this juxtaposition of conventional authority with his own self-authorizing speech. The protagonist points out that denying what one has vowed or disobeying commandments to which one has adhered is what got all of these saints into trouble, and he is in no way ready to let it pass. He first addresses St. Peter: "Mout fu petite vostre fois, / Quel renoiastes par trois fois / Que n'estiiés de sa compagne" ["Small was your faith when you denied three times that you were one of his companions"; vss. 37–39]. He then explains to St. Thomas, "Vos fesistes vo sairement! / Que vos ja ne le kerriiés, / Se vos les plaies ne veiés / ... faus fustes et mescreans!" ["You had sworn that you would not believe it until you saw the wounds ... you were false and disbelieving" vss. 68–73]. In this instance, the use of the word "sairement," meaning both sworn oath and sacrament, reveals the sacred nature of the spoken word in the peasant soul's lexicon. Later, while speaking to St. Paul, he will again accuse him of refuting an oath: "Sains Estevenes le compara, / Cui vos fesistes lapider. / Bien sai vo vie recorder: / Les commans a Deu desdegniés" ["Saint Stephen, whom you had stoned, paid for it dearly. I know how to recount your life very well: you disobeyed God's commands" vss. 92–95]. In order for the *vilain*'s argumentation to succeed, he must first establish a precedent of intolerance for going back on one's word and call for a single interpretation of what is said, while simultaneously playing on a tradition that calls for multiple interpretations of that which is written.

When it comes to theological exegesis, the truth, at least momentarily, lies in the mouth of the *vilain*. It is interesting to note that in taking on a figure such as St. Paul, the peasant soul is defying established Christian authority both directly and indirectly. By rendering these imaginary conversations possible, he is privileging the spoken over the written word within the logic of the text, while also questioning the validity of a dialectic system that reposes on spoken exchanges. The saints, unable to respond to the peasant soul, seem to be trapped in a textual world. Much as texts cannot explain themselves and, at least in the scholastic mode of thinking, necessitate exegesis through gloss, the saints are unable to defend their actions and respond to the *vilain*'s reading of them. His dialogue engages and subverts conclusions that were otherwise commented upon in glosses, underscoring the conventional nature of the written word and the verbal exchange's capacity for nuance and contradiction. Assuming the position of both oral commentator and hagiographer, he attempts to retell the saints' lives and says as much to St. Paul. The peasant ironically mocks St. Paul's ability to produce an authoritative discourse, exclaiming "Oh God, what a saint, and what a theologian!" (vs. 102).

However, once the peasant soul has given the saints a good tongue-lashing, God will remind him of his own verbal excesses. The *vilain*'s own sins are those of speech, but the truth value of his words is not called into question. Rather, what God accuses him of is his contesting of conventional authority: "Mes apostles as blastengiés / et avilliés et laidengiés: / Comment cuides ci remanoir?" ["You have blasphemed my apostles and insulted them and dishonored them: how could you think of staying here?" vss. 127–29]. The *vilain* refutes this observation not by illustrating his fidelity to his word but rather by enumerating the manners in which he has lived a just life previously, providing a form of empirical evidence that relies on "lived" experience rather than textual authority. The crux of his counterargument, however, rests on holding God himself to his word. Referring to his good Christian death, he reminds his Eminence, "Qui ensi muert, on nos sermone / que Deus ses pecciés li pardone. / Vos savés bien se j'ai voir dit!" ["Who dies in this manner, we are told in sermons, is forgiven his sins by God. You know full well I'm telling the truth" vss. 153–55]. That would seem, indeed, to be the problem: the *vilain* is telling the truth. By referring to a sole truth and one's ability to be truthful and faithful to the spoken word, the peasant soul is able to play on other truths, such as God's mercy regarding the saints, his argument being: "If they deserve it, why don't I?"

This is a valid, logical conclusion that even God is not prepared to deny. He refuses to engage in sophistry or provide a counterargument regarding *vilains* as a group. This particular *vilain* is exceptional because he can play off of his supposed lack of social value to demonstrate the potentially base act that God could commit by lying to him: "Vostre parole desdiroie, / car otroiés avés sans falle / Qui çaiens est, puis ne s'en alle. / Vos ne mentirés ja por moi" ["I will refute your word because you have declared that without fail he who enters here may not leave. You won't lie for the likes of me" vss. 158–61]. Consequently, God grants his request and comments on the peasant soul's ability to speak his mind, uttering the words that reorganize heavenly order: "Amis, fait Deus, et je t'otroi / Paradis; si m'as araisnié / Que par plaidier l'as desraisnié / Bien ses avant metre ta verbe!" ["Friend, says God, I will grant you Paradise; you have engaged me thoroughly and merit heaven with your plea. You surely have a way with words!" vss. 162–65]. In a form of *mouvance*, manuscripts *B* and *D* both present the same variant in God's remark to the peasant soul regarding his eloquence, attesting to an entirely different meaning and perhaps supporting the hypothesis that this fabliau's author was a cleric addressing a university audience and suggesting that the *vilain*'s sophistry is the product of nurture rather than nature. In these two versions, God's last remark is "Tu as esté a bone escole" ["You have been to a good school" *B* vs. 163 and *D* vs. 151], perhaps hinting at the university system of the day and the possible deviations of its rhetorical and logical instruction. If the peasant is well taught, what is the lesson?

This fabliau assumes as a philosophical point of departure the theological truth or convention, depending on one's point of view, that the saints have their place in heaven and, consequently, that God's judgment is irrefutable. The humor of the fabliau comes from embracing one form of logic in order to arrive at two distinct results (the *vilain's* interpretation and that of the saints) and from the *vilain's* capacity to dispute convention and win. The patent humor of the text is undeniable, whether this same convention is embraced by a contemporary audience or not, residing in the peasant soul's ability to beat the system and, to misquote Audre Lorde, "...use the master's tools to dismantle the master's house."[5] The soul's success also depends on the ability of the narrator to convince the audience to adhere momentarily to the saints' logic and conventional interpretation of their deeds, as they witness his performance with amusement and finally embrace the peasant soul's plea. The audience's position mirrors that of God's at the end of the tale, amused by the story and unable to argue with the logic contained therein. How, then, does one explain that texts about deception are really interested in the ability of language to approach truth?

Le Vilain qui conquist paradis par plait is founded on the premise that the sophismata, while providing the basis for rhetorical exercises such as the disputation, can undermine the very system they are meant to uphold. The audience does not necessarily need to be familiar with the disputation, its form and outcome, to appreciate the fabliau's comic effect. Readers or listeners, however, must be able to seize upon the fleeting nature of absolute truth and the tenuous project that lies behind authoritative discourse. In her study of vision and logic in two Old French and one Chaucerian fabliaux, Michelle Kohler comes to a similar conclusion, positing that such tales question the reliability of systems of knowledge in vogue at the time that still look very much like our own (147). *Le Vilain qui conquist paradis par plait* points to the disputation's goal of implementing a form of verbal authority that buttresses a written one, entailing some epistemological consequences. If *auctoritas* suddenly requires a verbal defense, does the system of textual authority begin to fail? Noomen and Van den

Boogaard posit an early thirteenth century composition for this fabliau, a date contemporaneous with the rise of the scholastic system. It could be inferred that the fabliau is the sign of an internal critique blossoming within that very same system. Much like the saints who are unable to truly "talk back" and demonstrate their ability to reason, the imposition of the peasant soul's "new" interpretation concerning the saints' condition represents the fragility of truth seeking discourses that rely on authority to arrive at binary answers, whether theological or worldly.

Kohler's conclusion can be taken a step further in this instance. In this fabliau, an improbable and, as such, humorous conclusion is arrived at through highly normative forms that were conceived for very conservative purposes and implemented by an unlikely candidate. The dialectic form of this fabliau could express not only a certain dissatisfaction or mild disbelief in the validity of scholastic methods to encounter divine truths, but also a contestation of the authority that lies behind those methods. Périgot's discussion of the disputation according to Thomas Aquinas defines a similar double status for this rhetorical practice, that of a rational tool at the service of a divine subject (69). She goes on to state that at the Paris Faculty of Theology, the exercise was slightly acrobatic, placing analyses pronounced by authorities on the same level as purely rational ones (69). *Le Vilain qui conquist paradis par plait* unravels the threads of a method that sought to produce authority while being authoritative. By questioning the language that founds authority, the *vilain* mirrors the process of deconstructing a logical fallacy, all while exposing that very same process to its own form of critique. It does not stand up to the test. The fabliau privileges worldly wit over conventional wisdom and experience over authority at a time when dialectical method intended for logic and authority to coincide neatly. This form of skepticism renders this fabliau perhaps a bit more "scandalous" than some others, prefiguring a form of questioning that will bring about the end of the scholastic system that seemingly already contained the seeds of its own demise. As such, scholasticism and the disputation will become fodder for the writings of Rabelais (as Périgot demonstrates) or of Chaucer: the *vilain*'s plea prefigures that of Alisoun, the Wife of Bath, who celebrates her worldly experience over the scholastic authority of young clerics who believe they have the corner on truth.[6] The peasant soul expresses a humanistic skepticism regarding the scholastic project and, like a disillusioned cleric, he provides empirical evidence of his own actions and experiences that will allow him to question the very system he embraces. Paradoxically, textual *auctoritas* is deprived of its authority when provided with a verbal defense.

As a result, the conclusion of the fabliau, seeking to reaffirm authority over matters of justice and express disapproval for the peasant soul's behavior, remains ineffectual.

"Noreture vaint mais nature / Fausetés amorce droiture / Tors va avant et drois a orce / Mels valt engiens que ne fait force" [Nurture conquers nature; injustice defeats justice; wrongfulness advances and righteousness is led astray; it is better to be crafty than mighty; vss. 169–72]. This moral seeks to re-establish the conservative spirit of the genre, yet fails to do so. The audience remains caught within a dialectical circle in which the weakness of the emerging scholastic philosophical system is aptly demonstrated, yet no satisfactory reply can be given. If anything, such a fabliau bears witness to the *esprit critique* of the scholastic institution, whose members may have been profoundly aware of the limits of their knowledge as well as of the capacity of the fabliaux as a genre to render intellectual skepticism humorous for the public at large, even *vilains*.

Notes

1. This study privileges use of the Old French *vilain*, a term rich in meaning and defined by Per Nykrog as a medieval social category including peasants, tradesmen, and bourgeois of varying degrees of wealth (127).

2. This form is shared by other fabliaux such as *Le Jugement des cons* (Noomen, IV, 23–33) or *Les Trois Dames qui troverent un vit* (Noomen, VIII, 269–81).

3. Social satire regarding *vilains* is a commonplace in the fabliaux, as is the belief that they are not welcome in heaven. The narrative premise of *Le Pet du vilain* by Rutebeuf depends on this very same commonplace. He provides a moral description of the *vilain* that asserts this belief:

> En paradiz l'esperitable
> Ont grant part la gent cheritable;
> Mais cil qu'en eulz n'ont charitei,
> Ne bien, ne foi, ne loiautei,
> Si ont failli a cele joie :
> Ne ne cuit que ja nuns en joie,
> S'il n'a en lui pitié humainne.
> Ce di je por la gent vilainne
> C'onques n'amerent clerc ne prestre:

>   Si ne cuit pas que Dieux lor preste
>   En paradix ne leu ne place [Noomen, V, 368, vss. 1–11].

[Charitable folks have a large share of celestial paradise, but those who have no charity within, nor goodness, nor peace, nor loyalty, have lost this pleasure. And I don't think that a single one enjoys it if he does not have within himself human pity. I say this for the likes of peasants that never a priest nor clergy member loved. I do not think that God grants them either place or space in Heaven.]

    4. "... the fabliaux are narratives about narration, it is also correct to conclude that, even before that, they are fundamentally language about language" (Lacy 95).

    5. Actual essay title "The Master's Tools Will Never Dismantle the Master's House."

    6. "Experience, though noon auctoritee / Were in this world, is right ynogh for me / To speke of wo that is in mariage" ["Experience, through no worldly authority of my own, gives me the right to speak of the woes of marriage" vss. 1–3]; "The Wife of Bath's Prologue," p. 105.

Works Cited

Chaucer, Geoffrey. *The Riverside Chaucer*, ed. Larry D. Benson. 3rd ed. Boston: Houghton Mifflin Company, 1987.

Lacy, Norris J. *Reading Fabliaux*. 1993; Birmingham, AL: Summa, 1999.

Lorde, Audrey. *Sister Outsider: Essays and Speeches*. Trumansburg, NY: Crossing Press, 1984.

Kohler, Michelle. "Vision, Logic, and the Comic Production of Reality in the *Merchant's Tale* and Two French Fabliaux." *The Chaucer Review*, 39.2 (2004), 137–50.

Montaiglon, Anatole de, and Gaston Raynaud, eds. *Recueil général et complet des fabliaux des XIIIe et XIVe siècles, imprimés ou inédits*. 6 vol. Paris: Librairie des bibliophiles, 1872–1890; rpt. Geneva: Slatkine, 1973.

Nykrog, Per. *Les Fabliaux*. Geneva: Droz, 1973.

Pearcy, Roy J. "Investigations into the Principles of Fabliau Structure." In *Versions of Medieval Comedy*, ed. Paul G. Ruggiers. Norman: University of Oklahoma Press, 1977. 67–100.

Périgot, Béatrice. *Dialectique et littérature: Les Avatars de la dispute entre Moyen Age et Renaissance*. Paris : Honoré Champion, 2005.

Togeby, Knud. "The Nature of the Fabliaux." In *The Humor of the Fabliaux: A Collection of Critical Essays*. Ed. Thomas D. Cooke and Benjamin L. Honeycutt. Columbia: University of Missouri Press, 1974. 7–13.

L'Esquiriel, *or What's in a Tail?*

Caroline Jewers

The squirrel family, *Sciuridae*, derives its name from Greek words meaning "shadow" and "tail," an eminently suitable derivation for my subject: the shadow-casting animal and appendage in *L'Esquiriel*, and further consideration of the critical debate about what this shady tale has in turn to tell us about language and gender.[1] It is a scurrilous fabliau, and the sequence of events will be important to the argument that follows: the adolescent daughter (in one version fourteen, and the other fifteen) of a rich *bourgeoise* from Rouen receives instruction from her mother about how women should behave. Specifically, she should avoid talking too much, and should never say the word that designates a man's penis (*vit*). The daughter is, of course, all agog to know what the word is and, when she has forced her mother to tell her, delights in its frequent repetition, at which her mother goes off weeping in sadness and frustration.

Their conversation has been overheard by a young man by the name of Robin (a rascally *pautoniers* [scoundrel; vs. 71]), who capitalizes on the girl's solitude and advances towards her with his hand down his trousers, engaging in some furtive, yet performative self-gratification. Keen to continue naming names, the girl asks what he has in his hand, and much to his continued pleasure, when he replies that he has a squirrel, she is eager to pet it, at his invitation. He explains that the squirrel was recently somewhat under the weather, and she is glad to note that he is now *toz vis* [quite well; vs. 97]. Continuing her explorations further, she finds two objects he says are eggs in the squirrel's nest, and further learns that the animal has marvellous therapeutic properties and likes nuts. She confesses to having eaten a handful earlier (under the circumstances an ironic "tot plain mon poing" [a full handful; vs. 119]), at which the young man declares that his squirrel will go and hunt for them, telling her he can reach her stomach via her vagina (*con*). Their intercourse takes its expected physical turn, and, with some vigorous attention paid to graphic detail, the young man and squirrel thus reach their vulgar climax: "Mal prist au cuer a l'escuiriel, / Si commence a plorer de l'uel / Et a vonchier et a crachier, / Et puis aprés a moloier" [The squirrel became queasy, and its eye begins to weep, vomit, and spit, and then to grow soft again; vss. 163–66]. But by this time the girl has found a taste for this lewd hide-and-seek and wants the squirrel to come out and play again. It is not to be, and the text ends on a deflatory "[i]l n'en vialt plus" [he no longer wants to; vs. 1183], and Robin departs.

Versions A and B, as compared by Noomen, are very similar, but differ slightly towards the end. In both versions the girl expresses concern that Robin has broken one of his eggs. Version B has her describe this simply as an *outrage* (vs. 174), but the A version includes a distasteful narrative description of the ejaculation that has taken place as the visibly runny *aubun* [albumen; vs. 196] of the egg on the girl's buttocks. The conclusions are also divergent: while the B text cuts off abruptly with "[d]e cest fablel est ce la fins" [that's the end of this fabliau; vs. 184], version A includes a moral peroration that comes too little and too late on the futility of chastening daughters, as any warnings only make it more likely that she will *mal fere* [do evil; vs. 206]. Such a coda seems like a hasty piece of *bricolage*, addressed to a hypothetical figure ("tels cuide bien chastier / Sa fille de dire folie" [he who thinks to admonish his daughter of the dangers of wrongful speech; vs. 202]). This may, of course, refer to a neutral "one"—but given that the only would-be educator in the the text is the girl's mother, although the excessive love of mother and father for the girl is mentioned at the beginning of the tale, the masculine *tels* strikes a slightly discordant note in context. The implication in both versions is that knowledge is a dangerous thing, and that women are insatiable.

There has been some judicious discussion of the evident *jouissance* of this text, which is often associated with a small group of fabliaux that have to do with knowledge or deprivation of language where women are concerned.[2] In considering *L'Esquiriel* Norris Lacy demonstrates the power of metaphor and language, showing how the fabliau uses verbal taboo, the girl's "flawed biology" (83), blatant misdirection, and rhetoric in order to lead the reader from speech act to sex act via the increasingly erotic power of linguistic artifice. He reminds us, as do Muscatine and others, that any consideration of the naming of parts should recall Raison's discussion of *coilles* [testicles] in the *Roman de la rose*, where she famously champions linguistic realism. Lacy states that "...the fabliau both confirms that view and offers an illustration of what happens when one refuses to call a spade a spade — or a *vit* a *vit*" (80). He rightly says that the girl's fascination with saying *vit* is to do with language, rather than any potential eroticism, and the result of the girl's naivety is her fate as a willing participant in her own seduction, with the depiction of graphic sex being all the more violent because of the euphemistic way in which it was set up.

Bloch alludes to the "verbal automatism" of *L'Esquiriel* and other language-based fabliaux, calling it "a play of the signifier divested of referent" (78), seeing this tale, *Porcelet,* and *C'est de la dame* as examples of body- and desire-based fabliaux that have castration anxiety at their core, as evidenced by their metonymic fixation on genitalia. Muscatine refers to *L'Esquiriel* as he marvels at the terms related to male and female sexuality (112–14), finding a positively Rabelaisian variety of invention when it comes to body parts. Ménard links *L'Esquiriel* with *Le Héron, La Pucelle qui vouloit voler,* and *De la demoiselle qui ne pooit oïr parler de foutre* as a grouping that deals specifically with the sexuality of young girls (22), and analyses the "grivoiserie et grossièreté" [licentiousness and crudeness] of sexual language (147–65). He considers Thomas Cooke's argument that certain fabliaux might be considered pornographic, but becomes an apologist for the worst offenders, by saying that scabrous passages are rare and short.[3] Cooke looks at the conventions of pornography and finds some similar traits in the fabliau: in an impersonal setting where erotic desire is always at the fore, we find masculine aggressiveness, a concentration on the phallus, a misogynistic vision of an inferior opposite sex, the conviction that women are to be dominated, that they are always ready to comply with male desire, and there is generally "a mechanistic attitude towards the sex organs" (140). Cooke makes a strong case, but like Ménard, he wants to avoid considering the explicit fabliaux like *L'Esquiriel* as going too far, finding them too good humored, realistic, and joyous to merit condemnation. He also claims that

> These tales characteristically end in a surprise that is so well prepared that the ending, the comic climax, is a deeply satisfying fulfillment. At the moment of the surprise ending, we see the relevance of all that has gone before, and when we see how the surprise balances the preparation, we are struck by the symmetry and harmony of the tale. This is true, I believe, no matter how farcical, crude, or even obscene the story has been [161].

There seems to be general agreement among commentators that "[i]n seduction stories like *La Demoiselle* ... or *L'Esquiriel* no one appears to be victimized" (Pearcy 177). Lacy says of the latter that we misunderstand the girl if we believe she has been tricked: her naivety is a sham, as although she is ignorant of some concepts, she knows what her *con* is.

No advice is given regarding the dangers of unscrupulous youths who inevitably have designs on the virtue of young women, whatever their level of education. I believe *L'Esquiriel* merits revisiting from a more gendered perspective, in order to shed some light on what is, essentially, a pornographic and highly misogynistic tale.[4] This is not to say that men are somehow championed: Robin is less than heroic, and the ending of *L'Esquiriel* leaves him a deflated figure. Loss of masculine desire signals the end of the narrative, and it is unclear whether Robin's inability to perform again is due to satiation or impotence. Whatever the case, the narrative set-up means us to snigger with him, and not at him, at the end. Indeed, *L'Esquiriel* is typical of what Sarah Melhado White states of the fabliaux in general, they are "...zero-sum games in which neither winners nor losers are much to be admired" (189). Even so, the girl is more the victim in this tale: she is, in fact, in a lose-lose situation.

She begins by being circumscribed by over-protective parents: in urging their daughter to speak carefully, and little, they take to heart the instructions of St. Paul, who in his first letter to Timothy states that women should learn in silence and with complete subjection.[5] She should avoid saying anything inappropriate "[c]ar mal puet en atorner / A feme quant en l'ot parler / Autrement que ele ne doit" [for bad things can happen to a woman when someone hears her speak other than they way she ought; vss. 19–21]. Her words are, of course, prophetic — but the lesson of *L'Esquiriel* is that things happen even if one does obey linguistic convention. In avoiding one kind of transgression, the girl finds another. Her fate cannot be ascribed to the fact that she learns what a *vit* is: her fate would have been the same had she continued to hypothesize, as she does to her mother, that it is a loach (vs. 30) or a grebe (A vs. 53, see Levy 65). No mention is made of what the "thing" does: the material point is that whatever the signifier, she cannot grasp the signified — and her lack of figurative grip will lead directly to the literal grasping of the "squirrel" shortly afterwards. The link between ignorance and female sexuality is familiar to twenty-first-century sensibilities in the form of the blonde joke: the blonde's inability to decode the world around her is in direct proportion to her suitability to provide unlimited sexual gratification to a male other. The blonde is put in her promiscuous place by, with, and for male desire. So it is in *L'Esquiriel*. Lacy asks, "...would it not have made far better sense for the mother to withhold the name or, on the contrary, to reveal it only to have the daughter react with revulsion at the word? Had that happened, the use of a euphemism in the seduction attempt would have been justified (in the former case) or essential (in the latter)" (81).

He is right, of course, but seen in a different light the girl's mother is at fault not because she concentrates on language, but because she fails to tell the girl about sex. The girl does not "ask for it": she is told. Had the girl known about the birds and bees, she would certainly not have had such curiosity or naivety about any more literal/metaphoric members of the animal kingdom. The fault lies not with the signifier or imparting it, but in omitting the advice on why this word can be dangerous, and what is signified by it. As Robin observes the conversation from his "leu secroi" [hiding place; vs. 65] his delight comes both from the girl's fascination with the word *vit*, and his realisation that she probably does not know the purpose it serves: she is at her maximum point of curiosity and minimal point of knowledge. The squirrel becomes the means by which she finds out, and it is thematically appropriate that Nature should furnish the means to the end.

The anonymous girl's knowledge of the natural world has already proven more picturesque than accurate when she asks if her father's appendage is a fish or bird, although the act of plunging into water points to more Freudian implications. She is most likely taunting her mother here with calculated absurdity, driven by her frustration: "Mout me poise quant je ne voi, / Par la foi que vos me devez / Ja soit ce qu'il soit deveez!" ["By the faith you owe me, it really bothers me when I can't see why it is that this is prohibited me" vss. 36–38]. The key here is that she wishes to see, to understand, to connect signifier to signified.

In contextualizing this important and hilarious scene, it is important to consider the scopic regime of this fabliau, and what can be seen by whom, and when. The narrator sets the scene for the audience, making them spectators to a private, domestic conversation. It soon becomes apparent that they are not the only voyeurs: Robin is quite literally watching the scene from his hiding place, and becomes aroused by it. This is a Victorian pornographic convention *avant la lettre*: for an instant he and we see the action almost through a key-hole cut-out. He has seen everything: but it is vital to how we interpret the tale to underline the fact that in what follows the girl cannot see the "squirrel," and we should not perhaps assume that she is aware of what she is doing. When Robin presents himself to the girl, we know what he is holding. Consistent with her theme of asking the names of things, she asks Robin what the concealed object is, and he replies with a term already familiar to her. This time, she knows both signifier and signified, but cannot see the animal in question. With the audience complicit in the joke, we know what it is, but she does not: it is kept "desoz ses dras" [under his clothes; vs. 72].

In this light, her desire to take the squirrel upstairs to her bedroom to play with and feed it takes on a different slant: it could be that she is innocent, in fact, and responding quite appropriately under the circumstances! If this fabliau is funny, its comic mechanism is more effective if she is ignorant of what she is touching: this section of the tale functions more like the fabliau of *La Crote,* being essentially a *devinette*, where the central question too is "what am I holding in my hand?" Treating her exploration as a real guessing-game makes the lexical choice all the more hilarious, since all her responses are from touch, and not sight: when she says the squirrel is hot (*chalt*, vs. 93, with all its sexual resonance), he says it was recently ill, making her declaration that it is now *toz vis* (vs. 97) another highly effective double-entendre, as the "squirrel" now starts moving and squirming. And then when we as the audience are most aware of Robin's tumescent masculinity, he dupes the unwitting girl further at the point where "ele avoit la coille sentue" [she had felt his balls; vs. 100, the very centre of the fabliau].[6]

When he tells her that the squirrel has a nest, and she declares there must be at least nine eggs in it, he corrects her by saying that squirrels can only ever have two eggs per month. Her reaction and his response belong to the rhetorical hyperbole that characterizes the way that genitalia are described in the fabliaux as disproportionately large and/or distended. The attention paid to the eggs at this juncture makes the manuscript A attention to the white of the egg at the end of the fabliau the most potent, as it were, of the two readings. Just a part of the joke is that squirrels do not lay eggs (though they do make nests): however, the crucial aspect to this piece of indirection is the implied gender change, since eggs connote the female of any given species. The eggs double the subterfuge, reinforce the sense of masculinity for those "in" on the joke, yet mislead the girl by presenting objects with yet another signifier and signified that do not match. Calling *coilles* eggs takes away their true signification and simultaneously neutralizes sexual threat, rendering them harmless. Similarly, the nuts the girl has eaten point more to masculinity than femininity, such that there is a sort of chiastic doubling of referents and mixing of sexually charged metaphors.[7]

There is something feminine about the squirrel too, perhaps because small rodents are mostly associated with the female pudenda. Such is the case in *La Sorisete des estopes*, for example, or in the ubiquitous image of the *connin* [rabbit] that stands for the *con*.[8]

The audience misses nothing in *L'Esquiriel*, and the girl misses seemingly everything: but the text is not done with her comic humiliation. It is also significant that the girl asks of the squirrel "[a] il nule mecine?" ["Has it any healing properties?" vs. 110], to which Robin replies it can cure wounds, women, and bladder dysfunctions. The degree to which it was thought squirrels could do this is impossible to confirm, but there are perhaps other inferences in the generic *noiz* preferred by them as food, and the *Tacuinum sanitatis* allows us to speculate that perhaps there may be some playful hidden meanings. Arano's account of the manuscript tradition tells us about the properties of some of the extended nut family: hearty, nourishing chestnuts are said to exert "an influence over coitus" (pl. V) and encourage it, despite being hard to digest, while acorns are said to prevent menstruation (p. XV).[9] In a similar vein, pine cones are said to stimulate the bladder, kidneys, and libido (pl. XXVII), thus continuing the connection between nut consumption and the *bas corporel*.

Petting the squirrel is thus promoted through transference as some kind of sexual healing, adding to the inherent comedy of the scene.

While the modest and appealing squirrel does not attract the same attention in art or bestiaries as other animals, it does have suitable emblematic properties for its eponymous fabliau.[10] Squirrels appear with some frequency in the margins of manuscripts. Herbert Friedmann notes that "...the squirrel was often considered, and frequently shown, as a creature habitually gnawing on an acorn or other nut, and that the nut, as first described by Adam of Saint Victor, was an image of Christ, the kernel within it standing for His hidden divinity, the squirrel almost automatically becomes a 'seeker after divinity'" (297).[11] Less sacred symbolism is apparent too, as Michael Camille notes of the Luttrell Psalter, where the bas-de-page of folio 33r shows a woman playing with a squirrel, evidently inviting it to run up her skirt (Camille, *Mirror in Parchment*, 299). Camille draws a useful parallel between this image and *L'Esquiriel*, and he also gives the example of a charming fifteenth-century ring bearing the image of a leashed squirrel on the inside, with the legend on the outside "une fame nominative a fait de moy son datiff par la parole genitive en depit de l'accusatif" with the words "mon amour est infinitive ge veu estre son relatif" on the inside ("A nominative lady has made her dative of me by the genitive word, in spite of the accusative ... my love is infinitive, and I want to be her relative," Camille, *Art of Love*, 103–04), speculating that this tamed squirrel, with its fondness for inflection and conjugation, might also double for the kind of pet we find in the fabliau. As well as for their industry, nimbleness, and inventiveness, the tameableness of squirrels may be important for interpreting *L'Esquiriel*.

There is also perhaps a literary analogy to be found in Guillaume de Blois's *Alda* (composed in the late 1160s), a comedy cited with reference to *Trubert* because of the shared elements of disguise (Gravdal 132, for example), or *La Demoiselle* because of Alda's simplicity in sexual matters (Brusegan 21). Alda is the daughter of a doting father who tries to protect her from the dangers of the world, only to have her seduced by Pyrrhus, who disguises himself as his sister, who is Alda's best friend. Alda believes she is kissing a woman, but is being seduced by a man without her knowing. Like the girl, she is unaware what the swelling member she can feel is: "Quid sit et unde, refer, tumor inguinis ille rigentis / Caudaque nescio que sic operosa tibi!" ["Where does it come from, tell me, that hard swelling rising up from your groin, that ... sort of tail that you work so hard?" vss. 485–86].[12] Pyrrhus explains that it is a tail that he bought in the market, where many were for sale of all sizes and prices. He bought a small one, as it was all he could afford, and declares that because of its size, it worked all the harder. The zoomorphic description he gives of the *cauda*'s activities is rather like the description of the squirrel's herculean labors. The animal is first proud, then ready for battle, then sweaty and exhausted, then shrinks and becomes withdrawn (vss. 501–16). As a result of spending a week with Pyrrhus, Alda becomes pregnant and marries him, and the coda tells us that it is useless for men to try and rule flighty women with wise counsel, and try and keep them from the vices that are inherent in them. Even leaving them in female company is unlikely to guarantee their safety. The use of the tail, the graphic description of the blows it gives, and the misogynistic lesson, are reminiscent, I think, of *L'Esquiriel*.

As the seduction scene unfolds, it is important to underline the fact that in scopic terms the girl still cannot see the "squirrel." Robin throws her down [Si l'a gitee tote enverse; vs. 133], and then pulls up her clothes. From this point, the action is in close-up, with the emphasis on his physical movement, balanced by the counterpoint of her verbal encouragement. The rhyme words, with their metaphorical references to hunting and eating, say it all: *trover, cerchier, mengier, cherchiez plus parfont, la o les noiz sont* (vss. 144–48), and here again, the comic mechanism is undoubtedly more effective if the audience sees the disjunction between what he does, and what she thinks she is doing. Like Alda, who calls the travestied Pyrrhus her *magistra* in love, the girl wants the lesson to go on, in spite of a momentary concern for the broken egg. Does the girl know by this time that something other than nut-hunting is going on? Maybe, but probably not until the very end, but even then it is not certain since the squirrel has disappeared, and she can register nothing beyond her own pleasure. There is a better than even chance she remains in ignorance. In version B, as soon as the girl wants more, Robin "n'i avoit que fere plus" [He had nothing more to do there; vs. 176], and the squirrel is no longer hungry, while in version A, before we get the moralizing ending, he is said to simply go off happily as he has done well [na mie failli a bien fere; vs. 200]. Has the squirrel been tamed? Do his interest and ardor wane because he is now put in the position of being pet or servant, rather than master, like the lovers in *Porcelet* and *La Dame qui aveine demandoit pour Morel*? Has he become impotent, as they do? Or simply taken his own pleasure, with scant regard to hers? What does this ending have to tell us about this tale and general traits in the fabliau?

One thing it tells us is that *L'Esquiriel* is not only about language, but also about registral clash, and scatological display — not that this was ever in doubt. One could almost call the girl courtly, and Robin *anticourtois* in behavior, although not in name (while it suggests a rougher social class than hers, we know that he is a prior's nephew). While there is anti-courtliness inherent in this seduction, which, with its opposing poles of high *éducation sentimentale* and low comedy, is reminiscent of characters like Perceval as they move from maternal wisdom to knowledge of the world through experience, the fabliau seems to tap into that other spirit, which is that of the bas-de-page, the misericord, and other totemic reflections of popular culture, where such physical display seems consistent and widespread. Mellinkoff and Randall give plenty of examples of manuscripts and buildings featuring various forms of sexual exhibitionism. Texts range from philosophical tracts and legal texts to romances, psalters, and books of hours, and to this we could add the astounding number of pilgrim badges featuring oversized and distorted genitalia, both male and female (Melinkoff, I, 141–45; McDonald 2–16), that supposedly offered fertility, prosperity, and luck to their holders. Whether the cultural display of such objects renders the erotic fabliaux less shocking is debatable, but there is certainly a link in terms of their iconography and subversive humor. Looking at how the narrative unfolds, from initial conversation, to graphic close-up shots, it is clear that this tale is about something other than language: it is about the display of masculinity, about sexual power that excludes women, as well as the hegemony of language, and the signifiers and signifieds comically conspire to celebrate, and comically undermine a myth, that of the phallus. The girl as passive recipient may take pleasure in the squirrel, but she is taken advantage of along the way, and only her conventional compliance keeps the seduction from being a rape. The tale of *L'Esquiriel* is undoubtedly about the nature of nature too: mediated through the animal world, it all comes down to Nature hammering at her forge. As far as language goes, function follows form, and the result is that knowing the words is not enough, with the text conspiring to keep important signifiers and signifieds apart, so that comedy can emerge from the ironic distance between the two. Whether she calls it a spade or a *vit*, the girl's ignorance of Mother Nature, combined with the masculinist gaze and rhetoric of the fabliau, can only lead to a protracted misogynistic farce. On a final note, what should we make of Cooke's conclusion that the fabliaux are not pornographic, but well-prepared, and their climactic endings deeply satisfying, surprising, and harmonious? In this case, perhaps Robin is the only one to claim the tale's plenitude, and as is often the case, one cannot overestimate the formulaic, predictable perorations to these funny, uproarious, and scandalous poems that end with both a bang and a whimper.

Notes

1. From the late Latin *scūriolus*, from *sciūrus*, derived from Greek ὀχίουρος, ὀχιά and οὐρά respectively. *L'Esquiriel* appears in Noomen, VI, 33–49, with notes on pp. 319–22.

2. Principally *Porcelet* (Noomen, VI, 185–91), *De la dame qui aveine demandoit pour Morel sa provende avoir* (Noomen, IX, 183–99), and *De la demoiselle qui ne pooit oïr parler de foutre* (Noomen, IV, 57–89).

3. "Mais ces passages choquants ne sont pas légion: une douzaine tout au plus. De surcroît, compte tenu de la brièveté des fabliaux ils n'emplissent pas des pages. Ils se limitent à quelques vers" (163).

4. Among those who redress the critical balance in regard to gender are Simon Gaunt, who says that "[s]ome fabliaux seem to tread a fine and ambiguous line between a misogynistic view of women as insatiable, and a less than complimentary portrayal of the virility of the men they encounter" (271). Lesley Johnson finds that in spite of their portrayal, women are "on top" in many fabliaux, thanks to their "cunning and high-spirits" (307).

5. Ch. 2, vss. 11–14:

> Mulier in silention discat cum omni subiectione
> docere autem mulieri non permitto neque dominari in virum sed
>   esse in silentio.
> Adam enim primus formatus est deinde Eva
> et Adam non est seductus mulier autem seducta in praevaricatione
>   fuit.

> [Let a woman learn in silence and with all subjection. But I do not permit a woman to teach, nor to dominate a man, but to be in silence. For man was formed first, and then Eve. And Adam was not seduced, but the seduced woman was in transgression.]

6. Noomen is quite right to privilege *sentue* over the *A* text, which gives *veue* (vs. 121), for all the reasons cited above.

7. The *D* text of *La Demoiselle qui ne pooit oïr de foutre* (Noomen, IV, 59–89) has another strange example of the same phenomenon, when the girl says of her own breasts "[c]e sont les coilles de mouton" [... they are sheep's testicles; vs. 147].

8. Noomen, VI, 173–83. In the case of *Porcelet* and *La Dame qui aveine demandoit pour Morel* women are associated with animals we might more readily associate with men, as they are the aggressors. Both the pig and black horse prove demanding and sexually aggressive, and are misogynistically rewarded by their lovers, Froment and Aveine respectively. When women become vocal about their demands, they are rewarded in the same flatulent way. There is also, of course, the "poulains" [colt] of *La Demoiselle* (vs. 61). Highlighting the playful and symbolic potential of animals, Guilhem IX's poem *Farai un vers qu'er covinen* (P-C 183,3) features the dilemma of a male speaker who has two horses (thinly veiled mistresses) he can saddle, but can only keep one, while the famous cat poem, *Farai un vers, pos mi sonelh* (P-C 183, 4) features an animal intermediary who suggests both chatte and aggressive tomcat.

9. Chestnuts are also reputed to cause headaches, which might explain why the girl exclaims "[s]e Dieus me garisse la teste / Mout a en vos soueve beste!' ["May God cure my head, he has a sweet beast in you!"]. vss. 149–50].

10. On the presence of lesser, but familiar animals in bestiaries: "Quant aux animaux de la faune occidentale, ils sont très inégalement representés. Certaines bêtes — et en particulier certaines bêtes sauvages pourtant encore nombreuses dans les forêts de l'Occident médiéval au XIIIe siècle — n'aparaissent que de manière épisodique ou pas du tout. C'est le cas, par exemple, du sanglier, de l'ours, du cerf ou du blaireau, mais également du lapin et de l'écureuil qui sont complètement ignorés" (Berlioz and Polo de Beaulieu 182).

11. As, for example, in *The Hours* of Mary of Burgundy, fol. 60v, where a bas-de-page squirrel eats an acorn, while in the top line of text we read "Benedicta tu in mulieribus et benedictus fructus ventris tui" [Blessed are you among women, and blessed the fruit of your womb]. A more secular tamed squirrel appears in a roundel with a trained ape in the Lansdowne Psalter 420, fol. 12v in Mellinkoff, II, p. 118. Squirrels also frequently appear in heraldry, and can signify retreat to the peace and quiet of the countryside, as well as ease and wealth.

12. Translated by Elliott (121).

Works Cited

Arano, Luisa Cogliati. *The Medieval Health Book: Tacuinum Sanitatis*. New York: George Braziller, 1976.

Bédier, Joseph. *Les Fabliaux: Etudes de littérature populaire et d'histoire littéraire du Moyen Age*. 1893; Paris: Champion, 1964.

Berlioz, Jacques, and Marie Anne Polo de Beaulieu. *L'Animal exemplaire au Moyen Age, Ve-XVe siècles*. Rennes: Presses Universitaires de Rennes, 1999.

Bloch, R. Howard. *The Scandal of the Fabliaux*. Chicago: University of Chicago Press, 1986.

Brusegan, Rosanna. "La Naïveté comique dans les fabliaux à séduction." In Danielle Buschinger and André Crépini, eds. *Comique, satire et parodie dans la tradition renardienne et les fabliaux: Actes du colloque des 15 et 16 janvier 1983*. Göppingen: Kümmerle, 1983. 19–30.

L'Esquiriel, *or What's in a Tail?* (Jewers)

Camille, Michael. *The Medieval Art of Love: Objects and Subjects of Desire.* New York: Harry N. Abrams, 1998.

———. *Mirror in Parchment: The Luttrell Psalter and the Making of Medieval England.* Chicago: University of Chicago Press, 1998.

Cohen, Gustave, ed. *La "Comédie" latine en France au XIIe siècle.* Paris: Les Belles Lettres, 1931.

Cooke, Thomas D. "Pornography, the Comic Spirit, and the Fabliaux." In Cooke and Honeycutt. eds. *The Humor of the Fabliaux.* Columbia: University of Missouri Press, 1974. 137–62.

———, and Benjamin L. Honeycutt, eds. *The Humor of the Fabliaux.* Columbia: University of Missouri Press, 1974.

Elliott, Alison Goddard, trans. *Seven Medieval Latin Comedies.* New York: Garland, 1984.

Fischer, Bonifatius, and Robert Weber. *Biblia sacra: iuxta Vulgatam versionem.* Stuttgart: Württembergische Bibelanstalt, 1969.

Friedmann, Herbert. *A Bestiary for Saint Jerome: Animal Symbolism in European Religious Art.* Washington, DC: Smithsonian Institution Press, 1980.

Gaunt, Simon. *Gender and Genre in Medieval French Literature.* Cambridge: Cambridge University Press, 1995.

Gravdal, Kathryn. *Vilain and Courtois: Transgressive Parody in French Literature of the Twelfth and Thirteenth Centuries.* Lincoln: University of Nebraska Press, 1989.

Inglis, Eric, ed. *The Hours of Mary of Burgundy: Codex Vindobonensis 1857, Vienna, Österreichische Nationalbibliothek.* London: Harvey Miller, 1995.

Johnson, Lesley. "Women on Top: Antifeminism in the Fabliaux." *Modern Language Review*, 78.2 (1983), 298–307.

Lacy, Norris J. *Reading Fabliaux*, esp. ch. VI. 1993; Birmingham, AL: Summa, 1999.

Levy, Brian J. *The Comic Text: Patterns and Images in the Old French Fabliaux.* Amsterdam: Rodopi, 2000.

McDonald, Nicola, ed. *Medieval Obscenities.* York: York Medieval Press, 2006.

Mellinkoff, Ruth. *Averting Demons: The Protective Power of Medieval Visual Motifs and Themes.* 2 vols. Los Angeles: Ruth Mellinkoff Publications, 2004.

Ménard, Philippe. *Les Fabliaux: Contes à rire du Moyen Age.* Paris: Presses Universitaires de France, 1983.

Muscatine, Charles. *The Old French Fabliaux.* New Haven: Yale University Press, 1986.

———. "Courtly Literature and Vulgar Language." In Glyn S. Burgess, ed. *Court and Poet: Selected Proceedings of the Third Congress of the International Courtly Literature Society (Liverpool 1980).* Liverpool: F. Cairns, 1981. 1–19.

Nykrog, Per. *Les Fabliaux: Etude d'histoire littéraire et de stylistique médiévale.* 1957; Geneva: Droz, 1973.

Pearcy, Roy. "Modes of Signification and the Humor of Obscene Diction in the Fabliaux." In Cooke and Honeycutt, eds. *The Humor of the Fabliaux.* Columbia: University of Missouri Press, 1974. 163–96.

Randall, Lilian M.C. *Images in the Margins of Gothic Manuscripts.* Berkeley: University of California Press, 1966.

White, Sarah Melhado. "Sexual Language and Human Conflict in Old French Fabliaux." *Comparative Studies in Society and History*, 24.2 (April 1982), 185–210.

Trickery, Trubertage, and the Limits of Laughter

NORRIS J. LACY

The thirteenth-century *Trubert* (Noomen, X, 143–262), by one Douin de Lavesne, is almost 3000 lines long. It is not often studied — perhaps not even often read — and when it is, the discussion almost invariably involves either the parodic character of the story or the question of genre. I confess that I do not see the work as parody, certainly not in the sense that *Aucassin et Nicolette* may parody idyllic or courtly romance, nor in the way a text such as *Audigier* is an obscene send-up of Old French epic conventions. The genre question is similarly vexed, though discussions of it may be even less productive: the usual question is whether a text this long and narratively complex can be classified as a fabliau. That will not concern us here; suffice it to say that I see no persuasive reason to exclude it from the fabliau corpus, and those who do so apparently base their decision on a prefabricated definition that prescribes brevity.[1]

But narratively complex it undeniably is. *Trubert* elaborates an astonishing number of themes, extending from cross-dressing to torture and murder, and including serial sex, deception, disguise, exhibitionism, cuckoldry, blackmail, debauchery, sadism, accusations of rape, gratuitous violence, mutilation of a corpse, and — by no means least, as we shall see — flatulence. Moreover, the presentation varies widely from episode to episode, ranging from the absurdly silly to the outrageously vicious. Whether the work is funny or not is naturally a matter of personal taste and reaction, and I confess that for me it falls somewhere short of hilarity;

but in any event, the violent vacillation of tones, textures, languages, and acts holds the key to the appeal of the text.

First, we must acknowledge that, however complex and diverse, even shapeless, the text may initially appear, it is in fact carefully structured, with episodes nicely organized into three broad sections, the second of which is itself divided into three parts, as follows:

Part I: Trubert, a simpleton ('*fou*' or '*sot*'), succeeds, whether through dumb luck or shrewdness, in making money in several business deals in which we might expect him to lose.

Part II: Trubert — first for money, then for fun — deceives a duke by impersonating a carpenter, then a physician, then a knight. Thereby he enriches himself, cuckolds the duke, and brutally beats him more than once.

Part III: To escape punishment, Trubert dresses as a woman and is taken into the service of the duke. He impregnates the duke's daughter, is married off to another man (Golias), and evades the consummation of the marriage by inflicting pain on the "husband."

Because the text is not well known, even to some fabliau scholars, analysis must follow from a considerably more extended indication of its content than is given by the preceding skeletal summary. The beginning section of the work is an elaboration of the common folktale type known as "The Youth Cheated Selling Oxen." Trubert, setting out to acquire money for his family, quickly exhibits his naiveté and lack of worldly experience when he sees a painted crucifix and is scandalized at what he assumes is the desecration of an actual corpse. However, this experience inspires him soon to buy a goat and pay to have it painted. This puzzling action seems to confirm his simplicity: he is apparently wasting some of his small sum of money merely because the idea of a painted body — whether of a savior or a goat — appeals to him, for no other reason, so far as we know, than that it is striking and pretty. Perhaps even at this point, though, we may suspect that he is more capable than he appears, a suspicion that is confirmed when he offers to sell the beautiful goat to a duchess for a bit of money and sexual gratification (specifically, five sous and a *foutre*—a nominal use of the verb: "a fuck"). Initially and understandably shocked, she eventually agrees: this is obviously an extremely appealing goat![2] However, after sleeping with her, Trubert refuses to leave when her servant announces the arrival of the duke. The duchess must bribe the young man to leave (further enriching him), after which he meets the duke and offers to sell the goat to him for five *sous* and, nonsensically, four hairs to be plucked from the duke's posterior (*poils du cul*). Obviously as impressed by the goat as the duchess had been, the duke eventually albeit reluctantly accepts the deal. When it is time to pluck the first hair, Trubert instead stabs the duke's rear with a stiletto or dagger (a *poinçon*), and to spare himself further pain, the duke pays him one hundred *sous*. Trubert returns home a much less poor man.

These events, remarkably, constitute only about 425 lines of the 3000 total. Yet, even at this point, the composition offers sufficient narrative closure to let it stand, had the author been inclined to do so, as a complete and finished fabliau. It resembles fabliaux such as the *Bouchier d'Abeville*, involving multiple acts of vengeance for an insult (Noomen, III, 237–335). In the *Bouchier*—to my mind one of the best of fabliaux—the butcher, rudely denied lodging by a rich priest, steals one of the priest's sheep and trades it to him for a night's lodging. They slaughter the sheep and share a feast. That night, by promising the sheepskin in turn to the priest's mistress and to his servant, he sleeps with each of them before selling the skin, the following morning, to the priest himself. The priest has thus lost a sheep, provided the hospitality he had first refused, furnished a rich repast, and then paid for the skin of his own sheep after his mistress and servant have slept with his guest. Revenge is richly taken; justice prevails and is further underlined when both his mistress and his servant claim the sheepskin.

Trubert too offers a sequence of deceptions, but there is a major difference between the two stories: the duke, unlike the irascible priest of the *Bouchier d'Abeville*, has done nothing to merit the pain inflicted on him; he has in fact treated Trubert well (as, indeed, had the duchess!). This will remain the case throughout: the physical violence is entirely gratuitous. In fact, the protagonist evinces, on several occasions, a gift for deception joined to a taste for unprovoked violence. Lacking a term to designate this curious combination, let us conveniently call it "trubertage" or, in French, *le trubertage* (modeled on *le pathelinage*, long a standard word in French).[3]

In any case, Trubert is just getting started. In the second large division of the work, he decides to visit the duke again to acquire more money. As noted, he assumes several consecutive roles: first as a master carpenter, then as a physician, finally as a knight. In the first of these, the duke engages Trubert's service to build a beautiful house, and the young man is given fine clothes and an opportunity to share a veritable feast with the duke, duchess, and their servant, Aude. Obviously, a great feast deserves a great fart, at least in the fabliau world if not indeed in our own; accordingly, Trubert "lesse un grant pet aler" [lets go a huge fart; vs. 524] and blames Aude for it. Since the narrator seems to linger over this episode and its preparation, it is worth asking whether the fart is, as it were, anything more than hot air. I shall return to that question in a moment.

Later that night Trubert surprisingly takes offense at being given a soft, comfortable bed — the kind to which he is not accustomed. However flimsy the excuse — and few excuses are too flimsy to incite a bout of *trubertage*— revenge is in order. He begins by presenting himself to the duchess, telling her (in the dark, of course) that he is the duke and repeatedly enjoying some very flagrant delight. Later, the duke finds himself in the mood for love (apparently an unusual event) and comes to the duchess's room. Postcoitally, she remarks that he has not been this good for a very long time (vs. 653), marveling that he can perform fourteen times in a single night. Oddly, his reaction to this observation is not recorded.

The next day, Trubert and the duke go into the forest; by tricking the duke, the young man ties him to a tree, beats him severely, and then identifies himself as the one who sold him the goat, cuckolded him thirteen times, stabbed him in the ass, and farted. Then he takes the duke's horse, later sells it, and then returns again to his (no doubt proud) mother.

What is most fascinating here is the lack of discrimination among his acts: cuckolding, stabbing, beating, and farting are all presented as equally offensive events or — depending on one's point of view — as morally neutral events or even as actions equally worthy of celebration.

When the duke is rescued, he obviously requires medical attention, and by a stroke of luck, the good Dr. Trubert happens to be in the vicinity (vss. 1062ff.). He brings a wonderful and very fragrant "ointment" with which he covers the duke's entire body. This miracle cure is actually dog droppings, *un estron de chien* (vs. 1088), that he had luckily found on the ground. After this pungent treatment, Trubert again ties him up and beats him, adding injury to insult, after which he again identifies himself (vs. 1314) and leaves. Notable in this episode, as in the preceding one, is the leveling effect that seems to imply an equation between punishments that we would ordinarily consider to be of entirely different orders. That is, nothing in the text or in narrative commentary suggests that physical brutality is any more — or less — serious an offense than is the application of dog shit to the duke's body.

The result, to my mind, is neither to inflate the gravity of the ointment scene nor to deflate that of physical punishment. Rather, if we can resist coloring our reading by our sensitivity to torture, the effect is rather to efface any moral or physical scale of punishment and suffering. Beatings and the mutilation of a corpse (see below) are on a narrative and moral par with farts and feces. The reader begins to consider that what happens to the duke is very nearly irrelevant, despite the fact, again, that the duke has done nothing to merit punishment: Trubert is a trickster out of control, intent only on exercising his natural but new-found talent for deception. He profits richly — and literally — from his tricks, but after the first time or two, there is no longer any indication that acquisitiveness is his goal. Instead, he deceives, copulates, punishes, and farts merely because he can and wants to.[4]

Incidentally, a bare plot summary might lead us to see this as something of a class war, with the poverty-stricken young man pitted against nobility in a contest that demonstrates Trubert's inventiveness, mental agility, and predictable victory. In fact, Kathryn Gravdal does speak of the "transgressive use of the vilain and courtois opposition,"[5] and she points out that Trubert switches between "two mimetic spaces" and "juxtaposes two languages (one vilain, the other courtois) ..." (119). However, if this story is at all about class conflicts, it is only incidentally so. Rather, the duke is originally the "mark" because he has the money that Trubert wants; later on, the young man continues to make money, but he seems less interested in the profit than in the joy of roguish behavior: the exercise of his skill in separating the duke from his cash and, in the process, inflicting pain.

His next trick occurs when the duke's men are searching for him to extract revenge; Trubert changes clothes with the duke's nephew, who is consequently mistaken for Trubert and promptly hanged (vs. 1645). No matter: this death appears to be a grave event only in the most literal sense: it is recounted routinely and quickly as just another price the duke must pay (for nothing!), and the narrator quickly moves on. Next, presenting himself as a courageous fighter named Hautdecuer (something of a medieval "Brave Heart," vs. 1761), Trubert proclaims himself more valiant than Roland (vs. 1761) and agrees to battle the latter's enemy, Golias. Before setting off for battle, he attends Mass, praying to the Virgin to let him return safe and sound, *wealthy*, and unrecognized (vss. 1783–88).

Soon, in the most shocking display of gratuitous violence (or rather of *trubertage*, since it also supplies the material for yet another deception of the duke), the new knight kills a passing woman, cuts out her private parts — specifically, the line says, with lilting rhyrhm, "Le cul et le con li coupa" [he cuts out her anus and cunt; vs. 1922] — and presents the trophy to the duke, identifying it as Golias's (bearded?) mouth and nostrils. Readers have to suspend a good deal of disbelief here, but the duke does not: he sees nothing amiss. In fact, he examines the gift and comments, "Par foi, je croi bien ... / Einsi faite bouche avoit il" [roughly, "Yes, that does look like his mouth," vss. 1965–66]. We may or may not find the absurdity and the violence amusing, but if we have retained the first part of the story in our mind, we must be struck by the contrast between this casual violence and Trubert's initial outrage at the crucifix, when he thought it was a painted human cadaver.

A great deal has already happened in this text, but only now have we made it to the two-thirds point in the work. As we begin the third section of the fabliau, the duke promises his daughter to the valiant knight — Trubert or Sir Hautdecoeur — who has apparently defeated his enemy. But he is chagrined, to say the least, to learn before long that Golias is still alive, that his own nephew has been hanged (by his own men), and that Trubert, once again, is responsible for it all. He consequently betroths his daughter to his former enemy and comes looking for Trubert, bent on revenge. (Significantly, this passage — vss. 2222ff. — represents the only time that the duke determines to take action, and it is the only event that might even remotely justify Trubert's cruel trickery; yet, the most shocking episodes of violence have already occurred.)

To evade capture, the young man assumes female attire, posing as his own sister (vs. 2374), whereupon he is promptly taken into the duke's household to serve his daughter. The charming new servant gives his/her name as Coillebaude (vs. 2399)—"coille" meaning testicles and "baude" meaning happy, bold, impudent, shameless, etc. (Gravdal translates Coillebaude as "Gayballs" [123]). Everyone enjoys a good laugh at this name, and it is suggested that it be used only in private whereas in public he/she should be called Florie.

So Trubert/Coillebaude/Florie is expected to serve the duke's daughter—and serve her he does. There follows an analogue of fabliaux such as *L'Esquiriel* (Noomen, VI, 33–49) and others that use euphemisms for sex organs to produce a predictable erotic result. In this case, while in bed with Coillebaude, the daughter asks the identity of that rampant object against her thigh. Trubert replies that it is a bunny—"petiz, mes molt est biaus" ["small but very beautiful"; vss. 2482–83]—a bunny that lives in Coillebaude's vagina. We cannot doubt that the daughter will invite it to visit hers, and she promptly does so: no subtle surprises here. I have previously argued that such references in fabliaux more often imply the woman's complicity than her gullibility (Lacy 78–90). That is doubtless the case here, but in any event the visit takes place, and the rabbit proves, then and on future occasions, to be both obliging and energetic. And as it turns out, it breeds like a rabbit, soon producing a pregnancy that the duke and duchess resolve by arranging the marriage of Golias to Trubert (still in drag) rather than to their daughter.[6]

On the trip to Golias's home, Trubert, for no apparent reason, displays his genitals to a shocked chaplain (vs. 2687), and when the latter reveals this scandal to Golias, Trubert accuses the chaplain of trying to seduce him (her). Believing his betrothed, Golias kills the chaplain, and the trip continues. There can be no explanation for Trubert's exhibitionism, beyond the fact that he knows that he can get away with it. And indeed he does.

When Golias first takes Trubert—"sa fame qui n'a pas con" [his wife who has no cunt; vs. 2786]—to bed (in the dark, obviously), the young man (woman) has concealed a purse between his legs.[7] Upon penetration—of the purse—by Golias, Trubert yanks so hard on the purse's drawstrings that her/his husband passes out from pain. Reviving, he comments that, as painful as that was for him, it must have been terrible for his bride. Trubert agrees. And finally, going out to relieve himself (*por pissier*, vs.

2869), Trubert stops by the bed of a servant, deflowers her, then sends her to the nuptial bed, where Golias, none the wiser, happily promises to make her queen. And suddenly the text breaks off. There is no moral; there is no indication of what Trubert did next, there is no suggestion that the duke continued to seek his tormentor. It just ends.

In studying and teaching this text, and in discussing it at a professional conference, I have noted that this is a fabliau in which, curiously, a summary may be more amusing than a reading of the actual text. My impression is that humorous effect is diffused by the work's length (2978 lines) and its narrative complexity, involving two familiar fabliau motifs — in the first and third parts — separated by a middle section composed of three disguise and torture scenes that are appealing in their symmetry but only modestly amusing in their content.[8]

Oddly, there is a quite slow build-up, with a fair amount of detail and texture, when the narrator is describing Trubert's initial deceptions and his later feasting, farting, and sex, and also, to an extent, when the duke is being deceived or beaten. But the text deals very briefly and casually with death (of the nephew, of the mutilated woman, of the chaplain). Thus, for example, the narrator uses 126 lines (vss. 487–612) to describe the dinner, the fart, the comfortable bed, and Trubert's decision to visit the duchess. Just the feast and the fart require forty-seven lines. Yet, when Trubert later sees a woman approaching, asks her to help him mount his horse, kills her, and mutilates the corpse, all of that is recounted in a mere eight lines.

I do not believe we can explain this modulation of tempo as an aversion to violence: the work abounds in that, and the narrator apparently delights in it. Instead, this seems to be a matter of focus, keeping emphasis on Trubert the trickster and on his victim, the duke. Kill a woman and cut up her corpse? Fine: the means is justified by the end (the literal end in this case), provided it is for a worthy cause, which is to play a good joke on the duke. The nephew's death is also a cruel blow to the duke. However, the chaplain's death, when he reports Trubert's exhibitionism, seems unmotivated and without consequence. It appears to be a death provoked by nothing other than Trubert's taste for violence combined with deceit, and by his confidence that he can escape with impunity from any situation.

The story also modifies its tone and texture repeatedly, often by shifts of register (e.g., selling the goat for five sous and a *foutre* but later resorting to euphemism to accomplish a seduction). Moreover, scenes of sometimes brutal realism (torture, punishment, murder) alternate with those of playfulness and fantasy. The latter include Trubert's disguises, dog droppings as medical miracle, the name Coillebaude, a very odd explanation for the daughter's pregnancy, etc.—all in the category of the far-fetched and fanciful, but all quite effective against the duke, who, obviously, is the ideal—which is to say, the easiest—mark. In fact, he is repeatedly victimized simply because he is available; Trubert does it simply because he can.

The work appears designed to produce admiration of Trubert's skill and ingenuity, and a certain amusement born of a peculiar brand of predictability; that is, the astonishing variety of ways in which Trubert can arrive at an entirely foreseeable result. And by now readers will surely have thought of Trubert's nearest relative, Renart (from the popular medieval *Roman de Renart*), with the duke in the role of Isengrin. It is in principle an infinitely extendible series of deceptions and punishments, and it needs to be noted, in fact, that at the end Trubert is free and absent and theoretically at liberty to resume tormenting the duke.

The duke is not only a good victim but also a good man, and the narrator, oddly, takes some pains to emphasize his goodness, fairness, and generosity. We should note again that the only act for which he might merit the slightest punishment (in a highly perverted system of judgment) is his offering Trubert a bed that was too comfortable. Otherwise, as the duke correctly says, "...je ne li ai riens forfet" ["I never did him any harm" vs. 2340].[9] If the author's intent was to elicit laughter, we might easily consider this emphasis on the duke's decency to be a narrative miscalculation. Some readers will not remain entirely indifferent to the pain and humiliation of a character depicted as generous and fair, and in those conditions, laughter is not easily generated.

I would argue, in fact, that this fabliau author does far less than most others to regulate reader response. In *Le Bouchier d'Abeville* and most other "revenge fabliaux," the narrator presents the victim as old, jealous, avaricious, or cruel, thereby preventing the generation of sympathy or pity. That does not occur in *Trubert*, and depending on our (perhaps subjective) degree of disengagement, we may delight in Trubert's tricks, condemn his unprovoked cruelty, or find ourselves poised ambivalently between the two reactions. It is that aspect of the work, and not its length, that is to my mind the most distinctive and significant feature of this fabliau.

In any event, this is not an account of justice exacted or appropriate revenge taken (as in many fabliaux, such as the *Borgoise d'Orliens* [Noomen, III, 337–74], in which a suspicious or cruel husband is punished). It is instead revenge for a *non*-offense, and as such it is not an entirely typical representative of its genre. It is an open-ended sequence of ruses crafted to demonstrate the virtuosity of Trubert, that of the narrator as well, and no doubt, too, the incorrigibly trusting nature of the duke, who remains irremediably dense and just as naïve as the hero had initially shown himself to be. From this vantage point, we can appreciate the work's accomplishments even if it fails to elicit laughter. It is, ultimately, a remarkably proficient demonstration of *trubertage*. And we can put down the text in full confidence that, were the story to continue, the duke would again be well and truly "truberted."

Notes

1. For example, Mary Jane Stearns Schenck simply says that the work's "length should set it outside the limits of a genre defined as a short narrative" (62).

2. More precisely, she either considers the goat appealing or begins to become interested in dalliance with Trubert. The latter explanation would be entirely unsurprising in a fabliau, and it is tempting here, but we lack textual support for it.

3. Obviously, *le pathelinage*, that is, the gift for deception demonstrated by the protagonist of the farce *Maistre Pathelin*, entered the language because of the broad familiarity of that work. Yet the eponym *le trubertage*, which, to the best of my knowledge, does not—or until now did not—exist, is at least as specific and complex as, and decidedly more distinctive than, *le pathelinage*.

4. By this time in the text, he is rarely described as *sot* or *fou*—and of course he no longer is that (though the formula recurs in vs. 1755). Curiously, though, even from an early point in the text—the first occurrence is at vs. 304—he is occasionally identified as "Trubert, qui de tot boise" [loosely, Trubert, who always plays tricks, or simply Trubert the trickster]; in addition to vs. 304, see vss. 775 and 2731. See also vs. 2756: "Trubert, qui molt set de guile" [Trubert, who is full of guile].

5. Pp. 11 and passim. True to her title, Gravdal emphasizes Trubert's "transgressive humor" and "the transgressive nature of Trubert" (120), though I cannot concur with her contention about the work's "combinational transgression, joining the roles of the wily trickster and the chivalric hero" (120). The clash of cultures is indeed one source of the humor—it is in the nature of the fabliaux to cast the "other" (whether priest, jealous husband, or occasionally a noble) in the role of object of revenge or pure trickery, but Trubert's one foray into chivalric "heroism" is pure burlesque.

6. The pregnancy is problematic only for practical reasons: the daughter's betrothal. Apart from that complication, her parents are pleased, because Coillebaude had informed them that their daughter had been filled by the Holy Spirit and that her body is full of little angels (vss. 2595–96).

7. The ruse is all the more interesting because *borse* [purse] is generally assumed to be a common euphemism for scrotum or testicles.

8. Even though, for my tastes, this is not among the most humorous of fabliaux, the central sequence is made reasonably appealing by its structural repetition: the duplication of successful disguises, of the victimization of the duke, and of his naïve failures to recognize either the danger or his antagonist.

9. We should recall also that the duke, early in the story, had the opportunity to cheat Trubert but refused to do so, insisting on honesty and fairness.

Works Cited

Gravdal, Kathryn. *Vilain and Courtois: Transgressive Parody in French Literature of the Twelfth and Thirteenth Centuries.* Lincoln: University of Nebraska Press, 1989.

Jodogne, Omer. "Audigier et la chanson de geste, avec une nouvelle édition du poème." *Le Moyen Age*, 66 (1960), 495–526.

Lacy, Norris J. *Reading Fabliaux.* 1993; Birmingham, AL: Summa, 1999.

Schenck, Mary Jane Stearns. *The Fabliaux: Tales of Wit and Deception.* Amsterdam: John Benjamins, 1987.

"No, No Nonete!": Reciting Jean de Condé's Virgin-less and Miracle-less Virgin Miracle

ADRIAN P. TUDOR

We are in the early years of the fourteenth century. The official minstrel to the court of Hainaut, Jean de Condé (ca. 1275–1345), is about to recite a poem. Much of his extant *œuvre* is allegorical and didactic; however today he is in playful mode. The style of his poetry will be no less elegant, but his voice and performance will be mischievous. This is the story of *La Nonete* (Noomen, X, 33–47):

> There is a convent where the women enjoy the delights of love. A young novice follows the example of her sisters, but the abbess fears scandal and imprisons her. One night the *nonete* spies a nun passing by with her own suitor. It is the prioress! She blackmails her into having her freed. The prioress and two companions go to see the abbess, but the abbess is in bed with a young abbot: he just manages to hide under the covers. Refusing to accede to their demand, the abbess sits up in bed and inadvertently puts on the abbot's breeches instead of her veil. The three visitors burst out laughing. The prioress tries to convince the abbess — who is unaware of her mistake — of the irresistible power of love, but this serves only to infuriate her superior. Eventually the abbess sees the breeches and must give in: the girl will be freed. When the nuns recognise the abbot, they know they will be able to behave however they wish.

Jean is too gifted a poet (and perhaps too aware of his position) to resort to filthy language and explicit sex scenes to elicit mirth. The "respectability" and courtly intertextuality of his fabliaux have long been established:

they are "downright courtly and learned," argues Busby; "their manuscript context may suggest a particular view of the form and function of the comic tale in Jean's aesthetic" ("The Respectable Fabliaux" 29). It could well be that a minstrel played *Nonete* almost straight throughout, relying on his courtly audience's ability to fill in the gaps and make the connections (cf. Ribard 87; Busby, "The Respectable Fabliaux" 30).

Some jongleurs, however, may have recited Jean's *Nonete* in an entirely more flamboyant manner (had it circulated more widely in this form, which the manuscript tradition, at least, does not seem to suggest). I will bear both the jongleur's art and the court minstrel's position in mind as I hypothesize for the fabliau what Levy termed a "performing script" ("Performing Fabliaux" 138). Levy neatly sets out the methodological and scholarly foundation for this conjectural approach, and doffs his cap, as do I, to the work of Noomen, Lacy, and Vitz ("Performing Fabliaux" 126; I must equally mention Payen's "storyboard" for the *Le Chevalier au barisel*). Lacy perfectly summarises much of this research: "It is entirely reasonable to speculate that performance would give different voices to different characters, that some actions ... would surely be indicated by gesture as well as word, and that emotions — anger, fear, grief — would be communicated in part by voice, facial expression, and gesture" (17).

Underpinning my "script" is the entirely plausible speculation that an additional intertextual echo — Virgin Miracles — might have had a particular resonance in some aspects of performance/recital and reception. My hypotheses regarding performance remain mere suggestions. However, they are supported by a narrative element, remark, or broad allusion in the text, leading to the possibility that the fun of *Nonete* might be as much a skit on Virgin Miracles as a typical (albeit late) continuation of the comic fabliau tradition; it might even be a pastiche of both traditions and a logical extension of Jean's own work.

Although the comic fabliau was waning by the turn of the fourteenth century, the tradition of Virgin Miracles was still flourishing. Gautier de Coinci — "the Virgin's *fableor*" (Levy, "'Or escoutez'" 333) — composed the most brilliant example of imaginative "literary" miracles — the *Miracles de Nostre Dame* — a hundred-or-so years before Jean de Condé, and they were still being copied; more faithful translations of Latin texts also flourished still (witness the *Rosarius*, ca. 1330). A recent development was the transposition of Virgin Miracles into dramatic pieces, the *Miracles de Nostre Dame par personnages*. Virgin Miracles in a variety of forms would remain popular to the end of the Middle Ages. Once infused into the vernacular textual tradition, these entertaining stories seemed quickly to merge with apparently less moralising pieces (just as did *exempla*), forming numerous stand-alone and collective, almost fablialesque narratives. It is hardly surprising to find *fableors* reverting to mock invocations to the Virgin for comic effect as is the case in two of Jean's works, *Nonete* and *Le Pliçon*.

It is inconceivable that our author was not in some way touched by the Marian Cult. As Busby notes, the aristocracy were commissioning manuscripts containing Virgin Miracles at exactly the time Jean composed *Nonete* (*Codex* 743–46) and indeed, Jean himself wrote a rhetorical piece entitled *Desour l'Ave Maria* (Scheler, XLIV, 129–33). Echoes of the Virgin Miracle tradition make themselves heard throughout *Nonete*. Narrative structures are very similar: in a miracle a devotee of the Virgin would typically disrupt the social order or break a contract and need the intervention of the Virgin for salvation/restoration of the initial situation. In *Nonete* all that is lacking is the Virgin: a devotee of Love who breaks the social order is unfairly punished, but finds a saviour — the prioress — to restore justice and the status quo.

My argument is not that Jean de Condé necessarily based *Nonete* on any particular Virgin Miracle story, rather that this fabliau in a general sense is (to borrow the term coined by Berthelot) an "anti-miracle" and that this adds much to the performer/reciter's toolkit. The ludic commentary on Virgin Miracles, in addition to the transposition of allegorical themes into this old-fashioned world, might have made *Nonete* a good deal funnier than it would otherwise have been. What effect might all of this have had on a reciter (for our purposes, Jean himself), and an audience? After all, Virgin Miracles require a degree of audience participation (song, prayer, etc); fabliaux likewise, although participation of a different type.

Finally, a word about our *dramatis personae*. It is likely that the regular clergy (particularly nuns) are uncommon in fabliaux because enclosure prevented contact with the laity — i.e., the audience — making them less funny. However, they were certainly not off-limits. Fabliaux mirrored Virgin Miracles, which had long ago developed into "situations familiar to the audience, which consisted not of monks or clerics but the unlet-

The Old French Fabliaux

tered" (Ward 164). The transferability of themes in medieval literature could do the rest. In short, there is no reason why Jean de Condé might not have had Virgin Miracles just as much in mind as more obviously courtly texts when he composed (and recited) *Nonete*. Our official court minstrel is about to amuse — and perhaps surprise — us with a short, frivolous piece which will inevitably press many buttons with his audience....

> The Prologue [vss. 1–13] warns us not to criticise others since we all have our faults [point to audience?]. Explanation of why reciter begins with this proverb: he is aware audience will have heard similar on many occasions, in both serious and comic contexts, so all is in the voice and performance [dead serious or overly ironic; after all, they are expecting an entertaining story]. Perhaps sound pitiful when speaking about the innocent actions of a fool [vss. 1–3]; more gestures towards audience when speaking about "teils hons" [such a man; vs. 4]; wag finger: a critical person can also be criticised [vss. 5–6] and all should aspire to do good [vss. 8–9]. Speed up excitedly, or yawn, upon words "sans atente" [without delay; vs. 10]; knowing smile or wink when insisting on truth of story [vss. 12–13].

The opening lines are firmly moralising in tone. It is not necessary in Virgin Miracles to stress that what follows will be the truth (although certainly not unheard of, for example Gautier, 1 Mir. 11, vs. 13). However, in a fabliau this is often both *de rigueur* and an integral part of the joke. Arguably, the very fact that there is such a "truth statement" might distance *Nonete* from a miracle. After all, in a different context, this prologue might be put to a different use: on the face of it, it reads perfectly seriously. But we are entering into the fabliaux world where nothing is as it seems: expectation for the story has been expertly cranked up.

> Now set the scene [vss. 14–28]: plenty of opportunity for fablialesque "business" — ironic/parodic touches — in telling of an abbey where the female community was "legiers com vens" [frivolous; vs. 16]. Reciter's language may be courtly but the tone of voice could be anything but, since this convent should not be a place where "Amours" [vs. 17] resides. When mentioning "couvens de dames" [community of women; vss. 15–16], abbess [vs. 19], prioress [vs. 23] and other residents of the community, perhaps mimic the female body with hands, or imitate mock piety, or nudge and wink. "Amour" reigns here, "healing" the abbess as

would her doctor [vss. 19–21]: any sort of sexual gesture, from modest wink to obscene gesticulation.

These lines set up the narrative and destroy any lingering possibility that what is about to follow could be "serious." (Even Ribard, whose reading is rather sober, sees that there is fun to be had in vss. 19–28 [259].) There are definite echoes of Virgin Miracles: for example, "J'ai bien oÿ ramentevoir / D'unne abbie dont li couvens / De dames iert legiers com vens" [I have heard tell of an abbey where the community of ladies was frivolous; vss. 14–16] contrasts sharply with a fairly typical passage such as: "Il fu, ce truis, une abbeÿe / Ou mout eut bele compaignie / Et biau convent de beles dames / Et si eut mout de saintes fames" [A delightful company of beautiful and saintly ladies was gathered within an abbey; Gautier, 1 Mir. 26, vss. 5–8]. As for Amour playing the role of the abbess's healer, the Virgin or God might ordinarily play this role: in Gautier's *Miracles* the Virgin-as-doctor is present in eleven miracles (Krause 49).

> The scene is set, the story begins (vss. 29–55): perhaps expect cheers when saying: "Or revenrai a mon pourpos" [I get back to my topic; vs. 29]. Then comes a cracking joke: the *nonete* has not come to the convent to pray, but "pour repos / Avoir" [for rest; vss. 30–31]. Imaginary prop: she has just taken the veil. Mock relief that love has ignored her; knowing smile, slowing of voice, mime or leer when mentioning the frequency of her love acts (vs. 39). The abbess notices this and forbids her from these pursuits (wag finger in displeasure): perhaps mimic shock/anger — after all, it is the abbess who notices such things — or illicit sympathy, since we know the abbess is just as guilty. Milk for all their worth the grief and sarcasm in the lines where the *nonete* is put "em prison" (vs. 46). Mime bolting door? Opportunity to overplay comic emotions when the imprisoned nun implores God and Saint Peter (prayerful gesture? raise voice? look heavenwards? or play for pathos? more "business" suggesting Saint Peter's keys?) and is in prison for over twenty days (slow pace on this line, sarcastic "wow" feature?). You (include audience) will now hear what happens to the pretty nun with the comely body (more lascivious gestures?).

The wonderful gag in vss. 30–31 recalls miracles such as Gautier's 1 Mir. 43 (with which our fabliau has many points of contact): vss. 12–21 of the miracle describe a model young woman taking the veil for exemplary reasons. Especially resonant of Virgin Miracles is the role of the strict/hypocritical abbess (that of the pregnant abbess had been circulating for perhaps 200 years before being made into a dramatic *Miracle par personnages* in 1340). Now, our *nonete's* actual crime remains somewhat unclear: is it simply her relationship with a man — adultery as a bride of Christ — or that she is caught, or that her indiscretion endangers this apparent paradise on earth? (Given the final two lines of the prioress's concluding, valedictory speech — "Et tout cil qui em parleront / En mal soient de Dieu maudit!" ["and may all who lack discretion (about abandoning themselves to pleasure) be cursed by God"; vss. 244–45] — the last possibility seems the most likely). It is only in vs. 52 where God and the key holder to heaven (the most logical saint to invoke in the circumstances) are mentioned in *Nonete*. We do not hear the nun's prayer directly, but this is an important stage in any pious narrative: a wrong is done, a saint is invoked, and the prayer will be answered.

> The plot now unravels (vss. 56–86): Perhaps with fingers make the shape of the hole through which the novice spies the prioress. Voice for ensuing ten-line blackmail speech may reflect mock innocence, or be faintly malicious, or pathetic ("De vostre vie vos passé / Mieus que de la moie ne faice!" ["you are living better than I am!" vss. 64–65], lines which also lend themselves to innuendo; whisper, since this is the dead of night; raise pitch of voice for the *nonete*. Upon the threat that the blackmailed nun's face will be bright red once the affair is revealed, point simultaneously to face and to an appropriate object (in audience?); mime turning a key since blackmailed nun might also be imprisoned. Shock/horror at revelation that blackmailed nun is the prioress! Creeping about as Prioress approaches where the *nonete* is being kept; change voice as she speaks (placating, perhaps lingering over mention of St. Martin in expectation of laughs). Re-modulate voice as *nonete* replies (sound naive or slightly threatening: "Puis que vous en couvent l'avés, / A vous m'en tieng comme a justice" ["since you have promised, I rely on you for justice" vss. 82–83 (cf. Noomen, X, 343)]. Mime prioress leaving the scene, with her lover, followed by suggestive gestures or knowing smile; although blackmailed, they go off to enjoy the pleasures of love....

The beautiful, clear night may not be miraculous, but it does answer the *nonete's* prayer. Dialogue allows for a good deal of "business" (at the reciter's discretion), and the mention of St. Martin might in itself give rise to laughter, given this particular saint's presence, random or otherwise (Cobby

175–79), in so many fabliaux. But despite the fun that can be had with the shifting emotions and the three characters present — the lover may not speak, but he is still "on stage" — and regardless of the juicy irony in the fact that the blackmailed prioress leaves the scene to continue her affair, there is a strange morality about everything, for the young nun is indeed imprisoned unfairly and her ruse will see justice done. The prioress, it seems, provides the answer to her prayer to find love once more.

> Prioress summons the help of two colleagues (vss. 87–101); perhaps crude gesture, or verbal lingering on beginning of word "*boursi*ère" [bursar; vs. 90, suggesting "bourse," scrotum. My italics]. More opportunity for mischief at description of prioress in full dress (vs. 88) and the brief plotting (a complicity shared with audience). Prioress's voice is not only that of a woman, but also of a senior (and supposedly holy) woman. Wring hands in mock grief during these words? The young nun has been in prison for so long: pronounce "longhement" (vs. 95) very slowly: twenty days she has gone without seeing her lover! When saying that it is amazing that she has not killed herself out of despair, stress the word "desespoir" [vs. 97].

This section allows for a great deal of fun in recital if required. Three properly attired religious women (the two offstage do not speak but can easily be brought on stage by a skilled minstrel) need no convincing to favor releasing the girl: the *nonete*'s skilful blackmail plays no further part in the story. The prioress's colleagues instantly, and correctly, as it happens, see that the situation is unjust (vss. 100–01) although there is nothing heavenly about their conclusion: the injustice is the girl's sexless isolation from her lover.

There is one interesting possible allusion to Virgin Miracles, the use of the word "desespoir." Despair is a serious sin, having great potential for damaging the soul. Pious literature is littered with sinners on the verge of despair, saved by divine intervention or the help of a saintly person; only very few who do despair gain salvation. It is a characteristic of Virgin Miracles that when a sinner is in danger of excluding the possibility of divine help — and thus in the time of greatest need — he or she remembers the Virgin and is rewarded for prior service. The Virgin is not invoked at this point but later in the fabliau, and in different circumstances. Would this absence have had significance for the audience of *Nonete*? Might this "prayerful" episode be especially charged with irony and sarcasm?

To the abbess's bedchamber (vss. 102–39). The prioress and her conspirators find the door open and enter dramatically with the greeting: "Dieus y soit!" ["God be with you!" vs. 104]. Knowing smile since abbess is not in bed alone. Hurried gesture to hide lover under covers; delicious opportunities for delivering the line: "n'estoit pas simples conviers, / Ains iert un biaus abbes jolis" [It wasn't just a simple lay brother but a handsome, good-looking abbot; vss. 110–11]. Reciter and audience complicit in the joke, but characters are not. The bed is surrounded by nuns falling to their knees to pray for their companion (gestures; during these exchanges an energetic jongleur could even repeatedly stand and kneel, depending on who is speaking). Haughty voice for abbess as she refuses their prayers. Great irony, if not smutty gestures, upon proverbial expression: "verge plus grosse et plus dure" [a thicker and harder rod; vs. 121]: audience will enjoy the double entendre ("verge" for punishment rod/penis). Expect expressions of disapproval from the audience as the abbess's hypocritical behaviour becomes more flagrant. Milk the irony when prioress tells abbess that she would be committing a sin to let the *nonete* die in prison (vss. 132–33). Mimic abbess's sudden anger: mime her sitting up in bed and putting on her cloak (imaginary prop).

These lines are full of dialogue and contrasting emotions (e.g., vss. 128–33, from pleading to authority to anger). The abbess is on top, but this will change in vss. 143–44, arguably the tipping point of the fabliau: the "'ballet' des acteurs" (Ribard 254) now begins in earnest. Still, for the moment she considers herself firmly in charge. The prioress is playing the role of the intercessor. Along with plentiful standard fablialesque *topoi* there is a profusion of religious expressions and gestures ready to be exploited. In Virgin Miracles, the audience may be expected to participate in a narrative prayer. Is it too much to imagine those listening to *Nonete* mimicking the prayerful words/gestures of the reciter/narrator/characters?

Another reassurance of the "truth" (knowing smile, nod or wink) and the real fun can begin (vss. 140–213). Mime the abbess putting on her "veil" and point to breeches (laugh? play straight? swaggering arrogance? imaginary or real prop?). Play contrasting emotions to the full: abbess is full of rage, fails to notice the mistake, and the nuns burst out in laughter (indicate straps hanging down from the abbess's head, point, guffaw or snigger). Mock solemnity of prioress's plea (vss. 156–71), in which there is an explicit admission of enjoying the pleasures of love (vss. 166–69). Anticipate polite or raucous laughter on lines 172–73 if reciter makes continued visual link to imaginary prop: "Se Dieus de chi lever me lest,/Pour moi n'iert hors de ceste anee" [just as God will let me get up, so if it's up to me she will not be free this year]. Adjustment in prioress's voice: adopt a more threatening tone (vss. 176–81), linger (eyes heavenwards?) over "Par le mere Dieu de Soissons" ["by Our Lady of Soissons"; vs. 180]. Build up pace during quick-fire verbal exchanges between abbess and prioress (vss. 182–91; two different women's voices, both very sure of themselves) but pause after mention of repenting (vs. 187). Exploit double meaning of vss. 188–89 (signalled by Noomen [345]). Adopt malicious voice and facial expression when prioress reveals abbess's mistake (vss. 192–95); gestures when explaining what the abbess has on her head is in fact "Çou de quoi on cuevre sen cul" [what you cover your arse with; vs. 195]. Spit out the curse (in style of fire and brimstone preacher?) that abbess might burn in hell if she goes against their wishes (vss. 200–03). Obscene gesture, or salacious tone of voice, or more nods, winks and nudges, when prioress speaks of abbess's sexual activity (204–05).

The opportunities for fablialesque "business" abound here (change of pace and pitch, gestures, imaginary or real props, mock invocations of God and the Virgin), ending with the revelation to the abbess of her mistake. Love has such power that it cannot be defeated, a statement sworn "par le corps Jhesucrist" ["by the body of Christ" vs. 156]. A courtly love tone mingles effortlessly with the religious setting and comic mockery in this topsy-turvy world. The prioress's first long speech (vss. 156–71), a shorter version of the long monologues common to miracles, is beautifully constructed for dramatic oral delivery: she again fulfils the role played by the Virgin in miracles, who may beg divine succour on behalf of a third party (but without the threat of blackmail).

Her invocation of Our Lady of Soissons is especially noteworthy, if not particularly exceptional. Soissons was one of the main centres of Marian devotion: Gautier's *Miracles* were composed for its community of nuns and contain many miracles and prayers specifically located in Soissons. The town is equally mentioned in, and is the setting for, a number of fabliaux. The mention of this particular Marian shrine, which has an intimate relationship with the vernacular tradition of Virgin Miracles, is thus far from fortuitous: it even more closely ties *Nonete* to a tradition of which the fabliau may be a gentle parody. It certainly invites mimicry and participation from both reciter and audience, in addition to the general fun that might be had throughout a performance of the fabliau. It might even be the reference for which the audience has been waiting (and made to wait). I can imagine the mood shifting very slightly, especially since a few lines later we learn that, if left in prison, the girl will suffer a miserable death for such a noble love (vss. 185–86)! Here the miracle story really has been turned on its head, since in the shadow of an invocation to Our Lady of Soissons, source of actual and textual miracles, the *nonete* will die for what, in Christian eyes, is anything but a noble love. The abbess acting against the wishes of the nuns, and her *démesure* (vs. 206), again recall those strict abbesses of Virgin Miracles. There is also an accumulation of reminders of the religious setting (vss. 156, 172, 180, 213, etc.). There are real grievances to be endured, since it is by now more than clear that the young nun is unjustly imprisoned. But the criticism is not of the abbess's sexual behaviour — as the audience of a standard Virgin Miracle would expect — rather of her unfair treatment of the *nonete*.

> We now approach the climax (vss. 214–45). The abbess is aware of her mistake: she leaps out of bed, takes the breeches off her head — continued use of invisible prop — and falls to her knees begging for mercy (facial gestures at realisation of her error, followed by action verb, then by pleading voice and gesture of supplication). Profusion of action and dramatic words present more opportunities for mime, gesture and mimicry: "sali" [leapt; vss. 216], "se tieste descuevre" [took the breeches off her head; vs. 218], "releva" [stood up; vs. 220], "cria mierchi" [begged for mercy; vss. 219, 222], "aiiés me moi pitei!" ["take pity on me!" vs. 225], "prissent le sarment" [swore an oath; vs. 226], "que durent vir le baceler" [they must see the young lad; vs. 228], "rebracie" [pulled back (the bed sheets); vs. 231], "embracie" [embrace; vs. 232], "baisa" [kissed; vs. 233], "s'abaissa" [bowed; vs. 234], "Vit l'abbé et le reconnut" [She saw the abbot and recognised him; vs. 235], "bawa" [interjection of surprise; vs. 236].... Plenty of changes of voice and pace (mock pathos, glee, etc). Final four lines before *queue* (vss. 242–45) to be delivered as mock-solemn homily.

The performance potential of vss. 214–45 is plain, but we are not necessarily ending where another fabliau might have ended (i.e., revelation of lover, winners and losers). The scene is one of the revelation of guilt and the witnessing of a "true" repentance, including a sort of penance. This is not without interest: in miracles, the pregnant abbess and the nun who left her abbey, amongst others, are spared public revelation of their guilt and shame thanks to the Virgin's intervention. Ironically, in *Nonete* the presence of the "viseteres" — the abbot charged with inspecting the morals of the convent — is the very cause of the abbess's sin; it is tempting to associate this character with the bishop and his retinue who perform "virginity checks" in stories such as that of the pregnant abbess.

The "repentance" is followed (as is right) by a formal salutary contract (which is usually between the penitent and the Virgin/God): do not spoil a cushy number for everyone. Much of this section might in fact be transposed into a miracle setting simply by changing the context and the characters: it is just a question of who is saying what. The religious references/echoes are striking throughout. For example, when the abbess realises she has been discovered, she falls to her knees and repents. This act of attrition, motivated by fear of punishment, is not uncommon in Virgin Miracles (as opposed to pious tales where a true act of contrition is required for redemption). The prioress is now firmly in charge, lifting the abbess from her knees: she is the abbess's only source of succour. In any miracle the same scenario might arise, but in *Nonete* the abbess is using the right words and gestures, including a promise never again to go against the prioress's wishes, to beg for mercy from the wrong person and on the wrong issue: this is the fabliau world, where anything goes. The cross that made Christ suffer, the tongue with which he spoke, the fires of hell, and the curse of God are all invoked in the prioress's final speech demanding heavenly justice for all those unwilling to abandon themselves to pleasure. The final two lines — "and may all who lack discretion [about abandoning themselves to pleasure] be cursed by God" — may show that she is aware that their behaviour transgresses the rules of society (if not God), although there is no indication that she considers their activities wrong, given her earlier eloquent defence of Amour.

Not only are vss. 214–45 redolent with performance potential of every kind, but also the proliferation of explicit religious expressions as well as implicit references and gestures brings the action of the narrative to an exciting, highly satirical and even ethical (in fabliaux terms) conclusion.

> The five-line *queue* can be delivered very much as a mock-solemn homily, perhaps following the frenetic action with a brief pause (or not), perhaps

with no change of voice, perhaps simply with a change of tone and a preacher's gesture. The audience will appreciate the twisting of proverbial and biblical lines and the repetition of the introduction, knowing that the recital is well and truly at an end.

* * *

Quite how the refined Jean de Condé might have recited *Nonete* cannot be known. It could be played entirely straight: it is not a blue tale, and Jean is an official minstrel whose family is established at court. If the poet did indeed place his five fabliaux at the extreme of, but still within, his didactic and moralising *œuvre*, then he might have toned down his performance, but there is no hard evidence to make us believe that he did so excessively (Busby, "The Respectable Fabliaux" 17). A more extravagant delivery — in his own terms, at least — cannot be excluded, for *Nonete* is brimming with traditional (and not-so-traditional) fablialesque performance potential. Jean's audience would have known his other works, and those of his father, and much about his life. The opportunities for self-allusive intertextual gags/self-parody/self-mocking seem almost endless (and inevitably inaccessible to modern readers). In the hands of another jongleur, the performance of this "respectable" fabliau could have been as vulgar as you like (although the manuscript tradition suggests that Jean's *Nonete* was not widely circulated, notwithstanding other versions of the story). Even a toned-down delivery could be hilarious: this dead-pan way of telling rude stories can be much funnier than using obscene words and gestures (nudge nudge, wink wink ...). My "performing script" hardly scratches at the surface of what fun could be had with our tale. Although not a typical fabliau, *Nonete* still offers the reciter every opportunity to ply his trade. One of the last fabliaux may well be one of the more refined, but it certainly pulls no punches.

The intertext plays a fundamental role in this fun. In any narrative the same scenario, or a similar scenario, can be told for a number of reasons and in a number of ways. Context is everything; all is in the telling. With just a few adjustments, the scenario of *Nonete* might easily be that of a miracle, or an improving or didactic tale, whilst the language and vocabulary are resolutely courtly. Miracles and fabliaux are far from dissimilar: reparation of a difficult situation, fulfilment of a need, rewards and punishments. Miracles are about salvation — and so is our fabliau. Much seems to parody Virgin Miracle themes and motifs — the classic AVE / EVA opposition — with Amour replacing God, and the prioress fulfilling the various functions of the Virgin. There is nothing scandalous about this, society by the mid-fourteenth century being infused with anti-clerical satire. Indeed, *Nonete* is mild satire at best, poking fun broadly at contemporary society and literary types. There are no virgins in this "miracle," and the Queen of Heaven's very absence allows fornication, which in a kind of absurd way seems an affirmation of the whole Virgin Miracle tradition. Rutebeuf's *Frere Denise* had already parodied hagiographic narratives to produce social satire; in *Nonete* Virgin Miracles are subject to gentle parody that serves, perhaps, to lampoon contemporary notions about monastic and lay society. Or to extend Jean's didactic *œuvre*. Or is just for fun. The genius of Jean de Condé's fabliau, perhaps in reading, recital, or performance above all, lies in its understatement: this is a Virgin-less and miracle-less Virgin Miracle, and it is perhaps just this which would produce the biggest laugh of all.

Works Cited

Berthelot, Anne. "Anti-miracle et anti-fabliau: La Subversion des genres." *Romania*, 106 (1985), 399–419.

Busby, Keith. "The Respectable Fabliaux: Jean Bodel, Rutebeuf, and Jean de Condé." *Reinardus*, 9 (1996), 15–31.

_____. *Codex and Context: Reading Old French Verse Narrative in Manuscript*. 2 vols. Amsterdam: Rodopi, 2002.

Cobby, Anne. "'Saint Amadour et Sainte Afflise': Calling upon the Saints in the Fabliaux." In Adrian P. Tudor and Alan Hindley, eds. *Grant risee? The Medieval Comic Presence/La Présence comique médiévale*. Turnhout: Brepols, 2006. 173–89.

Koenig, V. Frédéric, ed. *Gautier de Coinci: Les Miracles de Nostre Dame*. 4 vols. Geneva: Droz, 1955–70.

Krause, Kathy M. "Virgin, Saint, and Sinners: Women in Gautier de Coinci's *Miracles de Nostre Dame*." In Kathy M. Krause, ed. *Reassessing the Heroine in Medieval French Literature*. Gainesville: University Press of Florida, 2001. 26–52.

Lacy, Norris J. "Subject to Object: Performance and Observation in the Fabliaux." *Symposium*, 56 (2002), 17–24.

Levy, Brian J. "Performing Fabliaux." In Evelyn Birge Vitz, Marilyn Lawrence, and Nancy Freeman Regalado, eds. *Performing Medieval Narrative*. Cambridge: Brewer, 2005. 141–53.

_____. "'Or escoutez une merveille!' Parallel Paths: Gautier de Coinci and the Fabliaux." In Kathy Krause and Alison Stones, eds. *Gautier de Coinci: Miracles, Music and Manuscripts*. Turnhout: Brepols, 2006.

Payen, Jean-Charles. "Structure et sens du *Chevalier au barisel*," *Le Moyen Age*, 77 (1971), 239–62.

Raynaud, Gaston. "Une Nouvelle Version du fabliau de *La Nonnette*." *Romania*, 34 (1905), 279–83.

Ribard, Jacques. *Un Ménestrel du XIVe siècle: Jean de Condé*. Geneva: Droz, 1969.

Scheler, Auguste. *Dits et contes de Baudouin de Condé et de son fils Jean de Condé*. 3 vols. Brussels: Devaux, 1866–67.

Ward, Benedicta. *Miracles and the Medieval Mind: Theory, Record and Event 1000–1215*. Aldershot: Scolar Press, 1987.

Rhyme or Reason: Le Prestre comporté *and* Le Prestre et le chevalier

ANNE COBBY

In MS Paris, Bibliothèque nationale, fonds français 12603, *Le Prestre comporté* (hereafter *PCo*; Noomen, IX, 1–66) immediately precedes *Le Prestre et le chevalier* (*PCh*; Noomen, IX, 67–124). While the humour of these two understudied fabliaux is based on very different plots and devices, they recall each other in many aspects of their composition, to the extent that one could even wonder if they were by the same author. No other fabliau exceeds a thousand lines in length.[1] Both recount the events of a long night, give an important place to food, and have a leisurely pace interspersed with moments of hasty action and long sequences of dialogue. *PCo* tells of the wanderings of a corpse which is repeatedly hidden, found, and fearfully deposited elsewhere, while in *PCh* a priest attempts extortion on a knight by offering him hospitality and then charging for each ingredient, only to be out-tricked when the knight demands the household's sexual services. They are both well constructed and well written, with good distinction of dramatic voices, well-chosen circumstantial details, and a complex style including *enjambement*. But their use of rhyme is interestingly different.

It is obvious, and universally accepted in work on lyric poetry, that the choice and arrangement of rhyme-words are a significant part of poetic creation. Rhyme draws attention to words—especially useful and potent where delivery is oral—and sets up relations of connection or contrast between the sounds and concepts which it joins. Much less attention has been paid to rhyme in Old French narrative verse. An exception is the works of Chrétien de Troyes: J.C. Laidlaw's 1983 article on *Erec et Enide* has recently been followed by Ellen Thorington's on *Lancelot*, based upon the data of the *Charrette* Project at Princeton University. Laidlaw shows how Chrétien uses sequences of "ornate rhymes"[2] to emphasize content, to vary the rhythm of the romance, and to characterize and draw attention to certain sections of the text. Thorington classifies and counts the various kinds of ornate rhyme in *Lancelot* and shows how they help to characterize episodes and illuminate climactic moments of the narrative, while differences in technique distinguish Chrétien's work from his continuator's.

On the rhyming technique of the fabliaux, by contrast, almost no work has been done. Yet linguistic humour is fundamental to these texts, so we can expect that rhyme will contribute to that humour. We can also be confident that an audience used to oral delivery would have a sensitivity to rhyme and to complexity of rhyme that modern readers develop only with difficulty. More or less brief mention has been made of instances where the choice of rhyme-words or the ornateness of rhyme is used to support the theme of a fabliau (e.g., Butterfield 243–44; Cobby, "Understanding" 160–61, 167–68; Cobby, "Langage" 150–51). In this essay I shall undertake a somewhat more sustained study, comparing the ornate rhymes in *PCo* with those in *PCh*, exploring their contribution to these fabliaux, and arguing that attentiveness to rhyme can enhance our appreciation of the comic text. This is not to say that all rhyme is effective, in the corpus or even in these two fabliaux; facility in rhyme can co-exist with artistic exploitation. But we see more artistry when we attend to rhyme.

Ornate rhyme is far commoner in *PCo*, as this table shows.[3]

	PCo	*PCh*
Length — lines	1164	1357
Rich rhymes — couplets[3]	347	219
Percentage of rich rhymes	60%	32%
Sequences of 3 or more rich rhymes[4]	46	12
5 or more	16	1
4	11	4
3	19	7
2	27	33
Longest sequence	18	6
Passages of 3 or more couplets with no rich rhyme	16	70
Longest such passage	8	14

Rhyme or Reason (Cobby)

These figures suggest that in *PCh*, ornate rhyme is rare and therefore marked, whereas in *PCo* it is its absence which is marked. The difference in technique is evident from the beginning of the two texts. I cite *PCo* first:

> D'un priestre vous di et recort
> Ki avoit tourné son acort
> En luxure et en lecherie,
> En estreloi et en folie:
> Tout en apert se part clamoit.
> La femme d'un preudomme amoit,
> Dont il faisoit molt a blasmer.
> Chieus, ki ne s'en sot ou clamer,
> En est dolens et molt maris,
> Si com chieus ki n'est pas garis
> Del mal ki vient de jalousie:
> Et c'est la graindre derverie
> Del mont, si en vient mains anuis.
> Devant Noel, es longhes nuis
> D'ivier en la plus fort saison,
> Met un soir sa femme a raison
> Li preudons ... [*PCo*, vss. 1–17].

[I am telling you the story of a priest who had set himself to debauchery and lechery, to unlawful behaviour and foolishness: quite openly he claimed his share. He loved the wife of a decent man, for which he was much at fault. The man, who did not know where to complain, was very sad and grieved by it, for he was not spared the sickness which comes from jealousy: and it is the greatest folly in the world, and many troubles come from it. Before Christmas, in the long nights of winter in the harshest season, the man spoke to his wife one evening.]

> Traiiés en cha, s'oiiés un conte,
> Si com Milles d'Amiens le conte,
> D'un chevalier et d'un prevoire.
> Li contes fu mis en memore
> C'uns chevaliers mout povrement
> Repairoit du tournoiement,
> Si avoit tout perdu le sien;
> Et si avoit esté si bien

The Old French Fabliaux

> Batus que, s'il donnast cent saus,
> Ne trouvast il qui tant de cols
> Li donnast por cent saus contés.
> Laidement fu desbaretés,
> Si ot toute sa compaignie
> Perdue et toute sa mainsnie,
> Et son harnas et son conroi.
> Ensi s'en vint mout povrement
> Et un escuiers seulement [*PCh*, vss. 1–17].

> [Come this way, hear a tale, as Milon d'Amiens tells it, of a knight and a priest. The tale is handed down that a knight was returning in a very poor state from a tournament, and had lost all he had; and he had been so badly beaten that if he were to give a hundred shillings he would not find anyone to give him so many blows, not for a hundred shillings cash. He was ignominiously defeated, and had lost all his party and his retinue, his harness and his equipment. He came along in this very poor state, with just one squire.]

Prologues are always important in setting the scene and establishing expectations, so it is not surprising to find that both poets use ornate rhyme here, and each according to his own method. In the passages quoted, before the narrative proper begins, *PCo* has six ornate rhymes compared to *PCh*'s five, but in the first thirty lines *PCh* has ten to *PCo*'s eight. In the quotation *PCo*'s density of ornate rhyme is a little higher than the text's average (75 percent compared to 60 percent), but lower (53 percent) in the longer passage, whereas *PCh*'s is much higher in the short extract and even higher in the longer sample (62 percent and 71 percent compared to 32 percent). Both begin with a common feature, a rhyme (equivocal in *PCh*, merely rich in *PCo*) on the act of narration. *PCo* continues with a sequence of three ornate rhymes shortly followed by another two (vss. 5–10, 13–16). These set out the importance of narrative and desire, demand, love, and guilt, grief, night, and trouble. *Nuis / anuis*, which sum up the plot, will recur (vss. 736–37, 988–89). The ornate rhymes in vss. 17–30 introduce the themes of knowledge and truth — both important and elusive in the story — and delusion and distance, which we might relate to the nighttime wanderings of the corpse: *voir / savoir, songant / eslongant*. In his prologue, then, the author of *PCo* uses ornate rhymes to express several of his themes, but he neither uses equivocal rhyme, the most expressive kind of all, nor especially concentrates ornate rhyme in this important part of the text. It seems as if such rhyme is a natural part of his style.

In *PCh*, by contrast, there is a striking concentration of ornate rhyme in the prologue and especially as the narrative proper begins. The opening equivocal rhyme is very revealing: not only it this a tale which Milon d'Amiens is telling, but it is a tale about counting, accounting, and calculation. The strong introduction of the word *conte*, echoed in vss. 4 and 11, thus prepares all that will follow. Vs. 11 is particularly pregnant, introducing the monetary sense of *conter* so soon after the narrative sense, in conjunction with *cent saus* which will become a leitmotif, echoed at short distance and at the rhyme in vs. 9, albeit not an ornate rhyme. Later we will repeatedly find *saus* rhyming with *faus* [false] to express the treachery of the priest's financial dealings. The repeated and richly rhyming *povrement* stresses the hero's poverty, which makes him vulnerable to extortion. Most unusually for *PCh*, vss. 11–30 contain eight ornate rhymes, including a rare sequence of four. All this indicates that Milon, a sparing user of ornate rhyme, is using it here to focus attention on this crucial introductory passage, and to introduce essential themes and their interrelation. The author of *PCo*, on the other hand, while stressing themes by ornate rhyme, does not make greater use of it here than elsewhere, and does not call attention to what he is doing by unusual patterns, equivocal rhyme, or echo.

The differences in technique seen in the prologues continue throughout the two fabliaux. Since ornate rhyme is so common in *PCo*, I shall concentrate on sequences of at least five couplets, since such a density must surely have been intended and perceived. There are sixteen such sequences, and all but one occur at moments of dramatic and comic tension focused upon the corpse, beginning with the murder itself.

The first (vss. 69–84) tells how the priest-lover hides and then falls asleep in a bath, where the husband finds and quietly strangles him. The ornate rhymes highlight the scene's concerns: safety, fate, watching, seeing, rage, and two actions with the rope, obtaining it and making the noose. The dramatic intensity of this episode leads to the first moment of emotional intensity, marked by two sequences (vss. 126–45, 148–57). The woman, finding her lover but not knowing he is dead, addresses the body.

These sequences have several equivocal rhymes: *devin / de vin, point / point, mot / m'ot*, and soon also *a moi / a moi* (vss. 160–61). Several rhyme-words — though not the equivocal ones — relate to coming and going, bringing back, love and lover, being alive (*vis*, frequent at the rhyme, though this is a tale of death). This unmissable concentration of ornate rhyme — fifteen couplets out of sixteen — marks the point where the wanderings of the corpse are set in motion and puts a spotlight on many of the fabliau's themes. Above all, we cannot remain unaware of the poet's lavish use of ornate rhyme.

The fourth and fifth sequences (vss. 224–35, extended to 202–35 across single simple rhymes, and vss. 298–309) mark the next two crisis points, when the wife and her maid hide the corpse and then, thwarted by the husband, must hide it again. Here the themes are knowledge and truth, life, concealment, money; and again there are equivocal rhymes: *vis / vis* [alive / face], *afaire / a faire, abatre / a batre*. Then come two interesting absences. Vss. 310–19 are a rare instance of five consecutive couplets with no ornate rhyme. They immediately follow the dramatic second hiding of the corpse and announce the next upset to the wife's plans, which will necessitate the third concealment. This scene culminates in another sequence (vss. 340–49, extended to 340–57), referring to trouble, decision, and anger.

The following 160 lines (vss. 358–520), while not lacking ornate rhyme, have not a single sequence, in spite of the tension of the neighbours finding and recognising the corpse outside their door and disposing of it for the fourth time. This episode includes another ten lines with no ornate rhyme at all (vss. 471–80), a peaceful pastoral scene with a grazing mare upon which the corpse will shortly be tied. This suggests that passages without ornate rhyme — which are very rare and are found only where the corpse is not "on stage" — serve to set the scene for subsequent dramatic action. This episode is not devoid of drama and tension, yet there is no sequence of ornate rhyme until the corpse has been tied on the mare — because the following episode is far more dramatic and emotionally charged, and the scarcity of ornate rhyme preceding it throws the greater crisis into relief. Ornate rhyme returns when the mare's peasant owner, finding the priest's body on his beast, attacks it with his club, believes he has killed him and then recognizes his pastor, apostrophizes the corpse in horror at his action and sets about concealing it for the fifth time (vss. 535–44, extended to 521–44). The only equivocal rhyme is *porte / porte* [carry / gate], but to the carrying motif are added, in other ornate rhymes, recognition, perception, and blame.

This pattern is repeated in the next episode: there is no sequence of ornate rhyme when the peasant hides the corpse in a bacon-sack belonging to some thieves, then a peaceful scene at the inn with no ornate rhyme at all (vss. 600–09), and finally a long sequence when the innkeeper finds the body in the sack and animated speeches follow (vss. 658–79, including *rimes cloisonnées*). Rhyme-words feature forms and compounds of *venir*, stressing the arrival of the corpse, along with perception, truth, belief, betrayal. The next, vast sequence, follows very shortly (vss. 696–731, extended to 688–731 and, across *rimes cloisonnées* and single simple rhymes, into the following sequence). The innkeeper, who is blameless beyond his complicity with thieves, recognizes the priest and, like the peasant before him, is terrified. Though there are no equivocal rhymes, theme words abound: taking, hanging, punishment, carrying, finding, coming, and the pair *nuit / anuit* found in the prologue.

The next sequence (vss. 750–73) is quite different from the others. It describes the unwelcome visit of the bishop and his drunken retinue, and prepares the next action, a situation which, as we have seen, is normally characterized by either no ornate rhyme at all, or at least no long sequences. There are theme words, several uses of compounds of *prendre* [take], and verbs of motion. What this episode has in common with the other sequences is heightened emotion, albeit of a different kind, and on the part of the narrator rather than the characters. A second tavern scene follows, and then the next sequence (vss. 892–909), in which the second innkeeper takes the corpse to the prior's cell and the prior finds it. Again the rhymes speak of being (no longer) alive, finding, blame, coming back. Almost immediately afterwards the prior recognizes the priest and addresses him in anger and fear before making a plan, with rhymes on carrying, escaping, and finding, and two equivocal rhymes, *vis / vis* and *lais / lais* [ugly / lets] (vss. 918–31 or 912–69). He goes to the bishop, warns him there are stray dogs around and gives him a club; then, when the bishop is asleep, he places the priest's body on the bishop's feet. There is just one ornate sequence here, as he speaks to the bishop (vss. 986–99), but it extends across *rimes cloisonnées* and single simple rhymes to vs. 1045, when the bishop attacks the corpse with his club, taking it to be a dog. Theme words abound, as do equivocal rhymes: *entent / entent* (though better, from MS *J*, *atent / entent*), *lait / lait*, *esperis / Esperis* [woken / (Holy) Spirit], together with *nuit / anuit* and rhymes on *voir* [truth] and compounds of *faire, venir, prendre, porter*.

The emotional intensity of this passage is not of the same order as in the earlier sequences, but the dramatic and comic intensity is growing as the tale reaches its climax, and this is reflected by the concentration of ornate rhyme. After the violence there is a series of eight couplets with no ornate rhyme (vss. 1054-68), the longest absence in the text: not a peaceful scene as previously, as the bishop realizes the "dog" he has attacked is a man, but a respite, to cast into maximum relief the climax which is to follow. In the final long sequence (vss. 1069-90 or 1106), the concealment and subterfuge of the long night come to an end; the monks of the abbey gather around the bishop and recognize the body as a man, and as the priest, and bury him. The theme words we have met before recur here: seeing and seeming, (absence of) life, truth and knowledge, finding and taking. The concerns of each of the characters who find the body and, fearful of blame, hide it somewhere else, come together in this comic climax and public recognition which bring to an end the need to dissemble. The priest is buried at last, and the fear of blame which has followed his body around is defused by coming to rest on the bishop, whose status preserves him from criticism.

The epilogue to the fabliau (vss. 1107-58) has few ornate rhymes (eleven in twenty-six couplets, and never more than two together). This confirms the connection between sequences of ornate rhyme and dramatic moments, and between its absence or scarcity and undramatic moments, which are themselves rare. It also confirms that one or two ornate rhymes are not significant in this poet's expression. Nonetheless, the rhymes in this passage echo the sequences: coming, taking, hanging, carrying and finally, "Pour le siecle failli et vuit, / Qui mal se prouve et est prouvés, / Fu chius fabliaus fais et trouvés" [For the degenerate, empty world, which shows itself and is shown to be bad, this fabliau was made and composed; vss. 1156-58]. This is not the first time forms of *prouver* and *trouver* have rhymed together in this tale of finding (*trouver*) and finding out or revealing (*prouver*). In this concluding line the poet uses *trouver* in its other sense of literary composition to look back over the telling of a tale of finding, just as the first lines of *PCh* use the polysemic *conter* to announce a tale of calculation.

Study of the longest sequences of ornate rhyme in *PCo* has thus revealed that the author uses a vast amount of it in almost every part of his text, but in spite of this extensive use it retains potential as a dramatic, comic, and thematic marker. He draws attention to its presence by using it intensively in certain types of context — mostly moments of crisis — while forgoing it in others. Certain theme words recur in the long sequences and elsewhere in the text, though they rarely coincide with the subtler device of equivocal rhyme. Study of shorter sequences and specific words would surely add much more to our appreciation of the poet's technique.

As we saw earlier, *PCh* has a smaller proportion of ornate rhyme, fewer and shorter sequences, and longer intervals between ornate rhymes, so that their rarity enhances their potential for poetic and dramatic effect. Areas of striking density are clearly not how Milon d'Amiens uses ornate rhyme, so for his fabliau I shall focus rather on the rhyme-words themselves and on the concepts they express, while using the few, short sequences as a starting-point.[6] These occur at some — but by no means all — of the significant moments of the plot: the prologue, already discussed (vss. 16–30); the exposition of the knight's scheme to the audience (vss. 415–22) and to his squire (vss. 453–58); the priest's first attempt to buy him off, when he demands his niece Gille (vss. 518–23); several stages in the seduction of the priest's mistress Avinée: the priest's resistance and the knight's persistence (vss. 776–81, 792–803, 818–23), her meeting with the knight (vss. 944–49, 968–75), and her violent dispute with the priest (1020–27); the knight's demand for the priest himself (vss. 1082–87); and the final moment of revelation when the squire understands and sets out for the priest the logic of the knight's revenge (vss. 1132–37), as does Avinée later (vss. 1210–17). Important moments all, but so are many that have no ornate sequences. Isolated ornate rhymes are scattered throughout the text, but the sequences become more frequent as the knight's revenge upon the priest and the comic reversal approach their climax.

Rhyme-words are significant when they relate to the nub of the plot:

plotting, deceit, understanding, bargain, money, power, telling. In general, where such a word occurs repeatedly at the rhyme, and in ornate rhymes, it usually features in at least one sequence. In the first sequence after the prologue, when the knight lays out his plan of vengeance (vss. 409 or 415–22), every rhyme uses significant words: *se porpense / despense* (twice), *guille / Gille* (a telling pun if not technically an ornate rhyme), *lit / delit, Avinee / senee*. Gille and Avinée, the priest's niece and mistress, are the instruments of the knight's revenge, which he thinks up (*se porpense*) to cover his great expenditure (*despense*). *Gille / guille* and *lit / delit* are banal rhymes, frequently found elsewhere, but both sum up the knight's scheme: he works out his guile through Gille, and through demanding pleasure in bed. All these words recur at the rhyme at other stages of the reversal of power. *Despense* rhymes with compounds of *penser* when the priest thinks of offering money to the knight to save his own skin (vss. 1226–27) and when the squire reflects and realizes what his master is doing (vss. 1260–61). He continues to ponder: "Tantost li escuiers s'apense, / Et voit bien et bien s'aperchoit / Que li prevoires le dechoit" [At once the squire remembers and sees well and becomes well aware that the priest is deceiving him; vss. 1261–63]. Understanding deceit is the essence of this fabliau, and *dechoivre* rhymed equally eloquently with *reçoivre* as the priest made his plan (vss. 194–95), occurring again at the rhyme at the striking of the bargain (vs. 381) and in Avinée's dispute with the priest about it (vs. 836). Avinée rhymes *Gille* with *guille* when she acknowledges to the knight that he is turning the bargain to his advantage (vss. 912–13). *Lit* and *delit* rhyme several times, including twice when the knight sends for the priest (vss. 1048–49, 1114–15). *Avinee* rhymes with *destinee* [fortune, chance] when the knight sends for her (vss. 698–99, 720–21), when she leaves him (vss. 970–01, in a sequence), and when she gloats over the priest's distress (vss. 1184–85). These ornate rhymes, then, mark the stages in the knight's revenge, from its devising to its completion.

When the knight explains his plan to his squire, he speaks of service and knowledge, possession and inevitability, connections on which the fabliau relies, and most importantly of agreement and trust:

"De li tele est no couvenenche,
Dont j'ai sa foi et sa creance,

C'a mon talent servis seroie
De tous les mes que je savroie
Que il aroit en sa baillie.
Et ceste i estoit sans faillie!
Por ce le veus anuit avoir,
Qui qui le tiegne a non savoir" [vss. 451–58].

["She is part of our agreement, for which I have his faith and his assurance, that I should be served to my liking, with all the dishes which I should know he had in his possession. And she certainly was! Therefore I want to have her tonight, whoever may think it foolish."]

Vss. 453–55 quote the original bargain (vss. 228–30) verbatim. The squire will do the same later (vss. 1134–36, with vs. 1137 echoing vs. 456), when he at last grasps his master's scheme and its justice — how the bargain necessarily included the priest himself— and expresses his belated understanding by this repetition. Though not an ornate rhyme, *couvenenche / creance* prepares echoes which are: *couvent* rhymes with *avant* several times (vss. 1132–33, 1294–95, 1304–05, 1333–34) to recall the starting point which has led mercilessly to this point of reversal, and *foi* in vs. 452 recalls an equivocal rhyme on *foi* [faith, trust] at the establishment of the faithless bargain (vss. 226–27).

A frequent focus of equivocal rhyme, in and out of sequences, is the word *livres* [pounds, or books]. In conjunction with *saus / faus* [shillings / false], and rhyming with itself or with *delivres* [freed, in total], it sounds like a knell throughout the fabliau. It is always the priest, the false accountant (or the squire quoting him) who rhymes *saus* with *faus*, from when he calculates the bill (vss. 365–66), through his sacrifice of Gille (vss. 600–01), to his attempt to avoid sending Avinée to the knight (vss. 752–53, 808–09).[7] As his bribes rise, so *livres* takes over from *saus*, again mostly in the priest's voice, directly or indirectly. He swears on his books that he will offer seven pounds instead of Avinée (vss. 778–79, 796–97), but the knight refuses (*livres / delivres*, vss. 820–21; all three uses of *livres* in sequences). Finally, in a flurry of rhymes which show his desperation to be free and his reliance on his status as the owner of holy books, the priest resists the knight's demand for himself: *livres / delivres* (vss. 1158–59, 1228–29, 1284–85, 1302–03), *livres / livres* (vss. 1272–73, 1288–89). *Dis livres*, at the rhyme in these last two couplets, returns mid-verse in the very last line of the fabliau to draw it to a close.

As the fabliau ends with money so, as we saw, it begins with a rhyme-word, *conte*, which links its themes of accounting and recounting. This word too recurs in equivocal rhymes: at the knight's demand for Gille (vss. 506–07), the priest's refusal to go to him (vss. 1144–45), Avinée's reproaches (vss. 1214–15), and the final bribe (vss. 1280–81). Even where, as in the first and last instances, only the sense of narration applies, the early establishment of the polysemy brings the other sense irresistibly to mind. Other verbs of telling occur in ornate rhyme, particularly in the sequence when the squire tells the priest of the knight's final demand, where they focus attention on the scandalous fact and content of the message (vss. 1082–87 or 1091). All the ornate rhymes here are significant: *die / desdie, commande / mande* to convey the message and its force, *tiesniés / viegniés, n'i fallés / allés* to assert the link between adherence to the bargain and the priest's going to the knight. The squire rhymed *commande* with *mande* when he first demanded Gille (vss. 502–03, close to *conte / conte* vss. 506–07), while there was an equivocal rhyme *d'ire / dire* [anger / tell], when the knight asked for lodging (vss. 179–80). So the ornate and above all the equivocal rhymes in *PCh* accompany and reflect the unfolding of this tale of messages, money and understanding.

This inevitably very selective exploration of Milon d'Amiens's use of ornate, and especially equivocal, rhyme suggests that he uses it to focus attention on thematically significant words, concentrating it at some of the main stages of his comic narrative but using few uninterrupted sequences of ornate rhymes, and those short. Far more important are the echoes he sets up across his fabliau, and rhyme is one of the ways in which he calls attention to them and marks the stages in the unfolding of his comic intrigue. His anonymous colleague to whom we owe *PCo*, by contrast, uses much more ornate rhyme and gives us many long sequences at moments of heightened emotion, in which the rhyme-words sometimes but by no means always relate to the themes of the fabliau. This poet's rhymes too bring out the comedy of his tale, but since it is essentially episodic they do so by characterizing certain of its episodes. He is a virtuoso in the production of ornate rhyme, and his striking sequences draw attention to the exploitation of which he is capable. For Milon d'Amiens, ornateness of rhyme as such seems insignificant, but it illuminates the important words, concepts, and relations in his tale, above all where they offer themselves to the word-play of equivocal rhyme.

Notes

1. Except *Trubert*, which I and some others do not consider a fabliau because of its length and episodic nature. For that text see Norris Lacy's article in the present volume.
2. "All rhymes other than simple or sufficient rhyme; it thus embraces rich, leonine and equivocal rhyme" (Laidlaw 245, n. 7). I adopt this terminology and broad approach. For discussion of types of, and views on, rhyme in the Middle Ages and the varying terminology, see e.g., Lote II, 136–75.
3. Here and when identifying sequences, I count only rich rhymes, but I include in my discussion non-rich equivocal rhymes and *rimes cloisonnées* (leonine but for a non-identical consonant before the final syllable; Thorington 134) when, as often, they extend a sequence.
4. In *PCh* sometimes two out of a rhyme-group of three. *PCh* has several *vers orphelins* and approximate rhymes.
5. This is Laidlaw's minimum to exclude chance (131).
6. In *PCh* I take three as the minimum for a sequence.
7. In vss. 782–83 the priest's *saus* rhymes with *faus* applied to the squire, suggesting that this is an easy rhyme, ironic as it is elsewhere.

Works Cited

Butterfield, Ardis. "English, French and Anglo-French: Language and Nation in the Fabliau." *Zeitschrift für deutsche Philologie*, Beiheft 13 (2006), 238–59.
Cobby, Anne. "Langage du pouvoir, pouvoir du langage: *Constant du Hamel* et *Les Trois Aveugles de Compiegne*." *Reinardus*, 14 (2001), 131–51.
Cobby, A.E. "Understanding and Misunderstanding in *La Male Honte*." In Gillian Jondorf and D.N. Dumville, eds. *France and the British Isles in the Middle Ages and Renaissance: Essays by Members of Girton College, Cambridge, in Memory of Ruth Morgan*. Woodbridge: Boydell, 1991. 155–72.
Laidlaw, J.C. "Rhyme, Reason and Repetition in *Erec et Enide*." In P.B. Grout et al., eds. *The Legend of Arthur in the Middle Ages: Studies Presented to A.H. Diverres by Colleagues, Pupils and Friends*. Cambridge: D.S. Brewer, 1983. 129–37, 245–46.
Lote, Georges. *Histoire du vers français*. 7 vols. Paris: Boivin, Hatier; Aix-en-Provence: Université de Provence, 1949–92.
Thorington, Ellen. "'De conter un conte par rime': Rimes riches dans *Le Chevalier de la Charrette (Lancelot)*." *Œuvres & Critiques*, 27.1 (2002), 132–54.
The *Charrette* Project: <http://www.princeton.edu/~lancelot/>

The Non-Conformist Fabliau Genre and Its Transgressions: A Bakhtinian Analysis of Two Old French Fabliaux

Jean E. Jost

The Old French fabliaux insist on and delight in transgression of every conceivable form, a structural feature demarcating them from other medieval genres.[1] Although no single constrictive definition can contain this fluid, broadly based genre — which traverses a versatile spectrum of issues — its dissident political agenda, reversing conventional order and power, is a defining characteristic. Moreover, this counter-normative rebellion, crossing their narratives and even their styles, provides a unifying element to the tales.[2] Within the context of tensions of every sort, fabliau authors have established non-conformity by depicting transgressive actions, images, speech, behavior, and attitudes about bodies, dead and alive. They reverse traditional dominance while flaunting joyful hilarity or black humor. It is precisely this unrestrained joy in deviance that marks the fabliaux as Bakhtinian.[3]

Although little discussion of fabliau deviance, Bakhtinianism, or the use of literal, symbolic, and allegorical description has occurred, the notion of carnivalization proves particularly useful in studying the fabliaux. As David Murray notes, "Bakhtin sees the overturning of official unitary languages as coming from the unheard, unofficial voices generated in the less-recognized areas of society, and this life-enhancing debunking of the official he calls *carnivalization* after the model of medieval carnival with its release of folk energies" (116). The fabliaux partake of this phenomenon in multiple fashions, as they transgress the social order and applaud its life-enhancing Dionysian debunking. The joyfully sensual acceptance of the counter-normative and earthy is marked by the characteristics listed above (n. 3). Through those tropes, the tales are made aggressively anti-normative, countering accepted protocol, even being revolutionary. Tales negotiated in these fashions are rebellious and counter-normative.[4] Despite, or perhaps because of, the transgressive nature of the genre, unresolved problems and irresolution remain behind a façade of closure. Design, manipulation, and collusion invert power and bring down the superior, appropriately at the hands of the inferior, in Bakhtinian fashion. Whether they are cruel and justified or not, whether satisfaction is legitimate or not, these tales play on the jealousy of the have-nots, and their ribald and explosively creative ways of getting even. Schenck notes (ix) that here "dupers and victims engage in repeated acts of deception and misdeed, such as adultery, theft, or cheating. A cyclical pattern of aggression and retaliation may end in a pseudo-judicial scene or it may remain unsolved, but in no case does a heroic figure establish harmony or a just conclusion to the conflict." No traditional hero wins in a Bakhtinian topsy-turvy world of power inversion, which lowers the socially prominent and thereby raises the socially disempowered.

More concretely, victims are often rich, powerful males, privileged clergy, or aristocracy; victors may be women, the lower class, or the disenfranchised. *La Saineresse* and *Le Chevalier a la robe vermeille* are among the fabliaux that reveal the multiple methods of wily characters transgressing social and political mores and turning the social order topsy-turvy. Further, within the fabliaux, anti-normative behavior leads to humiliation, shame, physical and mental abuse, trickery, coarse bathroom humor, sexual degradation, castration, beating, and even murder done in the service of social, political, economic, and gender reversal. The language eschews polite refinement, using coarse vocabulary with a smirk, a nudge, or a wink. Subversion occurs in power reversal as wives supplant husbands, peasants supplant aristocrats, clerks supplant priests, and youth supplants age, cruelly encouraging ironic retribution. This drive for mutability, which Gaunt calls "a mistrust of fixed hierarchies" (235), defies established protocol.

Marital fabliaux offer counter-normative subversion by giving wives authority generally claimed by husbands, as in the deception of *La Saineresse* (Noomen, IV, 303–12). Here the foolish burgher who "boasted no woman could outsmart him" (vs. 3) is soundly outsmarted by his own wife.[5] Having overheard his bragging, the unnamed wife swears, "Qu'ele le fera mençongier" [that she would make him out to be a liar; vss. 6–7]. This vow is achieved by identity deception, a cross-dressing lover "Mout cointe et noble, et sambloit plus / Fame que homme la moitié, / Vestu d'un chainsse deliié, / D'une guimple bien safrenee" [... so all dolled up, he seemed by half / more like a woman than a male / in the loose-fitting gown and pale / wimple he wore of saffron yellow; vss. 14–17]. Reminiscent of Bakhtinian carnival, this scene reverses male and female roles, costume, and the empowered and disempowered. With Mardi Gras-like hilarity, the reversals performatively enact the narrative. The foolish burgher readily accepts the ploy of the cross-dressing "lovely lass" (vs. 24). The lover's occupation is equally feigned, since in yet another disguise, he carries cups for bleeding patients, although he is no healer. The naïve burgher, nevertheless, believes his wife's deceptive declaration to her cross-dressing lover:

> "Vous dites voir, ma douce amie.
> Montez lasus en cel solier;
> Il m'estuet de vostre mestier.
> ...
> J'ai goute es rains mout merveillouse,
> Et por ce que sui si goutouse,
> M'estuet il fere un poi sainier."

["Dear woman, you are not mistaken, / go on upstairs; wait for me there, / because I need a surgeon's care. / ... / My loins are swollen up with gout, / and I've been feeling down and out / and in need of a bleeder's skill; vss. 32–34; 37–39."]

Thus, she achieves power over him and turns the gender relationship upside down. After the tricksters' merriment, the still-deceived husband beseeches his wife to pay the "bewitching creature" (vs. 53) generously (vss. 56–57). The transgressive wife perversely details the "healer's" actions in amusingly ambiguous language, pointing out that she was

> "... [a] plus de cent cops ferue,
> Tant que je sui toute molue:
> ...

> Par trois rebinees me prist,
> Et a chascune foiz m'assist
> Sor mes rains deus de ses peçons;
> Et me feroit uns cops si lons...."

["more than a hundred times was battered, / and now I feel completely shattered. / ... / Three times I needed to be tapped, / and each time the blood-letter slapped / two instruments against my haunches / and struck at me with such deep punches ..." vss. 71–72, 75–78.]

Both subversive language — appearing true on the surface but not (allegory) — and actions and identity roles — seemingly valid but not (parody) — undo this marriage vow and reverse its social order. Adding insult to her husband's injury and indulging her pleasure at deception, she continues,

> "Et si ne vous en quier mentir:
> L'oingnement issoir d'un tuiel,
> Et si descendoit d'un forel
> D'une pel mout noire et hideuse,
> Mes mout par estoit savoreuse."

["Nor would I lie to you one bit / about the ointment: it came out / of a tube fashioned with a spout, / squeezed from a black and ugly pelt, / but ho! How wonderful it felt!" vss. 92–96]

Given the circumstances, his sympathetic response in equally ambiguous language is ironic: "... 'Ma bele amie, / ... / Bon oingnement avez eü!'" ["My lovely wife ... how fortunate you had that cream!" vss. 97, 99]. A powerful husband is thus tricked, metaphorically diseased through gender- and identity-deception by a supposed healer, through actions that are not as they seem, by a wife less honest than he believes. The balance of power is inverted by the less powerful wife, reversing their position with true Bakhtinian glee.[6]

La Saineresse illustrates several carnivalesque traits of the fabliaux. Subversion is found in challenges to social mores: action (subservient wives besting dominating husbands), crude anti-normative dialogue, unconventional narration, its representationality, its distance from reality, and its fictive nature. Punitive reprisal is levied against the powerful, as the subservient best them with jubilant, carnivalesque satisfaction. The fabliaux firmly eschew ethical grounding or morality. According to V.A. Kolve,

The Old French Fabliaux

"Characters in such stories live, for the most part, as though no moral imperatives existed beyond those intrinsic to the moment. They inhabit a world of cause and effect, pragmatic error and pragmatic punishment, that admits no goals beyond self-gratification, revenge, or social laughter — the comedic celebration of any selfishness clever enough to succeed" (160). The genre's content is amoral and anti-normative, ignoring, dismissing, or disregarding harm to others, much like children's cartoons bereft of consequences.

This same moral irresponsibility marks the topsy-turvy Bakhtinian world seeking a superior morality in its leveling of the high and low. Regardless of the outrage, hurt, or exploitation of words or actions, no consciousness of guilt or responsibility results. Rather, temporary irresponsibility and license are granted. Cleverness exonerates and elevates the perpetrator, who rarely suffers consequences of his immoral behavior, but often profits by it. The common good of the community or of its victimized members is disdained in Bakhtinian mode, reversing stereotypical hierarchy. Game, and not social welfare, is the narrative intent.[7]

As is the case in *La Saineresse*, few fabliau figures are named, perhaps to diminish the audience's emotional involvement and to maintain a comic mode and tone. More social reorganization may be effected if the inverted "types" remain universal. Unnamed stereotypes — husbands, wives, knights, travelers, clergy — populate the genre, and the victims are dismissively ignored: no pity is offered those who succumb to abuse in this unreal carnivalesque world.

The socially privileged is often an unworthy or unsavory character whose diminished status is gleefully applauded by the audience and allows the duping to be funny rather than pathetic. A fabliau world rejoices as the wife of a rich vavasor becomes a love object despite the transgression this would be in a romance or realistic world. Carnivalesque reversals seek a higher level of morality, equalizing the high and low, if sometimes only temporarily. Because characters are nameless types, tales are free to be more irreverent and invert authority.

Just as carnival's anti-normative inversion of social roles marks Mardi Gras festivities, so counter-cultural inversion of the fabliaux evokes humor by the putatively inappropriate distribution of power. Bakhtin suggests that "because of their sensuous character and their strong element of play, carnival images loosely resemble certain artistic forms, namely the spectacle" (7). The fabliaux share these elements, heightened by upheaval and reversals, making them simultaneously more humorous and more coldhearted.

The lack of any salvific dimension in the genre further alienates it from the normative and allies it with Bakhtin. Positing human nature as duplicitous and outrageous, ironic tales add to the anti-normative character and the audience's sense of alienation from people or plot. Thus fabliau writers use the pragmatic language of philosophy to counter social norms in their clever tales. The anti-normative amorality of the genre finally dominates our expectations. In addition, the tales display a kind of disreputableness, not only by their transgressive use of sexual and scatological words and deeds, but also because they do not offer a one-to-one correspondence to reality or a single, unequivocal meaning. Bloch suggests that "ultimately, the disreputableness of poetry lies in the mobility of its signs ... the poet as a 'quick-change artist,' a Faux-Semblant" (34). This is true of all poetry and its methods of displaying its wares: simile, metaphor, imagery, allegory. The very act of representation is *faux-semblant* [false seeming], but there is more "faux in fabliaux" than in other genres: falseness to an ontological world, a game-playing technique using deception in humorous or serious fashion — joyfully transgressive. Fabliau authors often seek to expose this quality of language.

Despite or because of its transgression, the genre has flourished. As Gaunt, paraphrasing Gabrielle Lyons, argues, "Successful characters in the fabliaux ... constantly use *savoir*, their wit and ingenuity, to determine the position of other characters who believe that their *avoir*, their place in a fixed social hierarchy, be it as a noble, a clerk or a husband, is god-given and unassailable" (235). The literary discipline accepts, encourages, and relies upon symbolism as a truth, a legitimate way of reading. But, since language itself is representational, literary critics forge on, symbolizing. If a genre contains an implicit or explicit moral, it "represents," suggesting by exemplifying a narrative. Analogy and imagery are an intricate game to open understanding, not a stumbling block to it.[8]

My second fabliau, *Le Chevalier a la robe vermeille* (Noomen, II, 241–308), is marked by many transgressive and normative elements. First, as Dubin notes, its locus is specifically 4 July, the day St.-Martin-le-

Bouillant's relics were brought to Tours,[9] in summer when nature's fecundity and fertility come to fruition. Clearly, this date is symbolic as well as literal since fertility and procreation are the matters of the tale. Further, a firm sense of place — the lovers' homes are two-and-a-half leagues apart — and time (pre-dawn) is established as expected. Deferral of the outcome heightens erotic suspense, allows transgression, prevents actions from being crimes of passion (since they are well considered), and furthers plot.

Le Chevalier a la robe vermeille posits an esteemed knight-lover who lived blamelessly. This honor is uncharacteristic, for the typical transgressive fabliau begins with a clever and duplicitous figure. The lover, who is neither, defies the usual expectation of being a disreputable scamp, although he is adulterous, cowardly, and an ostentatious dandy. As Dubin notes, "When he wears it, the red robe signals his vanity; when he doesn't, it signals cowardice" (7). Moreover, the tricked fabliau victim is often an unworthy or unsavory rogue, for whom the audience feels no empathy; hence the duping is funny, not pathetic. Thus the well-spoken, successful, prudent husband also violates the expected when he is duped.

Finally, the audience is presented with a beautiful "idealized" lady who might properly be a wife in medieval romance. However, in the fabliaux world, we accept her as the wife of a rich vavasor and as the knight's love-object. Additionally, she holds a transgressive role within the genre in that *her* quick-witted words, ingenious solution, and trickery, not the knight's, extricate them from trouble. Further reversal of genre expectations occur in the duper-dupee relationship. The knight-lover's higher social status gives him social superiority, although the *nouveau riche* husband is rapidly gaining status by virtue of his wealth. The social reversal violates the fabliaux norm that one of higher social class be duped by a social inferior. The inversion in this tale may indicate historic changes in social class — that the author and/or audience affiliate themselves with a man of lower station who now, at least here, has the greater power and wins the game.

We are told that the wife "devint s'amie" (that is, became the knight's lover, vs. 7). In Dubin's translation, she gave the knight her heart, but the story reveals that she also gave much more: the heart metonymically represents her body and emotions. This structure defies the usual social-class disruption, placing adversaries closer than generic expectations would by aligning knight-lover and vavasor-husband: both are thought worthy, well-spoken, and well-off, but are still rivals. Whereas the lover recalls jurisprudence and court decisions, the husband speaks with prudence and skill. The lover is called a talker and doer but is not so here; the husband is both a talker and a man of action. The lover is a man of emotion, the husband a man of reason, though not always reasonable. This parallel set of virtues deviates from the usual fabliau husbands — foolish, duped, and unsympathetic. Here the husband is quite respectable, verbally astute, and prudent. Nevertheless, when the exceedingly clever wife wins, we cheer.

In addition, the lover's royal ermine-lined red robe embodies representation; it inscribes his identity as the Knight of the Red Robe. Its color, weight, and substance signify his wealth, arrogance, and passion. Second, the color red is blatant rather than surreptitious or sly, signifying the knight who attempts no demure sneaking in, but offers an arrogant and even challenging announcement of his arrival. (This ostentation, atypical in fabliaux, may result from his aristocratic standing.) Third, red symbolizes passion, excitement, and unbridled lust, duly reinforced by his actions — the speed with which he mounts his horse and dashes off to meet his love, the desire to hop into bed clothed, the rapidity of stripping and jumping into bed. The patient, unclad, waiting wife contrasts with the impatient, clothed, dashing lover.

Bloch notes of another tale that the robe itself is an inadequate garment, leaving the wearer only partially covered or protected.[10] Its loose-fitting nature suggests its inability to repel shame, inclement weather, or other bodily threats. It masks the figure by its loose cut, not conforming to body shape, often preventing recognition of its wearer. It provides a hiding place if used as a blanket. Not being tailored to a particular wearer, it could fit anyone, thus providing anonymity. Like the knight's passion, the robe is new. It is made of high-priced wool lined in ermine, representing royalty or aristocracy, which may display arrogance. He feels no need to be discreet (hide his belongings), but may be defensive or fearful of loss in the home of a *nouveau riche* vavasor. He needs to mark his territory (the wife's house), his noble station (the robe), and his sexual property (the wife's body). Second, ermine represents sensuousness in its smooth erotic texture, like smooth bare skin. Moreover, ermine suggests the feminine — with associations of mice, rabbit, beaver and furry places. As Bloch suggests, the coat is also the fabliau; it is linguistic property, "a metaphoric equation of language and clothing, the insufficiency of both to cover what is conceived (as presence) to be the naked body of Nature, and the inherent scandal associated with the cover-up of such a failure" (34). Just as language does not "cover" what is conceived, but is allowed to reveal it, so the robe does not cover what is bare, leaving visible what a reader will inevitably find. Thus it is scandalous and rebellious, transgressive in overthrowing existing hierarchy.

When the non-aristocratic husband discovers the robe, the resourceful wife's suggestion that this aristocratic marker/symbol is a gift to him is carnivalesque. The robe must be returned to the knight, its owner, which violates the wife's promise to her husband that he will have it; since the robe is a representation of aristocracy or nobility, it symbolizes the man wearing it. When the wife first gives her husband the coat, she metaphorically gives him nobility and the role of lover, but when she takes it from him, he loses both. Homosociality is evident here even though it is the wife who entwines the men. The lover's brash display is not aimed at attracting the husband, but it does so. Also, the men temporarily share the same signifiers — wife, bed (the lover lies back against the wall under blankets when the husband crawls in), and clothing. When the knight inadvertently leaves the robe on the chest as he dresses, he abdicates it; this symbol of social class and the role of lover is symbolically left in place of the lost member, a carnivalesque exchange. The wife has pilfered the member, the robe, and the fabliau, and gives the robe to her husband, who temporarily possesses the robe, its chivalric class, and the identity of "lover." Nothing is inadvertent, insignificant, or innocent: at some subconscious psychological level, all action is meaningful and acknowledges unspoken drives. Ultimately, the knight reclaims robe, spurs, sparrowhawk, and dogs, but momentarily loses the wife, bed, and connection to the husband. The vavasor gains nothing that was promised and loses the game by being cuckolded. The lover reclaims his property, and thus his dignity and identity, from the rich vavasor. Although the husband is indeed cuckolded, no one is publicly disgraced, since the infidelity remains secret.

The knight's prominence, indicated by his red robe, is reinforced by his golden spurs, his sparrow hawk, and his dogs. The golden spurs, perhaps phallic, are valuable and eye-catching, a symbol of opulence. Spurs are instruments to encourage a horse to run faster; for a man they are a "tool" to spur on passion. This molting sparrow-hawk is also losing his robe/feathers at a time of adolescence,[11] when he is likely to be fertile and ready to breed. Young dogs accompanying the Knight are good lark-hunters: animalistic, energetic predators. Such extravagant, obtrusive signs would impress his lady, but a clandestine lover should be unobtrusive, so in one sense, he is more stupid than the traditional stupid husband. Taking no pains to conceal anything, he rashly ties his horse in plain view, sets his sparrow-hawk on a perch, places his clothing on a chest visible to all, and hops in bed. This is the man unconcerned with blame, the man of worth and power.

In this tale, the robe-as-inadequate-covering is exacerbated since the knight fails to wear anything on his legs on this hot day (no doubt a phallic reference), although he wears the heavy ostentatious robe. Symbolically, the knight is vulnerable: sexually, to the wife and her bare legs; physically, to her husband who might beat either the lover's or the wife's legs; and psychologically, in his overconfidence and lack of discretion. This may signify overcompensation for a deeper defensive feeling: that lower classes are usurping his noble position. Too blatantly he makes his sexual presence known at his beloved's home. His bareness is an erotic sign, a readiness to find his pleasure. The narrator claims that he does not wear leggings because it is hot, an epistemological passion-marker.

The fabliau is disreputable not for its transgressively blatant use of sexual and scatological words and actions, but for its quality of representation, not "being" but "indicating" other level of meanings, and refusing a one-to-one correspondence with reality. At the heart of this tale is false language or vow-breaking by the wife, infidelity against a husband who appears undeserving of this offense. She promises him the knight's paraphernalia, symbols inappropriate to the husband, even if he is worthy. She then breaks that promise by retracting the gifts, thus committing a double offense. The tale, if not the marriage, is saved by the offending wife's cleverness, however. If words are inherently deceptive in their representational character, her use of them makes them doubly so. The "blameless," "worthy" lover slips impotently behind the bed while the wily wife sneakily deceives her worthy husband with aplomb. The husband has a chance to capitalize on events and trump the lover, but he relinquishes it by falling asleep. He too becomes impotent.

The lady's use of language, a series of verbal infidelities, reinforces her physical unfaithfulness in bed. She systematically tells one lie after another. Ingenious though the falsehoods be, her infidelity is not diminished, but multiplied. She describes all the lover's accoutrements as her brother's gifts to her husband. Her diction is interesting: "Mes onques por mon serement / Ne por rien que seüse dire / Ne poi son voleir escondire!" ["Neither for oath nor argument," she tells her lawyer husband — she who has broken her own oath — "would (her brother) abandon his intent" (to gift the husband); vss. 121–23]. She has thus broken her second promise, never intending to offer anything to her husband. His accusation of her venality is more true than he knows, as the audience realizes in an instance of dramatic irony.

The wife's justification, that it is good to receive, for only receivers are givers, is to be read sexually as well. Her quick words are precisely what the vavasor-husband, who himself uses them well, would value and accept. She solves her last problem, to sneak the concealed lover out the door, by lulling her husband to sleep. The lover, however, collects his belongings, invalidating the wife's explanation for their presence and leaving her to deal with the fallout. Her quick wit extends her lying when she appeals to her husband's pride and vanity: he wouldn't wear hand-me-downs! "Forment vos abesiez," the lady swears; Dubin translates it as "You're lowering yourself" (vs. 205). Besides, she claims that her brother is not to be emulated. With the household properly informed and in collusion with the wife, the husband cannot win. Ironically, he is undone by her speech: he is not so smart after all. She swears, "Sire, foi que je doi mon pere, / Il a bien deus mois et demi / Ou plus que mon frere ne vi!" ["Sire, on my father's soul, it has been over two months since I've seen my brother," vss. 245–47]; she thus contradicts her previous claim that her brother brought the robe that very day, and insists he is fantasizing, being foolish or illogical, and "Ce deüst dire uns fous, uns ivres!" ["A fool or a drunk might make that claim!" vs. 252]. Her aggression increases when she accuses him of being deranged: "...vos estes tieus atornez / Que touz les ieus avez troublez! / ... / ... vos estes enfantomez" ["your mind is so turned around / Your sight is troubled and unsound. / ... / By some demon you're possessed" (260–61, 274).

The wife's final tirade cajoling God to return the husband's senses (vs. 283) ironically concludes with an accusation of promise-breaking, precisely her sin. Like May who convinces January in *The Merchant's Tale* that what he saw was not what he saw, "and made the truth appear a dream" (vs. 307), the wife gets rid of her unwanted vavasor by sending him on a pilgrimage. Dubin notes, "she makes for a convincing witness, and, before you know it, their roles have reversed, and she has taken charge of the investigation" (4). What his senses tell him is true is actually false: the contest between ontological and epistemological truth occurs throughout the genre. Men are recurrently faced with their own perceptions, epistemological reality, which their wives regularly contradict, trying to convince them that ontologically they are mistaken.

Manifesting their ordinary middle-class expression, characters may be shockingly blatant, crude, or crass. Rhymed speech is counter-normative in its bare-bones treatment, seemingly defying protocol and good taste. Contrasting ordinary speech with its taboo topics adds another dimension to fabliau complexity. Because the genre eschews responsibility for hurt or blame, acting on immediate impulse and self-gratification, it uses what Kolve calls "a narrative that is not only funny but oddly innocent and imaginatively gay" (161). This irresponsibility and freedom from judgment, blithely skipping all unpleasant consequences of one's actions, allow for a frivolous dismissal of cruelty and pain. Such a lack of social affiliation, empathy or responsibility produces a strangely detached narrative, devoid of normative reinforcement while approving more equitable social realignment: wifely superiority over husbands, churls' conquest of knights, and husbands besting clerics. This overturning of the powerful promotes a joyous Baktinian celebration and raucous pleasure.

In many ways, fabliaux are fully normative: in colloquial expression, curses and aphorisms, speech-imitating rhymed couplets, ordinary life situations lived by undignified or unremarkable characters, and refusal to move from the baldly realistic to the idealistic. However, their anti-hierarchic and anti-hieratic value system and Bakhtinian carnivalesque inversions defiantly infuse plot, characters, dialogue, and language. We can thus consider Bakhtinian deviance and subversion to be marks or structural pillars of the genre on which the narrative is overlaid and crafted. As Gaunt comments, "writers of *fabliaux* revel in the dismantling of the discourses, structures, and hierarchies through which the culture in which they lived made sense of its world and sought to justify its inequalities with morally ordered, divinely ordained schemes of human life and death" (239). Inverting social and moral worlds to right social inequities, the genre espouses, accepts, and rejoices in the non-normative: the Bakhtinian transgressive, conventionally unacceptable, offers greater creative freedom, simple comic joy, socio-cultural revolution, and a redistribution of newly appropriated power.

Notes

1. For more on the transgressive aspects of the fabliaux, see especially Simon Gaunt (235), Lynette R. Muir (87), and Mary Jane Schenck (x).

2. Gaunt and Norris Lacy, among others, have noted the difficulty in defining the fabliaux corpus. Like Gaunt, I assume the genre's "existence and homogeneity" (234) without defining and hence limiting it.

3. The theories of Mikhail Bakhtin (1895-1975) have exerted strong influence on modern criticism. Particularly notable are his ideas on "carnival," from which the present essay draws. Among Bakhtinian characteristics of the fabliaux I find the following: 1) role-playing or disguise, including parody of people or events (e.g., Noah's flood), and conceivably being allegorical; 2) role-reversals, especially of the *vilain* and the *courtois*, the dispossessed and the powerful, as at Mardi Gras; 3) intrigue, surprise, danger, adventure, or thrills; 4) deception and trickery, especially of a person of a higher social order; 5) game-playing and ritual repetition (often three instances or three times three, as in folktales); 6) a Dionysian sense of unrestraint or license; 7) joyful satisfaction in upsetting the social order; 8) temporary social disruption accepted as exciting and wondrous, not cataclysmic; 9) a tension between actual and perceived reality, and a willing acceptance of the absurd, unlikely, or impossible; 10) vengeance revealing an underlying hostility and rejection of the social order; 11) acceptance of cruelty and disdain, hence a needed emotional distance; often using sex as punishment; anti-feminist and anti-politically correct; 12) use of long-held traditional/ritual "events"; 13) of the common people, their bawdy language and actions; joyfully undignified with an unbridled life-affirming energy, and celebration at being the winners; 14) a controlled perspective or point of view as the narrator poses and postures; 15) comic manipulation through narrative over-determination, carefully orchestrated timing, happenstance; controlled authorial pacing; 16) a return to the status quo at the end, often hastily concluded with no more fanfare than a joyful carnivalesque celebration of victory.

4. Howard Bloch emphasizes the tales' rebellious nature, claiming "one is ... forced to accept the scandal of the fabliaux — the excessiveness of their sexual and scatological obscenity, their anti-clericalism, anti-feminism, anti-courtliness, the consistency with which they indulge the senses, whet the appetites (erotic, gastronomic, economic) and affirm what Bakhtin identifies as the 'celebration of lower body parts'" (11).

5. All translations of fabliau passages in this essay are by Nathaniel Dubin (1998). I am grateful to him for his extensive assistance and humorous translations, to Howard

Bloch and members of the 2003 National Endowment for the Humanities Seminar at Yale for their contributions to this project, and to this volume's co-editors for excellent editorial advice.

6. I thus view the fabliaux in a different light than does Lacy, who suggests "that behind the illicit relationships, cruel deceptions, and outrageous jokes there lurks a fundamentally conservative spirit that endorses what is simple, natural, and direct and that urges the maintenance of the status quo in relationships between classes and sexes" (xiii–iv).

7. Schenck argues that the fabliaux are didactic as well as entertaining (x). However, I question their didactic intent, since deception, changes of fortune, and retribution are not always warranted, do not always result from wrongdoing, and may be enacted against innocents without repercussions.

8. However, contrary to its counter-normative content, fabliau vocabulary level, sentence structure, diction, style, and all-pervasive rhyme are determinedly normative: purposely colloquial and unsophisticated. Its ordinary speech patterns in rhymed couplets border on sing-song doggerel. Formulaic cliches, aphorisms, oaths, curses, and sacred or profane prayers, color characters' dialogue.

9. Nathaniel Dubin, e-mail correspondence, 13 February 2007.

10. Bloch 22, 26, and passim, speaking of *La Vieille Truande* and others.

11. My thanks to Judith Tschann for this insight.

Works Cited

Bakhtin, Mikail. *Rabelais and His World*, trans. Helen Iswolsky. Bloomington: Indiana University Press, 1984.

Bloch, R. Howard. *The Scandal of the Fabliaux*. Chicago: University of Chicago Press, 1986.

Cooke, Thomas D. *The Old French and Chaucerian Fabliaux: A Study of their Comic Climax*. Columbia: University of Missouri Press, 1978.

Dubin, Nathaniel. "Who Is the Knight of the Red Robe, and Why Does(n't) He Wear It?" Unpublished paper, International Conference on Medieval Studies, Kalamazoo, MI, May 1995.

Gaunt, Simon. *Gender and Genre in Medieval French Literature*. Cambridge: Cambridge University Press, 1995.

Kolve, V.A. *Chaucer and the Image of Narrative: The First Five Canterbury Tales*. Stanford, CA: Stanford University Press, 1984.

Lacy, Norris J. *Reading Fabliaux*. 1993; Birmingham, AL: Summa, 1999.

Lyons, Gabrielle. "'Avoir' and 'Savoir:' A Strategic Approach to the Old French *Fabliaux*." Ph.D. dissertation, Cambridge University, 1992.

Muir, Lynette, R. *Literature and Society in Medieval France: The Mirror and the Image 1100–1500*. New York: St. Martin's Press, 1985.

Murray, David. "Dialogics: Joseph Conrad, *Heart of Darkness*." In *Literary Theory at Work: Three Texts*, ed. Douglas Tallack. London: B.T. Batsford, 1987. 115–34.

Schenck, Mary Jane Stearns. *The Fabliaux: Tales of Wit and Deception*. Amsterdam: John Benjamins, 1987.

The *"Fin Humour"* of Guillaume au faucon

Joan Tasker Grimbert

The fabliau genre has generally resisted attempts to assign it a precise definition, and many have fallen back on Joseph Bédier's famously concise formulation of *conte à rire* (11), a funny story.[1] Yet, when we consider humor in the fabliaux, *Guillaume au faucon* (Noomen, VIII, 229–45) does not come readily to mind. Indeed, some scholars do not even count it as a fabliau,[2] and those who do justify its inclusion in their collections and discussions because, first, the author himself refers to it as a fabliau (vs. 614) in his epilogue, and second, a prime role in the denouement is played by an obscene pun that is generally thought to move the narrative abruptly to the register of the fabliau from that of the courtly lai (the latter genre implied by the authorial narrator's statement in vs. 1 that he means to treat an "aventure").[3]

Guillaume au faucon is preserved in a single manuscript (BnF fr. 19152), an anthology apparently conceived as such, containing sixty-one diverse pieces — popular proverbs, translations from Latin, fabliaux, and courtly, didactic, and burlesque poems (Faral 10). In the Middle Ages, of course, the notion of genre was not as clear-cut as was once thought, but surely audiences then had "certain generic assumptions," especially as they related to "the more generalized creation of comic and other expectations."[4] It is from this perspective that I would like to reconsider the comic aspects of *Guillaume au faucon*, which are more pervasive than most critics have claimed and are hardly relegated to the surprise ending.[5] The *fin humour* [subtle humor] of this fabliau, which depends precisely on audience expectations, is urbane and easily overlooked by anyone unfamiliar with literary conventions associated with *fin'amor*, especially with lyric (chanson d'amour, jeu-parti, chanson de malmariée), lai, and courtly romance. While it is perfectly possible to enjoy our fabliau without picking up the abundant intertextual allusions — nods to various genres and apparent winks to specific works — an informed reading will elicit numerous *sourires* along the way to the final *rire*.

Roger Dubuis (262) sees *Guillaume au faucon* as a pastiche of the traditional theme — treated as well in Jean Renart's *Lai de l'ombre* (also in BnF fr. 19152) — in which a married woman confronted with an ardent suitor drives him to despair by her expressed determination to remain true to her husband.[6] In both this lai and our fabliau, the lady abruptly changes her mind, although there are signs throughout each text that point to such an evolution. But the similarity in plot ends there. In Renart's lai, the lady is seduced by the knight's cunning (and charming) gesture of offering his ring to her by tossing it into the well where her face is reflected; in our fabliau, it is the lady herself who seizes upon a clever ruse — dependent on a pun — that will justify her surrender in a manner effectively authorized by her unsuspecting husband. The audience for *Guillaume au faucon* may well have known Renart's lai and found particularly funny the contrast in the way the impasse is resolved. But there are many more implicit references to texts and to various genres that set up expectations whose delicious disappointment would have been a keen source of enjoyment. The subtle humor of *Guillaume au faucon* results, in my opinion, from the effect of these allusions and the artful alternation of courtly and fabliau elements.

The characterization of the two main characters, Guillaume and his lady, conforms to the general conventions of lyric — the ardent suitor and the resistant (often married) noble *dame*— but the two are fleshed out in a way that makes them quite complex. The lady's characterization is full of contradictions. She is beautiful, of course, but, oddly enough, the detailed description of her physical person and her clothing corresponds — in places word-for-word!— to Chrétien's portrait of Blancheflor. The close resemblance between the two portraits would not by itself have been a source of laughter if not for the single original — and striking — element added by the narrator, who compares the lady's beauty, when she was elegantly dressed, to that of a molted falcon (vss. 69–70).[7] This detail is important in that it foreshadows the denouement, in which her lord's falcon will play a crucial role (Eichmann 75).

Morally, the chatelaine could not be more different from Blancheflor. She is a sophisticated, married woman, her castle is not under siege, and it is hard to imagine her making advances to her husband's amorous squire in the way the rather desperate Blancheflor dares to come on to Perceval (Chrétien, *Perceval*, vss. 1960–2069). Is she then the haughty Lady of lyric? The narrator's moralizing misogynist commentary (vss. 32–48), which effectively undermines the courtly setting, seems calculated to make us think so. Observing that if she had known how Guillaume felt, she would have refrained from talking to him, like a "feme trop mal aprise" [very rude woman; vs. 30] he launches into a tirade against the capricious behavior of the typical *belle dame sans merci*, who refuses even to talk to a man on discovering he loves her. The clear implication is that Guillaume's lady is the same sort of woman. Yet, as the story evolves, her character seems much more nuanced. She will resist her suitor's advances in part no doubt because he is yet only a squire but also because she appears to be a faithful and loving wife, hardly a *malmariée*— at least until her husband pushes her into that role.

In fabliaux, where anonymity is the rule, names can be significant. The suitor is the only character in this fabliau who bears a name, and "Guillaume" is richly evocative, as it is associated with the verb 'guiler,' to trick or seduce, and with the nouns 'guilant' and 'guileor,' a deceiver.[8] Guillaume definitely deals in deceit, but this trait is masked by his earnestness and what seems initially to be a disarming naïveté. A young, noble squire in love with his lord's wife, he has waited seven years to speak out, and indeed has delayed learning arms in order to remain at the chatelaine's side. When one day he declines her husband's invitation to accompany him on the tourney circuit, Guillaume finally makes his move, and this subtle comedy is launched.

The amicable relationship the squire apparently enjoys with the chatelaine helps to set the stage for a comic misunderstanding once he completes his love *complainte* and heads for the lady's chamber. When he enters, she greets him with a look of tender consideration ("La dame fait un doz regart," vs. 185). Smiling, she begs him to sit down, calling him "beaus amis chiers" ["dear fair friend" vs. 193], a variant on "biaus doux amis" [fair sweet friend], a frequent form of address in women's songs. The chatelaine is entirely unaware of having encouraged the squire by addressing him thus, and the audience may well have been reminded of comic situations in other works involving the ambiguity of the term "ami" [friend / beloved]. For example, in *Cligés*, Soredamors is truly stymied by the mere question of how to address Alixandre. Should she call him "Ami"? No! She dares not, but his name is too long to utter; calling him "ami" would be so much easier. Even "mes dolz amis" [my dear friend] would be better, she is musing when the Queen arrives and nonchalantly greets him as "Amis" (Chrétien, *Cligés*, vss. 1378–420).

The intimate setting in the chatelaine's chamber is inviting. As the squire and his lady sit side-by-side, laughing, joking, and speaking of this and that, Guillaume requests a *conseil* [advice] that the lady agrees to give. If a man has loved a woman for seven years without revealing that love, he asks, has he been foolish or wise? The audience would have recognized this situation as the kind found in the jeu-parti, a courtly genre that flourished in the thirteenth century in which one partner asks the other to choose between two options in a particular situation. But the choice usually depends on the specification of important socio-economic data (class, power, wealth) and of moral traits (generosity, arrogance).[9] Guillaume's hilariously all-inclusive manner of characterizing the social status of the "protagonists" in this hypothetical situation empties it of all the particulars needed to make an informed choice.

"Se clers ou chevaliers amoit,
Borjois, vallez, qui que il soit,
Ou escuiers meïsme ensanble,
Dites moi que il vos en senble—
S'il amoit dame ou damoisele,
Reïne, contesse ou pucele,
De quele guise qu'ele soit,
De haut liu ou de bas endroit—"[vss. 208–15].

["If a clerk or knight were in love, or a bourgeois, a young man of whatever condition, or even a squire, tell me your opinion: if he loved a lady or maiden, a queen, countess, or young girl of whatever rank, from the highest to the lowest ..."].

Guillaume begins his list of male protagonists with the most likely categories and ends with his own (unlikely) case. By running the whole gamut of possible male and female classes, he reduces the situation to one question: is it foolish or wise to hide one's love?[10]

The lady, no doubt charmed to be asked for advice, neglects to enquire about specifics and falls headlong into the trap — and into the comic role reserved for her. A man in love would not be wise to conceal his feelings when he has the chance to speak, she opines. If she happens not to love him, she will still show him *merci*. She clearly means that the lady would be merciful in her refusal, but in troubadour lyric, this term was highly coded, signifying the ultimate gift of the Lady's body, whereas in much of Old French literature, it simply meant "pity" or "mercy." In what follows, from the moment the chatelaine refuses to grant Guillaume the *merci* he seeks up to the point that she gives in, the author plays delightfully on the ambiguity of the word.

The chatelaine becomes even more immersed in this comedy when she confidently cites another reason for encouraging the hypothetical male to speak out: Love does not esteem cowards. Rising to the occasion, she is categorical in her judgment:

> "Amors demande hardement!
> Un jugement droit vos en faz:
> Cil que Amors a pris au laz
> Ne doit pas estre acoardi,
> Seürs doit estre et hardi.
> Se ge ere d'amor esprise,
> Foi que ge doi a saint Denise,
> Diroie li comme hardie.
> Itant li lo ge que li die:
> S'ele le velt amer, si l'aint" [vss. 241–50].

["Love requires daring. Here is my just sentence: he whom Love has ensnared must not be a coward, but rather confident and bold. If I were in love, I swear by St. Denis I would not hesitate to speak out. I counsel him thus to declare himself. If she wishes to love him, let her do so."]

By saying that she herself would follow her own counsel, she graciously extends her "jugement" to include the situation of a *woman* in love.[11] In

The "Fin Humour" of Guillaume au faucon (Grimbert)

this scene, we are reminded again of *Cligés*, as we recall the anguish that Alixandre and Soredamors endured while fretting about whether to speak out, and the Queen's subsequent warning that they are only harming themselves by not doing so. But of course Alixandre and Soredamors are perfectly matched, and when the Queen counsels them, she already knows their feelings are mutual.

Although Guillaume is hardly in the same situation as Chrétien's lovers, the chatelaine's forceful counsel encourages him to confess immediately that he is the very one who has languished so long—and for her love alone. Adopting the stance of the perfect courtly lover (in a scene reminiscent of Yvain's initial declaration of love to Laudine[12]), the squire puts himself totally in his lady's power, assuring her that he has always been and will forever be hers, and exhorting her to heal his "wound" by granting him the gift of her love. He naturally assumes she will be sympathetic even if she happens not to love him, since she has assured him that a lady will show *merci* to a man who confesses his love. But of course she had been operating in the abstract, and now that Guillaume has furnished the specifics, she is incensed by his impertinent proposition.

The narrator's report of her brutal reaction is frankly comical after Guillaume's exceedingly courtly speech: "La dame entent bien que il dit, / Mais tot ce prise molt petit" [The lady understands well what he is saying, but she assigns very little value to it; vss. 275-76]—"Not a cent's worth" (vs. 278), specifies the narrator. Initiating a hurtful tirade (vss. 281-304), she actually asks him if this is a joke ("gas"), claims never to have been the butt of a joke ("gabee"), and tells him to address his jokes elsewhere ("Vos gaberoiz encor autrui!"). If the audience could have anticipated this response, it would only be because the romance situations that the previous interview recalls concern totally different sets of characters. To be sure, the narrator's earlier misogynous complaint about women who refuse even to speak to men that they learn are devoted to them could have alerted us to the chatelaine's abrupt change of humor and her stern warning never to broach this matter again (Lacy 55). She justifies her attitude by claiming to know nothing of love or of anything he is requesting and threatens to report his conduct to her husband.

The spell is definitely broken, but have we left the realm of the courtly lyric? Perhaps not, because if only we were privy to the manner in which the resisting Lady in troubadour lyric might have formulated her refusal, we could imagine hearing similar language, especially since, although the chatelaine curses Guillaume roundly ("'Mal dahez ait parmi le col'" ["A curse on him (who brought you here)"][13]; vs. 302]), she continues to use the same courteous address that had initially encouraged him, even as she exhorts him to depart: "'Baus sire, quar vos en alez!'" ["Fair sir, leave!" vs. 292]; "'Beaus amis, traez vous en la!'" ["Fair friend, get out of here!" vs. 304]. The troubadour lover would no doubt have persisted, as does the narrator/lover in Chrétien's song, *Amors tençon et bataille*. So, too, does Guillaume, who, though he feels "dolenz et esbahiz" [grieved and upset] and justifiably "trahiz" [betrayed; vss. 309–10], knows he must not give up. True to the lover persona he has assumed, he vows never to eat another morsel until she takes pity on him. Curiously, he puts on the same plane the two gifts (*dons*) he asks her to grant: his right to abstain from eating and her *merci* (Leclanche 167, n. 4). The ensuing tug-of-war is delightful, but from here on in, the courtly ambiance is undermined by the gradual intrusion of the husband's presence. Guillaume, as good as his word, pleads for *merci* from his lady, who he claims is his health and salvation, whereas she remains inflexible as she attempts to persuade him to end his hunger strike by reminding him of the fidelity he owes his lord and threatening to expose to her husband what has transpired during his absence.

The humor at this point lies in the striking contrast between Guillaume's exaggerated claims, dictated by his love sickness (he even hallucinates that he is holding her in his arms[14]), and the chatelaine's reasoned language governed by common sense. The lady appears caught between her friendship for the squire and her determination to hold her ground. At this point in the story, she seems the polar opposite of the lusty, deceitful wife of numerous fabliaux or the *malmariée* of so many women's songs. But the fact that she expends so much energy trying to bring Guillaume to reason indicates that she somehow enjoys the "game" they are playing and hints at an eventual change of heart, as does (paradoxically) her emphatic contention — thrice repeated in the space of fifteen lines — that he will never have what he seeks:

> "Guillaumes, foi que ge vos doi,
> Vos n'avrez ja merci par moi

The "Fin Humour" of Guillaume au faucon (Grimbert)

> En tel maniere com vos dites.
> ...
> Ja ne porroiz veoir le jor
> Que vos m'aiez en vo baillie!
> ...
> Quant vos ainsi vos ociez,
> La vostre ame sera perie,
> Quar ge ne vos donroie mie
> Le don que vos me demandez" [vss. 412–14; 419–20; 423–26].
>
> ["Guillaume, I swear you will never have 'merci' from me in the way you mean." ... "Never will you see the day when you will have me in your power!" ... "If you kill yourself in this way, your soul will be lost, for I would never grant you the gift you request of me."]

As we endeavor to uncover clues indicating the chatelaine's eventual surrender, it is well to recall that in the *Lai de l'ombre*, Renart prepares the lady's change of heart as the logical conclusion to the evolution in both protagonists' thoughts, which he records in detail for his audience. The lady, we learn, is impressed with the suit of this most perfect of knights, and she realizes that she would never find a more worthy lover. She is charmed by his gesture of entrusting his ring to "the woman he loves best after her"—her reflection in the well. The narrator of our fabliau, on the contrary, provides no such commentary, keeping us guessing as to the effect that the squire's suit is actually having on the chatelaine.

The narrator changes his strategy when the knight returns from his tourneying, and the manner in which he creates a sense of mounting suspense accounts for a good part of the humor in the second half of the story. So, too, does the play on generic expectations, for with the introduction of the husband as an active "partner" in this triangle, the audience can foresee that this apparently courtly lai may well turn into a fabliau. The lady has already threatened to expose Guillaume's faithless behavior, and upon her husband's return home, she makes one more attempt to knock sense into the squire—in vain: the narrator notes wryly that she leaves his room "sanz estre amie" [without agreeing to be his beloved; vs. 443]. A real stand-off, it will end badly, or so we are led to believe. The chatelaine's response to her husband's inquiry about Guillaume's absence from the table seems categorical: "'Il est malades d'un tel mal / Dont ja n'avra medecinal, / Sicom ge cuit, en nule guise'" ["He is sick with a malady for which, I do believe, he will never ever have medicine"; vss. 466–68]. When her lord expresses sympathy, the narrator's muscular commentary compels us to anticipate a veritable showdown:

> Mais s'il seüst bien l'aquoison
> Por quoi Guillaumes se geüst,
> Ja du lit ne se remeüst!
> Il ne le set encore pas;
> Il i a un molt fort trespas:
> Ge cuit a toz tens le savra,
> Que la dame li contera
> La parole, s'il ne menjue,
> Par quoi la teste avra perdue [vss. 471–79].

[But if he knew the reason why Guillaume was in bed, never from that bed would he rise again! He does not yet know it. A very grave fault has been committed, and I think he will learn about it at any moment now because, if Guillaume refuses to eat, the lady will tell him — and Guillaume will lose his head.]

The audience's expectations at this point are dictated not only by its knowledge of the brutality that generally characterizes the confrontation between a husband and his wife's lover in countless fabliaux but also by the expressed intransigence of the chatelaine and the unreliable narrator's grossly misleading commentary. As husband and wife head for Guillaume's room,[15] we anticipate that all hell will break loose, but it does not, because neither the Lady nor her lord acts in a manner consistent with our expectations. The husband actually kneels at his squire's feet and gently inquires why he is ill. The wife, irritated no doubt by this show of tender affection, coupled with Guillaume's adamant refusal to modify his behavior in response either to his lord's inquiries or to his lady's escalating threats, is led to the brink of an explanation. But she gets no further than mentioning Guillaume's visit to her bedroom and threatening (for Guillaume's benefit) to expose "'la grant honte et la deshenor'" ["the great shame and dishonor"; vs. 540] when her husband interrupts her, flying into the canonical fabliau rage. Yet, contrary to the narrator's earlier prediction, his anger is directed toward his wife rather than Guillaume. Does this detail — the courtly knight's abrupt metamorphosis into a wife-berating husband — help tip the balance in favor of the love-sick suitor? The poor woman

The *"Fin Humour" of* Guillaume au faucon *(Grimbert)*

issues one last threat, and then, apparently moved by Guillaume's steadfast refusal to end his fast even in the face of impending violence, she has a change of heart:

> Lors en ot la dame pitié
> Et a son seignor respondi:
> "Sire, Guillaumes que vez ci
> Si me requist vostre faucon,
> Et ge ne l'en voil faire don;
> Si vos dirai par quel maniere:
> Qu'en voz oiseaus n'ai ge que faire" [vss. 559–65].

[Then the lady had pity on him and gave her lord this response: "Sire, Guillaume, whom you see here asked me for your falcon. I did not want to make him a present of it, and I'll tell you why: your birds are none of my affair."]

The lady's show of mercy at this point is not the only surprise, for the knight's generous response demonstrates once more his great affection for Guillaume. But again he is kinder to his squire than to his wife. Telling her he is not pleased with her handling of the situation, he asserts that he would rather Guillaume have all his birds than that he be sick in bed for even one day. "Bien l'a la dame deceü!" [Truly, the lady has deceived him! vs. 571], exults the narrator. The lady agrees to give Guillaume the falcon, as her husband has instructed, virtually "authorizing" her to be false or unfaithful to him.[16] She proceeds to do so, but not before Love has pierced her with its arrow.

The moment at which the Lady suddenly takes pity on Guillaume is generally considered the pivot of this text — the point at which it is transformed from a courtly lai into a fabliau by means of an obscene pun. On handing over the falcon/"faux con" [false cunt], the chatelaine notes that Guillaume has received two (valuable) things for the price of one (vss. 606–07), and the narrator confirms that the squire has, in effect, killed two birds with one stone, adding: "Et cil si ot ainz l'endemain / Le faucon dont il ot tel faim, / Et de la dame son deduit, / Qu'il ama mielz que autre fruit" [And before the next day he had the falcon/false cunt for which he had so hungered, and his enjoyment of the lady, which he liked better than any fruit; vss. 610–13]. But does this pun, which fabliau scholars

143

before Jodogne do not seem even to have recognized,[17] really have enough shock value to signal at this point a sudden change of registers? We have seen that fabliau elements had already been introduced with the intrusion of the husband. Moreover, the chatelaine's change of heart is not as abrupt or unforeseen as has been claimed. Nor is it inexplicable; not only is it the logical result of Guillaume's devotion, it is a natural response to her husband's thoughtless treatment of her. How poorly he has rewarded her steadfastness, her confidelity, so to speak!

We have seen that this work includes elements of both the courtly lai and the fabliau, and that most of the humor comes *not* from the pun that finally breaks the deadlock between Guillaume and the lady, but from the clever play on expectations raised either by allusions to other works/genres or by the narrator's misleading commentary. In the epilogue, the authorial narrator underscores the mixture of genres that we have noted. By means of this "flabel" [fabliau; vs. 614] he has illustrated an "essanple novel" [brand-new lesson; vs. 615] addressed to young men in love; if they are bold and persevering in their suit, they cannot help succeeding. The advice returns us to Guillaume's original jeu-parti and proves that the lady gave him excellent advice indeed!

Notes

1. See Ménard's discussion and conclusion (36–45).

2. Voicing the common view, Muscatine calls it "a predominantly courtly poem that barely qualifies as a fabliau by virtue of tonal irregularities at its very end" (65).

3. In both these respects *Guillaume au faucon* resembles another fabliau, *Du chevalier qui recovra l'amor de sa dame*, which also seems essentially courtly until the surprising ending (Lacy 46–55).

4. Lacy 53; see also 18–34.

5. Nor is *forme* [form] really privileged over *fond* [content], as Dubuis has asserted (262).

6. Tudor dates Renart's lai to 1217–22 or 1201–04 (9) and notes that some scholars have also seen it as poking fun at courtly love (12). See Jodogne's insightful comparison of these two texts (1044–45).

7. Reid (199, n. 67) lists the verses in the fabliau (vss. 68, 71–90, 91–97, 112–13) that correspond to the *Roman de Perceval*, vss. 1796–827. Vss. 69–70 are inserted into the description of Blancheflor's elegance, which is said to surpass that of a sparrowhawk or parrot (vss. 1795–97).

8. The noun 'guillaume' does not appear in the Old French dictionaries of Godefroy, Greimas, or Tobler-Lommatzsch, but it may have been forged later. In *La Farce de Maistre Pathelin*, when the cloth merchant suspects Pathelin's deceit, he muses,

The "Fin Humour" of Guillaume au faucon (Grimbert)

"Et tient il les gens pour Guillaumes" (772). The word is glossed as 'sot' [fool] by Picot, who reminds us that the name of the cloth merchant (who tries to deceive and is himself deceived) is Guillaume (117).

9. The various "cases" put before Marie de Champagne in Andreas Capellanus's famous treatise also define the classes scrupulously.

10. See Långfors VI for a *jeu-parti* on this same theme.

11. Leclanche believes she is simply putting herself in the situation of a male suitor (163, n. 2), but one question raised in jeux-partis that had women participants was whether it was acceptable for a woman to reveal her love first if the man were too reticent (see, for example, Doss-Quinby, 74–78). Soredamors also considers this question (Chrétien, *Cligés*, vss. 992–1046).

12. Chrétien, *Yvain*, vss. 1976–2038. Yvain's avowal is similarly exaggerated, but his lady responds well to it, since it is in her interest to accept his suit.

13. This curse seems illogical since it was Guillaume himself who "brought" him there (Leclanche, 167, n. 1), but it has the merit of recalling the moment when Lunete blames Yvain, in almost the same terms, for remaining silent when brought into the presence of his lady (Chrétien, *Yvain*, vss. 1961–65). The irony is that Yvain is reproached not for speaking out but for failing to do so.

14. In *Cligés*, Alis, drugged by Thessala's potion, dreams he is making love to Fenice (vss. 3307–50). The knight in the *Lai de l'ombre* also dreams that he is holding his beloved (Renart, vss. 178–79), but it is before he even formulates his declaration.

15. This moment is the most exciting from both the narrative and dramatic viewpoint "because the episode itself and the nature of the tale are held in suspense" (Eichmann 75).

16. Nykrog considers this work a fabliau because the "indulgent husband" is a fabliau type (17), but since the husband fails to grasp the pun, he does not really authorize his wife's adultery (Jodogne 1044, n. 4).

17. The pun is not remarked upon by Reid or Nykrog (Muscatine 115). Dubuis (262, n. 31) finds it curious that Bédier, normally so sensitive to obscenity, praises this fabliau's elegance (11), delicacy (246), exquisite sentimentality, and noble essence (322).

Works Cited

Andreas Capellanus. *The Art of Courtly Love*, trans. John Jay Parry. 1941; New York: Columbia University Press, 1969.

Bédier, Joseph. *Les Fabliaux: Etudes de littérature populaire et d'histoire littéraire du Moyen Age*. 1893; Paris: Champion, 1964.

Chrétien de Troyes. *Cligés*, ed. Stewart Gregory and Claude Luttrell. Cambridge: D.S. Brewer, 1993.

———. *Le Chevalier au lion ou Le Roman d'Yvain*, ed. David F. Hult. Paris: Librairie Générale Française, 1994.

———. *Le Roman de Perceval, ou Le Conte du Graal: Edition critique d'après tous les manuscrits*, ed. Keith Busby. Tübingen: Max Niemeyer, 1993.

Doss-Quinby, Eglal, Joan Tasker Grimbert, Wendy Pfeffer, and Elizabeth Aubrey, eds. *Songs of the Women Trouvères*. New Haven: Yale University Press, 2001.

Dubuis, Roger. *"Les Cent Nouvelles Nouvelles" et la tradition de la nouvelle en France au Moyen Age*. Grenoble: Presses Universitaires de Grenoble, 1973.

The Old French Fabliaux

Eichmann, Raymond. "The Failure of Literary Language in *Guillaume au faucon*." *Reinardus*, 1 (1998), 72–78.
La Farce de Maistre Pathelin, ed. Guillaume Picot. Paris: Larousse, 1972.
Faral, Edmond. *Le Manuscrit 19152 du fond français de la Bibliothèque nationale*. Paris: Droz, 1934.
Jodogne, Omer. "Considérations sur le fabliau." In Pierre Gallais and Yves-Jean Riou, eds. *Mélanges offerts à René Crozet*. 2 vols. Poitiers: Société d'études médiévales, 1966. II, 1043–55.
Lacy, Norris J. *Reading Fabliaux*. 1993; Birmingham, AL: Summa, 1999.
Långfors, Arthur, ed. *Recueil général des jeux-partis français*. Paris: Librairie Ancienne Edouard Champion, 1926.
Leclanche, Jean-Luc. *Chevalerie et Grivoiserie. Fabliaux de chevalerie*. Paris: Champion, 2003.
Ménard, Philippe. *Les Fabliaux: Contes à rire du Moyen Age*. Paris: Presses Universitaires de France, 1983.
Mucatine, Charles. *The Old French Fabliaux*. New Haven: Yale University Press, 1986.
Nykrog, Per. *Les Fabliaux: Etude d'histoire littéraire et de stylistique médiévale*. 1957; Geneva: Droz, 1973.
Reid, T.B.W., ed. *Twelve Fabliaux*. Manchester: Manchester University Press, 1958.
Renart, Jehan. *Le Lai de l'ombre*, trans. and introduction by Adrian P. Tudor; text ed. by Alan Hindley and Brian J. Levy. Liverpool Online Series. Liverpool: School of Modern Languages, 2004.

Modern Dirty Jokes and the Old French Fabliaux

Logan E. Whalen

Scholarly discussions of the literary corpus that we now collectively call the Old French fabliaux often raise more questions than they answer.[1] Even agreeing on which of these texts from the end of the twelfth through the first half of the fourteenth centuries should be classified as fabliaux remains one of the most problematic issues of genre in our discipline. In fact, Norris J. Lacy proposes the use of "nexus" rather than "genre" when discussing the fabliaux to broaden the boundaries of definition (*Reading Fabliaux* 33). The delicate nature of classification is reflected in the variation of texts counted as fabliaux from one critical edition to the next, ranging anywhere from 127 with the recent work of Willem Noomen and Nico van den Boogaard, to 147 in Joseph Bédier's 1893 study, to the 160 proposed by Per Nykrog in 1957. Although all of the relatively brief tales that fall into this category share some common structural elements, such as their composition in octosyllabic rhymed couplets and their narrative as opposed to lyric form, their themes vary and are broad in scope: antifeminism, anticlericalism, deception, adultery, sexual obsession, and scatology. Some, like *Trubert* (Noomen, X, 143–262) and *Berangier au long cul* (Noomen, VI, 245–77), represent intricately constructed compositions whose literary value rivals that of the more serious courtly genres of lai and romance, but the simple, playful nature of others make them little more than medieval dirty jokes (Lacy, "Fabliau" 333).

In considering fabliaux in the latter category, this article relies on oral evidence in contemporary popular culture alongside written scholarly sources to focus on the way in which certain texts echo, through both their structure and themes, modern dirty jokes that permeate all social classes and cross linguistic, cultural, and geographic borders.[2] In his preface to Marie-Thérèse Lorcin's book on the fabliaux, *Façons de sentir et de penser: les fabliaux français*, Georges Duby notes that these Old French texts may not have described medieval life as it should have been, or even life as it really was. Rather, they offered more of an intersection of these two ideas: "…ils empruntent à la vie les éléments d'une intrigue simplette et d'un décor, l'un et l'autre ajustés à la 'mentalité' des dominants de la société féodale. La valeur pour nous de tels écrits tient précisément à ce mélange de vérité et d'allusion" (vi). The humorous appeal of these stories remains as relevant in our day as it was to the bourgeois and courtly circles of medieval France, and modern dirty jokes play on episodes from real daily life as easily as they embrace and promote the urban legend.

When I teach fabliaux in both undergraduate and graduate courses, students immediately recognize the similarity of texts like *Cele qui se fist foutre sur la fosse de son mari* (Noomen, III, 375–403) and *De la crote* (Noomen, VI, 25–32) to jokes they heard and told as adolescents. In specifying how the fabliaux recall contemporary anecdotes, students invariably mention thematic and structural concerns, but perhaps even more engaging than their responses about the relationships between Old French fabliaux and modern dirty stories is their disagreement at times over exactly what constitutes a joke in the modern sense of the term. These classroom discussions regularly reveal that it can be just as challenging to classify a joke as it can be to identify which brief medieval narratives should count as fabliaux. Some students distinguish between, say, riddles, anecdotes, limericks, and longer fabricated narratives, while others simply lump together all humorous stories as jokes. Lacy has commented on the element of humor as it pertains to the similarity between the modern joke and the fabliau:

> I once suggested that the modern form most closely related to the fabliau is the joke. I would still defend that position, but with an important reservation: we can take the joke as a close relative of the fabliau, but not as its equivalent, because that too would assume that humor is the single necessary ingredient. An acceptable synonym of "fabliau" may instead be "anecdote," for the term suggests the restricted form and content, while

allowing for a range of intents and effects, from bawdy humor to amusing portraits and even, conceivably, to moral lessons [*Reading Fabliaux* 30].

Since this study focuses on the thematic relationship between modern dirty jokes and fabliaux, I limit my discussion here to texts that contain bawdy themes and argue that they are, for all intents and purposes, what we would consider as dirty jokes in contemporary society.

Like some fabliaux, some jokes are complex short narratives that require the audience to follow a carefully constructed storyline before the punch line is delivered, while other jokes amount to nothing more than a simple question and answer. For example, there is the question, "What's black and white and re[a]d all over?" and its response, "a newspaper," a joke because it is humorous, or is it just a trick question intended to demonstrate the homophonous play on "red," the color, and "read," the past participle of the verb "to read"? I believe most of us would put this riddle in the joke category, as well as all the racist, sexist, gory, obscene, and sacrilegious variations it has engendered throughout the years. In the same way, are limericks still limericks when they take on a "dirty" character, or can we say that they become at that point dirty jokes? I recall from my youth a bawdy limerick that began, "I knew a girl from Old Kentuck / She couldn't cook, but she sure could fuck." As adolescents we referred to this poem as a dirty joke long before we even knew what the definition of a limerick was. Furthermore, some brief jokes have become so codified in our culture that they do not even require a question to solicit a response. Utter the simple onomatopoeia, "Knock, Knock," anywhere in the United States and one is guaranteed to prompt her or his interlocutor to respond, "Who's there?"

The point is that modern dirty jokes, just like their medieval counterparts, can be short expressions or more complex narratives, but are still known broadly as "jokes." The third edition of *The American Heritage Dictionary of the English Language* defines a joke as "Something said or done to evoke laughter or amusement, especially an amusing story with a punch line.... Joke can be traced back to the Latin *iocus*, or 'jest, sport, laughingstock, trifle,' which in turn can be traced back to the Indo-European root *yek-*, meaning 'to speak....'" The common element of all jokes appears to be their intention to amuse, or evoke laughter, and in this respect, they share an aim identical to many of the Old French fabliaux. Most scholars interested in the fabliaux recognize that all the texts in the corpus, regardless of whose list one follows, represent a desire to amuse the audience for which they are destined. As Lacy notes, "Even when the authors draw logical moral conclusions from their anecdotes, their primary purpose is in a broad sense entertainment" ("Fabliau" 334).

Yet another common trait between fabliaux and the modern joke lies in the mode of presentation to their audience, specifically, whether the person telling the story wants those who are receiving it to know in advance that what they are about to hear is a joke, or whether she or he hopes to introduce the first elements as though they were real events in order to offer the punch line as a surprise. Take for example the modern one-line joke: "I used to have a friend who was into sado-masochism, necrophilia, and bestiality, [insert a pause here] but then he realized he was just beating a dead horse." Without an introduction, this line has quite a different effect than if the person presenting the joke first said, "I've got a joke for you: I used to have a friend who was into sado-masochism, necrophilia, and bestiality...." The former presentation plays on the credibility of the line as seen from the perspective of the audience — it is entirely conceivable that someone could have a friend who was obsessed with such sexually aberrant behavior, causing the audience to hesitate over the punch line before realizing what they just heard was a joke — whereas the latter presentation clearly proposes a joke. Even the more subtle introduction, "This guy walks into a bar," has become, at least in American culture, a sure marker to alert the audience to a forthcoming punch line and is seldom confused with the actual beginning of a true story.

In the same fashion, about half of the Old French fabliaux do not announce themselves as such, while around seventy of the tales employ a form of the word "fabliau" in the first few verses to signal to the audience that what one is about to hear is a joke or anecdote and that they should expect a punch line or comic ending (Lacy, "Fabliau" 333; Nykrog 21–25). Furthermore, in the same way that the modern fixed introduction, "This guy walks into a bar," announces a joke, the very mention of a jongleur's or author's name in the exordia of some fabliaux may have in fact served as a sign to the audience. For instance, Keith Busby speculates ("Courtly Literature" 67) that the name Garin, which appears at the beginning of six texts, could have aided the audience in identifying each tale as a fabliau. As Nykrog's list shows us, the same could be true for any other author who composed more than a few fabliaux and whose name appears in the poem (325).

Many fabliaux are not as straightforward in their presentation and begin as though one could be listening to an account of actual events, the narrative material having been arranged in such a way as to reveal slowly the fact that the story in question amounts to a joke of sorts. This paradigm opens the text of *Le Vilain Asnier* (Noomen, VIII, 207–14):

> Il avint ja a Montpellier
> C'un vilein estoit costumier
> De fiens charigier et amasser
> A deus asnes terre fumer.
> Un jor ot ses asnes chargiez;
> Maintenant ne s'est atargiez,
> El borc entra, ses asnes maine
> Devant lui chaçoit a grant paine:
> Souvent le estuet dire: "Hez!" [vss. 1–9].

> [There was at Montpellier a peasant whose custom was to load his two donkeys with manure. One day he loaded them and did not waste any time heading to town, all the while following after them and saying, "Giddy up!"]

Containing no mention of the word "fabliau," this passage represents a perfectly normal and believable scenario in which a worker is going about his everyday job. However, the audience becomes a bit suspicious about the veracity of the events being recounted as the narrator soon reveals that the peasant faints from the agreeable odors of the spice merchants when he walks by their stands and that the crowd believes he is dead. The audience realizes what they are hearing is undoubtedly a joke as the narrator delivers the punch line: a passerby revives the peasant by holding a clump of manure under his nose.

Turning now to specific examples of Old French fabliaux that bear remarkable thematic similarities to modern dirty jokes, one notices implications of the popularity of some of these tales vis-à-vis their possible intended audience. *Les Quatre Souhais Saint Martin* represents what Nykrog identifies as a "fabliau classique," a text that is found in three or more manuscripts (324–25).[3] In addition to its inclusion in the late thirteenth- or early fourteenth-century Paris, BnF, fr. 837 that contains fifty-eight fabliaux, the most preserved in any codex (Busby, *Codex*, I, 439–43), this fabliau is also recorded in three other manuscripts.[4] The story recounts the adventures of a peasant couple that are granted four wishes by Saint Martin because of the husband's dedication to the saint. The wife first wishes that her husband will be covered in pricks ("vit"), since just one is not enough for her, and he immediately sprouts them from his head to his feet:

> Et sitost con ele l'ot dit,
> Si saillent do vilain li vit,
> Li vit li saillent par lo nes,
> Et par la boche de delez.
> Or poez oïr granz mervoilles:
> Li vit li saillent des oroilles,
> Darriere, aval et amont,
> Et par devant en mi lo front;
> Tot contreval, desi q'as piez,
> Fu li vilains de viz chargiez [vss. 103–12].

[As soon as she spoke, pricks sprouted all over the peasant. Now hear what a sight it was to behold. They sprang forth from his nose, mouth, forehead and ears. He was completely covered in pricks from his head to his feet.]

In revenge, the husband quickly wishes the same misfortune on his wife and she immediately grows cunts ("con") all over her body:

> Dit li vilains: "Ce poise moi:
> Or sohaiderai, par ma foi!
> Je resohait, fait li bons hons,
> Que tu raies autretant cons
> Comme je ai de viz sor moi:
> Autretant cons raies sor toi!"
> Lors fu la fame bien connue:
> Ele ot un con en la veüe,
> Quatre en ot el front, coste a coste,
> Et con detrés et con encoste,
> Et con devant et con darriere [vss. 141–51].

[The peasant said, "Oh no! Now I will make a wish! I wish," said the man, "that you have as many cunts as I have pricks. May you have as many cunts!" The woman found straight away cunts on her face, four on her forehead side by side, and cunts all over her front and back.]

In haste, and foolishly, the husband wishes that the genitalia be removed from him and his wife, and the wish is granted:

> Et li prodom sohaide et dit
> Q'ele n'ait con ne il n'ait vit.
> Lors fu la jantis dame irie
> C'on de son con ne trova mie,
> Et li prodom, qant il revit
> Qu'il n'avoit mie de son vit,
> Refu de l'autre part iriez [vss. 181–87].

[And the man wished that she would have no cunts and he no pricks. The lady then became upset when she noticed that she didn't have a cunt at all, and the man, in his turn, was angry when he saw that he had no prick.]

Unfortunately, this means that they must use their last wish to return them to their original physical state:

> "Sire, fait ele, sohaidiez
> — Lo cart soait encor avon —
> Que vos aiez vit et je con:
> Puis si seron comme devant,
> Si n'i avron perdu noiant."
> Et li prodom resohaida;
> Si n'i perdi ne gaaigna,
> Car ses viz li est revenuz,
> Mais ses soaiz a il perduz... [vss. 188–96].

["My lord," she said, "wish that you have a prick and I a cunt for we have one more wish. Then we will be like we were before and will not have lost anything." Then the man wished again, with nothing lost or gained, for his prick was returned, but he had lost his wishes.]

There are, of course, many possibilities of theoretical analysis here, and this text has already been thoroughly treated during the past twenty years.[5]

Notwithstanding the useful insights made into this and other fabliaux under discussion here, my concern in this study lies in the resemblance of this text to the myriad "genie jokes" circulating today. In one popular version of the genie joke, a man sits down at a bar, puts a paper sack in front of him, orders a drink, and then begins to cry quietly. The bartender brings his drink, notices the tears, and asks him if he is okay. The patron replies that he should be happy because he ran into a genie earlier in the day who granted him just one wish, a wish that would give him anything he wanted. He begins to cry harder and points toward the sack. The bartender asks if it contains what he wished for, and the man nods his head yes. Consumed with curiosity, the bartender asks to see the contents of the bag so the man reaches inside, pulls out a tiny baby grand piano, places it on the bar, then reaches back inside and pulls out a little man and places him on the bar in front of the piano. The miniature man immediately sits down at the piano and begins to play skillfully. The bartender exclaims that he has never seen anything like that before and cannot believe that the patron is sad for this gift from the genie. The patron looks up at him and replies, "Do you honestly think that I wished for a ten-inch pianist?" In the modern version of this joke the saint is replaced by the genie, but the general theme remains somewhat similar to the one in the fabliau.

Le Chevalier qui fist parler les cons (Noomen, III, 45–174), a tale by the aforementioned Garin, was among the most popular Old French fabliaux based on the surviving manuscripts, seven of which contain this text. According to Noomen's research, only one other fabliau, *Auberée* (Noomen, I, 161–312), is recorded in more manuscripts — eight — and two others, *La Couille noire* (Noomen, V, 163–89) and *Le Sacristain* (Noomen, VII, 1–189), are also preserved in seven manuscripts. The popularity of this tale during the Middle Ages, like that of *Les Quatre Souhais Saint Martin*, may seem surprising given their overtly lewd sexual content. In fact, most of the thirty "classic" fabliaux would probably make the Christian Coalition's banned book list today and earn an NC17 or higher rating by the motion picture industry.

In this tale, a knight helps three fairies in distress and is rewarded by each of them with a different miraculous power: 1) he will always be shown good hospitality wherever he travels, 2) he will be able to speak to the vagina of any woman or female beast and it will have to respond, and 3) if the vagina cannot respond for any reason, he can command the anus to speak in its place. Over the course of the 618 verses he uses each of these gifts, including during the final episode in which he is warmly received at a castle by the count and countess. After dinner, the countess asks one of her ladies in waiting to slip into the knight's bed since she herself cannot go. As the knight touches the lady in waiting's vagina he is reminded of his power and commands the sexual organ to speak:

> "Sire cons, or parlez a moi!
> Ge vos vueil demander por quoi
> Vostre dame est venue ci.
> –Sire, ce dit li cons, merci!
> Quar la contesse l'i envoie
> Por vos faire soulaz et joie,
> Ce ne vos quier ge ja celer" [vss. 419–24].

["Lord Cunt, speak to me! I want to ask you why your lady came here." "Lord," said the cunt, "thank you!" "I will hide it from you no longer: the countess sent me here to bring you pleasure."]

Dismayed when her sex responds, the woman flees the room to tell the countess what she has seen and heard. The countess does not believe her and challenges the knight the next day, wagering that he will be unable to prove his powers on her. He accepts the wager, she goes to her room and stuffs her vagina with cloth, then returns to the hall. The knight orders her vagina to speak, but begins to lose heart when there is no response. His squire quickly reminds him of his third power, and the knight immediately asks the anus to tell him why the vagina would not speak:

> Le cul apele maintenant,
> Si le conjure et si li prie
> Que tost la verité li die
> Du con, qui parole ne muet.
> Ce dit li cus: "Quar il ne puet,
> Qu'il a la gueule tote plaine
> Ne sai de queton ou de laine,
> Que ma dame orainz i bouta,
> Quant en sa chambre s'en entra" [vss. 570–78].

[He now addressed the ass and asked it to tell him the truth about the cunt, why it would not speak. The ass responded, "It cannot because its mouth is stuffed with either cotton or wool — I am not sure which — that my lady put in there when she went to her room."]

After learning that the countess had stuffed herself with cotton or wool, the knight complains to the count, who makes his wife remove the cloth. This time when asked, the genital replies:

> Li chevaliers au con parole,
> Si li demande que devoit
> Que tost respondu ne l'avoit.
> Ce dit li cons: "Ge ne pooie,
> Por ce que enconbrez estoie
> Du coton que ma dame i mist" [vss. 598–603].

[The knight spoke to the cunt and asked it why it had not replied earlier. The cunt said, "I could not, for I was stuffed with cotton my lady had put there."]

Le Chevalier qui fist parler les cons resonates with matter found in modern versions of dirty jokes in which the vagina is personified, material that perpetuates the misogynist theme of the *vagina dentata*, the hungry vagina, or the talking genitalia.

Preserved in only one manuscript, the famous Paris, BnF, fr. 837, *Du Con qui fu fait a la besche* (Noomen, IV, 13–22) tells how the Devil, at God's command, created the vagina:

> Trestoz les feremenz esgarde
> Un a un, que point ne s'i tarde;
> Et quant il a trestout veü,
> Si a mout bien aperceü
> Que la besche est assez trenchant,
> S'en puet on fere maintenant
> Une grande fosse et parfonde:
> Il dist qu'il n'a si bone el monde.
> La besche prent et si s'afiche,
> Toute enz jusqu'au manche la fiche:
> Ainsi fist le con a la besche [vss. 53–63].

[The Devil did not waste any time looking over all the tools before him one by one. After he had seen each one, he realized that the shovel was rather sharp, and that one could dig a big and deep hole with it. He said that there was nothing better in the world, so he took the shovel, stood in position, and buried it up to the handle: thus the cunt was made with the shovel.]

This anecdote contains elements that bear noticeable similarity to a poem I often heard recited in junior high school. Like the fabliau it resembles, this modern poem participates in the objectification of a woman through her genitalia as it recounts how the vagina was made by seven men from various professions — carpenter, blacksmith, tailor, hunter, doctor, fisherman, and priest — each responsible for a different aspect of its construction. The first few verses suffice to demonstrate the similarity: "Seven wise men made up their minds / to make a cunt of their own design. / First was a carpenter full of wit, / with a hammer and chisel he made the split...." While the modern text focuses exclusively on the description of the sexual organ, the fabliau is more misogynist in the verses quoted here and in the rest of the text. The tale implies that a woman's sexual organ is evil — it is made by the Devil and not by God — and explicitly states elsewhere that she talks incessantly, is responsible for a man's financial woes, and should be beaten regularly.

In the end, I am not arguing for direct transmission of exact versions of Old French fabliaux from the Middle Ages to the modern era, although that may have been the case with a few of the 150 or so fabliaux, such as *La Damoisele qui ne pooit oïr parler de foutre* (Noomen, IV, 57–89), a tale almost thematically identical to the ubiquitous modern farmer/daughter and euphemism jokes. Rather, I see ancient origins in the themes themselves that reappear in subsequent generations, producing modern jokes that resemble their medieval counterparts, a sort of *translatio ioci* (to adapt the concept of *translatio studii*), the transfer of knowledge from one generation and culture to the next. In this paradigm *Ur*-jokes possibly passed from Ancient Greece and Rome to the continent, then to England, and ultimately across the Atlantic Ocean to the United States. I do not propose that this transmission necessarily took place with the Mayflower, but perhaps occurred even within the last century, when these tales that had survived in Europe from the Middle Ages may have eventually made their way into our own culture through stand-up comedians, films, other media in pop culture, and most recently the internet.

The Old French Fabliaux

I agree with Lacy, as cited above, that instead of considering fabliaux as a genre we may instead need to think of them as a nexus of texts that share common linguistic and thematic traits. I suggest that most of the texts that belong to this nexus of fabliaux are jokes of one kind or another in the way that we use the term today and in the sense that I have argued above. That is to say, they are different from lai, romance, or even fables, and are texts whose principal function remains to entertain, more often than not through humor, a humor that is frequently scurrilous in nature, but not at all lost on its audience 700 years later. Whatever didactic elements the fabliaux contained, it appears that medieval society sought to entertain itself through these primarily humorous stories by juxtaposing them with more serious performances or readings in much the same way that we use jokes in our own contemporary culture to remind ourselves that life doesn't always have to be serious.

Notes

1. I thank my research assistant, Brett Anderson, for his valuable insights and collaboration on this project.
2. Although this study concentrates on jokes that remain current in North American culture, specifically in the United States, I have witnessed that similarities in the structure, content, and humor of the modern stories under consideration here exist in other countries, even at times in the form of the same joke, *mutatis mutandis*.
3. He does not include this tale in his list although it qualifies according to his own criterion.
4. See the *Inventaire des manuscrits* at the beginning of any of Noomen's volumes: Berne, Bibliothèque de la Bourgeoisie, 354, Paris, BnF, fr. 12603, and Oxford, Bodleian Library, Digby 86.
5. For example, E. Jane Burns cogently argues that this text serves as an example "in which female characters might be heard as resisting, speaking against, and dissenting from, the very discourses that construct female nature" ("This Prick" 195).

Works Cited

Bédier, Joseph. *Les Fabliaux: Etude de littérature populaire et d'histoire littéraire au Moyen Age*. 1893; Paris: Champion, 1964.

Burns, E. Jane. "This Prick Which Is Not One: How Women Talk Back in Old French Fabliaux." In Linda Lomperis and Sarah Stanbury, eds. *Feminist Approaches to the Body in Medieval Literature*. Philadelphia: University of Pennsylvania Press, 1993. 188–212.

Busby, Keith. *Codex and Context: Reading Old French Verse Narrative in Manuscript*. 2 vols. Amsterdam: Rodopi, 2002.

———. "Courtly Literature and the Fabliaux: Some Instances of Parody." *Zeitschrift für romanische Philologie*, 102 (1986), 67–87.
Lacy, Norris J. *Reading Fabliaux*. 1993; Birmingham, AL: Summa, 1999.
———. "Fabliau." In William W. Kibler and Grover Zinn, eds. *Medieval France: An Encyclopedia*. New York: Garland, 1995. 332–34.
Lorcin, Marie-Thérèse. *Façons de sentir et de penser: Les Fabliaux français*. Paris: Champion, 1979.
Nykrog, Per. *Les Fabliaux: Etude d'histoire littéraire et de stylistique médiévale*. 1957; Geneva: Droz, 1973.

Esprit gaulois *for the English:*
The Humour of the
Anglo-Norman fabliau

KEITH BUSBY

One of the most remarkable features of Middle English literature is the almost total absence of fabliaux. Outside of Chaucer's *Canterbury Tales*, the only poem universally accepted by scholars as a fabliau is that known as *Dame Sirith and the Weeping Bitch*, preserved, not by chance, I would contend, in Oxford, Bodl., Digby 86, one of the well-known English literary manuscripts examined in this article. I will not go over the arguments regarding *The Canterbury Tales* as a repository of representative genres or the idea that the compiler of Digby 86, like Chaucer, was trying to give French narrative the *entrée* into Middle English, although I believe such arguments to be persuasive as at least a partial explanation of the situation (cf. Busby, "Conspicuous by its Absence").

In earlier studies of the fabliaux (esp. Busby, *Codex and Context*, I, 437–63), I suggested that reading these short narratives in the local context of their major manuscripts (such as Paris, BnF, fr. 837 and fr. 19152; Bern, Burgerbibl. 354; Berlin, Staatsbibl., Hamilton 257) added much to their meaning and a specific dimension to their general intertextuality. I will look here at some Anglo-Norman fabliaux, mainly in two important trilingual manuscripts, Digby 86, and London, BL, Harley 2253, and show how their general and immediate contexts create both meaning and humour.[1] I reject any suggestion that either of these books is a "miscellany" if such a term implies random selection and ordering of contents, or "provincial," except in the literal sense of the word. Indeed, one of the most extraordinary features of both of these two books is the fact that even though they were produced and owned far from London, they contain quite sophisticated and canonical works in all three languages. These are not the books of the merchant classes but rather of the aristocracy of the West Midlands, whose cultural and personal connections were with the highest royal courtly circles. Digby 86 was produced in the Worcester area between 1272 and 1282, and probably copied by its first owner, Richard II de Grimhill (Tschann and Parkes lvii), while Harley 2253 was produced around 1340 by a professional scribe in the Ludlow area of Shropshire, possibly for the Ludlows of Stokesay (Revard). Although the Grimhills were less elevated socially than the Ludlows, members of the family are well-attested in the documents, linked to the Beauchamps of Warwick, were appointed to royal commissions and involved in disputes with the Despensers (Miller). Such a socio-historical context does not exclude humour, even of the most vulgar kind. Indeed, looking at the whole corpus of fabliaux, those contained in Anglo-Norman manuscripts are among the most shocking to modern sensibilities. The general dearth of fabliaux in England is therefore more apparent than real as the genre seems to have been regarded as more appropriately expressed in French rather than English.

Ian Short and Roy J. Pearcy have recently published eighteen texts, including four tales from the *Ysopet* of Marie de France and seven from an Anglo-Norman version of the *Disciplina Clericalis* of Petrus Alfonsus, as the corpus of Anglo-Norman fabliaux.[2] I do not dispute their inclusion of these tales in the corpus, particularly in light of the presence of the *Disciplina* text in Digby 86, but will restrict myself here to the poems independent of a formal framework. The principle of structuring and ordering a collection of fables or moral tales within a defined space may, however, have provided an example for manuscript planners and compilers to follow on a larger scale and with texts of different genres.

Before coming to the two principal manuscripts, I should like to consider briefly the two Anglo-Norman fabliaux preserved elsewhere. Little can be said of the context of *Le Héron* (a euphemistic variant of the continental *Cele qui fu foutue et desfoutue*) in Clermont-Ferrand, Archives Départementales du Puy-de-Dôme F2 (s. 13$^{ex.}$) as the manuscript is fragmentary (Noomen, IV, 151–88), but *De un chivaler e de sa dame e de un clerk* (Noomen, X, 117–42) in Cambridge, Corpus Christi College 50 (s. 13$^{2/2}$) affords general insight into the place of the fabliau in the French genre-system as perceived by the planners of English manuscripts. Without going into the detail of any specific intertextualities, the goings-on between the knight, his lady, his sister, and the clerk stand brazenly in between Wace's *Brut* and a list of English kings on the one hand, and *Amis et Amiloun*, *Les Quatre Filles de Dieu*, and *Gui de Warewic* on the other (description in Wilkins 26–32). There is no obvious sense of codicological incompatibility, and the bedding and beating of the fabliau become more outrageously funny as a prologue to the two quasi-hagiographical romances and the allegory of God's daughters.

The text of *Les Quatre Sohais Saint Martin* in Digby 86 begins on f. 113r, at vs. 44 of the most recent edition (Noomen, IV, 199–210) owing to a number of missing quires (probably four, judging from the signatures). The texts that immediately preceded *Les Quatre Sohais* cannot therefore be established, although it would be possible, even tempting, to read the manuscript as it now stands. This is especially appealing as the ff. 74r–112v contain, in addition to the *Chastoiement* (made up of individual short tales) and Raoul's hellish dream-vision, the suggestively titled "De vn vallet qui soutint dames et dammaiseles" (ff. 102v–103v), *La Complainte de Jerusalem* by Huon de Saint-Quentin (ff. 103v–105r), Robert Biket's *Le Lai du cor* (ff. 105r–109v), "Le Fablel del gelous" (ff. 109v–110r), *La Prière Nostre Dame* by Thibaut d'Amiens (ff. 110r–111r), and *La Bestournee* by a certain Richard (incomplete, ff. 111r–112v). What we see here, I would argue, is an alternation of the frivolous and the serious, the spiritual and the secular, which creates humour by juxtaposition and *Stimmungsbrechung* within the first two longer texts in the sequence and between the shorter ones which follow. This is exactly what is found in the larger continental books mentioned above and authorizes us to read the *Quatre Sohais* and the texts that follow it in the same manner.

What is probably the earliest fabliau to be preserved in an Anglo-Norman manuscript is a shocker. Its obscene and surreal *merveilleux* borders on the sacrilegious as the fractious husband and wife squander the wishes granted them by St. Martin by first conjuring up and eliminating a profusion of pudenda before having to use the final wish to return to a state of normality. It even surpasses in its breathtaking and detailed cornucopia of both kinds of genitalia the display of male organs in *Le Sohait des vez* (Noomen, VI, 259–72), and stands out, as it were, in a corpus of texts where three-letter words are par for the course. The intertextuality of these two hallucinatory poems outside of their manuscript contexts is underlined by the fact that both are predicated on the notion of wishing, one moral of the first obviously being that you should be careful what you wish for; the second is that a man cannot trust his wife with something so important. Taken on its own, *Les Quatre Sohais Saint Martin* is humourous enough with its portrait of the gullible husband, his harridan of a wife, and their mutual panic at the situation into which they have wished each other. Much of the humour also derives from the nature of this particular fabliau as a parodic variant of the miracle tale or the kind of story related at the end of a saint's life as evidence of sanctity.

The version of *Les Quatre Sohais Saint Martin* in Digby 86, however, does not end with the short moral of the continental version. Its redactor moves seamlessly into an extract of thirty-six lines from *Le Blasme des femmes* into which he inserts another twenty from *Le Chastiemusart* (transcribed in Noomen and Van den Boogaard's apparatus to vol. IV, 409–11). Whoever was responsible for this (and it may have been Richard de Grimhill) therefore had at his disposal full texts of both of these anti-feminist pieces, the first of which appears in full in Harley 2253 (ff. 111rb–vb). The *mise en page* of Digby 86 makes it clear that the text up to and including the first line of f. 114rb is meant to be read uninterrupted. No *titulus* separates the narrative of *Les Quatre Sohais* from its synthetic conclusion, the following heading being "La vie d'un vallet amerous" on the second line of the column; *tituli* are the general rule in Digby 86. The only indication of the factitious conclusion is the compressed appearance of the alexandrines of *Le Chastiemusart* in columns more suited to the octosyllable of the rest of the text.

Although these excerpts from *Le Blasme des femmes* and *Le Chastiemusart* are quite apposite as an extension of the anti-feminist moral of *Les Quatre Sohais Saint Martin*, their humour may derive more from their excessive length than from their suitability. No other fabliau, however openly edifying, has a concluding diatribe of fifty-six lines to sober up the reader or listener after the compulsive hilarity of the tale itself. What starts out as a mere corroboration of the lesson becomes a ranting anaphora of female vices and character defects that finally ends with the simplest of advice to men: "Qi li donast poy a manjer, / E mal a vester e a chaucer, / E batust menu e sovent, / Dounke freit fenme a soun talent" (ff. 113vb–114ra). Keep your woman ill-fed, ill-clothed, ill-shod, well-beaten, and she will obey you. Yet despite all the anti-feminism, so familiar to us from so many medieval sources, we must wonder whether the overkill of the conclusion does not have the opposite effect of making us in the end laugh as much or more at the weakness of the husband.

Given the apparent familiarity of the Worcestershire milieu with a whole range of French texts, it is likely that the Grimhills and their immediate circle would have recognized the intertextual game being played here. There is little doubt that the kind of quotation and wholesale appropriation that marks the ending of *Les Quatre Sohais Saint Martin* in Digby 86 is elsewhere part of a ludic collusion between author and audience, between scribe and reader, the point of which is to spot the source and appreciate the author's skill in identifying and incorporating extraneous material. If that is the case here, the truly perspicacious might have pricked up their ears at the following couplet from *Le Blasme des femmes*: "Pur ceo vus di par seint Martin / Que femmes sount de mal engin" [This is why I tell you, by Saint Martin, that women are full of evil tricks; f. 113vb.] The saint, having witnessed the squandering of his gift by the foolish couple (that is to say, by the wife) would surely be in a position to know. And is the saint also blind to the foolishness of the husband? The textual history of the *Blasme* is obscure (Fiero, Pfeffer, and Allain 12–16), but the redactor of the Digby extract must surely have been attracted to the rhyme "Martin : engin" by its suitability in the context. In an interesting modification to a rhyme in the list of men deceived by wicked women (Solomon, Sampson, Constantine, Hippocrates), the last-mentioned is said in the B version of *Blasme* (Wright, *Reliquiæ Antiquæ*, II, 223)[3] to be well-versed in medicine "Qe tant savoit de medicyne artz" [Who knew so much of the art of medicine]; in Digby 86, the line is entirely renardian and reads: "Qui taunt savoit d'engin et d'ars" [Who knew so much of trickery and cleverness; f. 113vb]. Even Renart can be deceived by Hersent. The echo of *Le Roman de Renart* is confirmed by the veritable bestiary contained in a single line of the excerpt from *Le Chastiemusart*: "Leoun, lepart, gopil, singe, chat, e chen" [Lion, leopard, fox, monkey, cat, and dog; f. 114ra]. These can all be tamed and controlled. Not so a wicked woman.

Esprit gaulois *for the English* (Busby)

The next poem in Digby 86 is an obscene *unicum*, entitled in the manuscrit itself *La Vie de vn vallet amerous* (ff. 114rb–116va), of which I will forego a lengthy summary.[4] Suffice it to say that its young male narrator appears to suffer from a not unusual hormonal imbalance that only sexual activity can cure. Once he has successfully followed his brother's advice on how to arouse and seduce his "amie," he finds her malodorous, overweight, and physically repugnant. Rejecting tall and skinny women, he concludes that petite women, pliant and compliant, with a sweet disposition, are the only ones for him. He cannot resist attempting to seduce any woman who fits the bill, irrespective of her social origins. However, the prospect of fatherhood terrifies him, not just because of mewling infants in the house, but also because women use children as a means of dominating men. He is therefore determined to run the gamut of women until he finds one who is not only beautiful (and presumably petite) but also infertile. Only such a woman will he marry. He concludes by beseeching Saints John, Thomas, and Alban to transmit his request to God, whom he also begs to forgive him his sins so he may gain eternal life.

Clearly, this poem continues where the extended anti-feminist conclusion of *Les Quatre Sohais Saint Martin* leaves off, but moves in a very unusual direction towards quite a unique conclusion. The link between *La Vie de vn vallet amerous* and the fabliau that precedes it is the intercession, actual and invoked, of saints in everyday life. It is comic in the *Quatre Sohais* because of the obscene use to which it is put, and in the young man's tale because of the breathtaking unlikelihood that John, Thomas, or Alban would ever agree to pass on this outrageous and hubristic appeal to God above, let alone that God would ever grant his prayer. Saint Martin apparently has a lot to answer for, because when the young man asks his brother's advice towards the beginning of the poem, he invokes the patron saint of Tours:

> "De moun estat li fist saver
> Tout la fin,
> Si priay pour Saint Martin
> Cunseil de luy,
> Coment puray moun ennuy
> Meuz chever" [f. 114rb].

["I informed him all about my condition, and begged him, for Saint Martin's sake, to advise me how I could put an end to my distress."]

The Old French Fabliaux

In the last instance, however, it is the faithful who abuse the goodwill of the saint, the couple by stupidly squandering the four wishes, the young man's brother by offering cynical advice in Martin's name, and the young man himself by following the advice and his own selfish sexual inclinations. The users of Digby 86 could hardly have ignored the repeated appeals to Saint Martin and might in retrospect even have attributed the surreal profusion of pudenda in *Les Quatre Sohais* to the feverish imaginings of the *vallet amerous*. And as the young man expresses his desire to repent eventually at the end of his life, so the compiler of Digby 86 makes amends for including the two scurrilous and anti-feminist poems by next copying a section of Robert Grosseteste's *Château d'amour* about the four daughters of God (also present in CCCC 50), women of a different kind altogether (Murray 94–101).

The section of Harley 2253 I wish to examine here is ff. 107v–127v, not because its beginning and end correspond to gatherings, but rather because it contains all of the manuscript's fabliaux and is framed by two poems featuring an aristocrat and a minstrel,[5] *Le Jongleur d'Ely et le roi d'Angleterre* (ff. 107va–109vb) and a poem in Middle English concerning the Countess of Dunbar and Thomas of Erceldoune (otherwise known as Thomas the Rhymer, ff. 127rb–va); Harley 2253 does not usually attribute titles or rubrics to its individual pieces. The *Jongleur d'Ely*[6] is a dialogue between the minstrel and his king, whose humour depends to a large degree on puns and the ambiguity of language, in which the latter, to his obviously increasing frustration, rarely gets a straight answer. After a short description of his carefree, unsavoury, and precarious lifestyle (of which the king heartily disapproves), the jongleur launches into a long discourse on how appearance and behaviour are always interpreted perversely by contrarious and petty-minded persons. Like language, social status and human activity can be deceptive.

The verbal humour of the *Jongleur d'Ely* and its topsy-turvy world where virtue is vice and wisdom is folly prepare us for a local manuscript context where anything goes. The last voice in the poem is that of the jongleur himself: "Car um poet oyr sovent / Un fol parler sagement. / Sage est qe parle sagement, / Fol come parle folement" [For you can often hear a fool speak wisely. A wise man speaks wisely, just as a fool speaks foolishly; f. 109vb].

The opening of the next poem, the fabliau of *Les Trois Dames qui troverent un vit* (ff. 110ra–va; Noomen, VIII, 274–77), continues the discourse in the first person: "Puis que de fabler ay comencé, / Ja ny ert pur moun travail lessé" [Since I have begun to tell tales, want of effort will not make me stop; f. 110ra]. The narrator of the *fabliau* is thus the jongleur from Ely, a "rybaud" by his own admission and in the eyes of the king of England, whose very livelihood depends on the kind of shameless verbal trickery to which the king fell victim: "'Je di bourde pur fere gent ryre, / Et je vous en countray, bel douz syre'" ["I tell jokes to make people laugh, and I'll tell you some, fair gentle lord"; f. 108rb].[7] In this light, the point of *Les Trois Dames* becomes not merely one of anti-feminism, but whether the object found on the path is indeed what it at first appears to be or whether it is the bolt of the abbey door or a relic, all three of which possibilities are offered for our consideration in the text. In the end, the female pilgrims, the abbess, and Dame Eleyne see in the item in question exactly what they want to see. The former are easily distracted from their spiritual journey to Mont St. Michel, while the latter two are not as free of carnal desires as they ought to be.

Much of the humour in the fabliau is generated by carrying over lessons learned from the *Jongleur d'Ely*, but the play of narrators may be even more complex. Per Nykrog was the first to point out that the opening couplet of *Les Trois Dames* is a lightly retouched variant of the first two lines of Marie de France's lai of *Yonec* (84). The narrator's preferred genre is now fabliau instead of lai, but are we dealing with Marie or the jongleur from Ely? Things may not be what they seem. Even a fleeting suspicion that Marie is behind *Les Trois Dames* would cause a sharp intake of breath. Although Marie's *Equitan* borders on the fabliau genre by virtue of its plot and cruel dénouement, and despite the classification of some of her fables as fabliaux, Marie is never guilty of indiscretion or vulgarity. Her incompatibility with the abbess of *Les Trois Dames*, in light of her own possible station in life and favourable treatment of convents and their inhabitants in the *Lais*, is stridently humourous.

The same question regarding the identity of the narrator now has to be posed, with no prospect of resolution, at the beginning of the next poem, the so-called *Dit des femmes* (ff. 110vb–111rb; ed. Wright, *Reliquiæ antiquæ*, II, 218–21), which calls a halt to the vilification of the female sex.

The Old French Fabliaux

Women are beautiful, sweet, and virtuous; those who malign them are "de vileyne natioun" [of a boorish race; f. 111ra]. And "Qy a femme fet vyleynie, / Dieu ly doynt male vie" [May God bring a bad life to him who does ill to women; f. 111ra.]. Of women are born all men: "Roys, countz, e barouns, / Evesques, freres que fount sermounz, / Prestres, moygnes, e abbés" [Kings, counts, barons, bishops, friars who deliver sermons, priests, monks, and abbots; f. 111ra]. Women inspire deeds of arms, virtue, and love: "De femmes vienent les pruesses, / Les honeurs, e les hautesses, / Tote bounté e drywerye" [From women come deeds of prowess, honours, and lofty deeds, all goodness and love; f. 111rb]. There is a switch of narrator here, perhaps to a female one, possibly even someone like Marie de France, but the apology for women is short-lived, for *Le Blasme des femmes* (ff. 111rb–vb; ed. from this manuscript by Wright, *Reliquiæ antiquæ*, II, 221–23, and Jubinal, *Nouveau Recueil*, II, 330–33) restores the underlying anti-feminism of the sequence; this is the same poem on which the redactor of *Les Quatre Sohais saint Martin* in Digby 86 drew for his lengthy concluding moral. This contrasting pair operates on more than just a general level, for the *Blasme* responds in detail to some of the female virtues trumpeted in the *Dit*. Just to give one example: rather than inspire prowess, women are the origin of wars, death, destruction of cities and castles, quarrels and duels, and cause men to leave religious orders (f. 111va). The woman-centred sequence terminates with *Femmes a la pye* (f. 112ra–b; ed. Wright, *Specimens of Lyric Poetry* 107–09), an anti-feminist strophic poem stressing the unfortunate similarity between women and magpies.

The text of *Urbain le courtois* in Harley 2253 (ff. 112rb–113vb)[8] would appear at first sight to have little to do with the fabliaux in its immediate vicinity. Space precludes more than a passing mention of it here, but it is surely significant that its allusions to romance and epic place it fairly and squarely in the mainstream of vernacular literature rather than in the obscure category of "didactic treatise":

> Qe unqe ly noble Rodlaund
> Ne valsist le demy tant
> Come il fet a son quider,
> E si ne valt il mye Olyver,
> E plus quide estre plus beals
> Qe Absolon ly juvenceals

Esprit gaulois *for the English* (Busby)

> Ou Ypomedes estoit,
> Qe totes beautés avoit,
> E plus estre cortois e seyn
> Qe ne fust sire Gaweyn,
> Ou que Milanqe⁹ ne fu,
> E si est ledement descu [ff. 112rb–va].

[For noble Roland was never worth half as much as him, so the proud man thought, but he was never as worthy as Oliver, and he thought he was more handsome than young Absalom or Ypomedon, who was possessed of all beauty, and considered himself more courtly and upstanding than Sir Gawain or Milanqe, and thus badly deluded himself.]

Specifically, the reference to Gawain links *Urbain* to the text of the French version of *De conjuge non ducenda* (ff. 117ra–118rb), a poem in which a certain "Gawein" cautions his readers or listeners against the perils of marriage (Wright, *The Latin Poems* 292–94). The suitability of placing such anti-matrimonial advice in the mouth of the most notorious, unmarried, ladies' man of Arthurian romance (the English "whitewashing" of whose character was not yet complete) would not have escaped the attention of the well-informed readership of Harley 2253.

Preceding this poem is the fabliau of *Le Chevalier a la corbeille* (ff. 115va–117ra; Noomen, IX, 267–68), where it functions as prefatory illustration of the wisdom of Gawain's advice, just as *La Gageure* (ff. 118rb–vb; Noomen, X, 3–10) vindicates the *De conjuge* as its postface. Much of the humour in this sequence is generated, of course, by its apparently standard anti-feminism, but the real outrage lies in the fact that in *Le Chevalier à la corbeille*, it is the devious knight who devises the basket-trick, and in *La Gageure*, the ingenious squire, cheered on by his elder brother, who thwarts the female plot.

The fourth fabliau in Harley 2253 is the Anglo-Norman version of *Le Chevalier qui fist parler les cons* (ff. 122vb–124va; Noomen, III, 57–155), preceded by the *Ordre de bel ayse* (ff. 121ra–122va) and followed by a Middle English *Satire on the Retinues of the Great* (ff. 124va–125r). *L'Ordre de bel ayse* (Aspin, *Anglo-Norman Political Songs* 130–42) is a satire on various religious orders in England, dating from ca. 1300, a kind of precursor of Rabelais's Abbaye de Thélème. Among other prescriptions, the order's foundations must have no walls, and the inhabitants, monks and nuns, should be well-dressed and shod, eat and drink well, sleep late after hangovers, and may make love up to three times daily (assured of privacy and without fear of censure). This is in most respects a very different poem to the *Chevalier qui fist parler*, but the repeated use of the word "ordre" surely suggests that religious order is beginning to resemble the secular order of knighthood. Moreover, the vocabulary in general ("delitous e bel," "robes bien avenauntz," "solacer," "fere le giw d'amour," "enclos privement," etc.) is often that of courtly literature, and consequently of the kind of text parodied in *Le Chevalier qui fist parler*.

As regards vulgarity, the sexual relations between the monks and nuns are exactly what we see in numerous fabliaux, the use of euphemism also being characteristic of the genre: "De taunt est nostre ordre dyvers / Qe nos sueres deyvent envers / Gysyr e orer countre mount, / Par grant devocioun le fount" [In so far is our order divergent that our sisters must lie on their backs and pray facing upwards; they do it by great devoutness; f. 122ra (trans. Aspin)]. Euphemism is not a striking feature of *Le Chevalier qui fist parler*, whose brazen use of the words "cul" and "coun," not to mention the startling eloquence of the organs in question, stands in shrill and vocal contrast to the discreet activity of *L'ordre de bel ayse*. The word "trufle" at the beginning of *Le Chevalier qui fist* takes us all the way back to its use as generic designator at the end of *Le Jongleur d'Ely et le roi d'Angleterre*.

The opening of the satire that follows confirms the nature of the poems we have just been reading or listening to: "Of rybaudz y ryme and rede o mi rolle" [Of rogues I rhyme and read off my roll; f. 124va]. The use of the French word "rybaudz" makes the transition between Anglo-Norman and Middle English seamless and reminds us of the jongleur of Ely at the beginning of the sequence under consideration here. Like *L'Ordre de bel ayse*, the satire on retinues (Robbins 27–29) is a poem with a specifically English historical context and import but which is linked thematically and lexically to an insular version of a continental fabliau. In the voice of a minstrel, bilingual perhaps, the satire focuses on young grooms to whom the unscrupulous squire Huet in the fabliau bears more than a passing resemblance.

A fuller commentary on this section of Harley 2253 would not ignore, as I have had to do here, such poems as *Trailbaston* (ff. 113vb–114v, noting its bucolic courtly setting), the Middle English *Man in the Moon* (ff.

114v–115r, with its theme of deception), the Middle English dream-book (ff. 119ra–121-ra, are the fabliaux comic visions?), *The Proverbs of Hendyng* (ff. 125ra–127ra, which provide the proverbial endings generally missing in the Harley fabliaux), the prophecy of Thomas of Erceldoune (ff. 127rb-va, which completes the minstrel frame of the section) and more besides. Such a commentary would also treat in more detail the verbal and thematic links between all those poems I have discussed and show how they help structure Harley 2253 both locally and globally.

The humour of the Anglo-Norman fabliaux is not essentially different from much of that found in the larger corpus of continental texts, but a great deal of it is generated by the specific context in which the poems are found. It depends not only on the spontaneous humour and vulgar laughter that arise during each reading of each story, but also on the listener's or reader's ability to recall elements of preceding items and make links back and forth across pairs and groups of texts, sometimes at a distance of several folios or hundreds of lines. The scribe or compiler decides on the codicological comic potential of arranging the items included in the codex before the informed reader or listener, familiar with the corpus of texts within and without the manuscript, generates the intertextual humour of the fabliaux.

Notes

1. Both manuscripts are accessible in facsimile form, Digby 86 by Tschann and Parkes, and Harley 2253 by Ker. The bibliography on both is considerable and cannot be cited in its entirety. Most relevant material and bibliographical details are to be found in Fein. Important work on Harley 2253 has been done by Carter Revard, to whom I am much indebted, and whose e-mails are proof that the Internet has not killed the art of letter-writing.

2. This is an excellent complement to Noomen and Van den Boogaard, but all references here will be to the latter, in conformity with the usage of this volume.

3. This line is extant only in Harley 2253, f. 111vb. It is not in the text from Cambridge, UL, Gg. I. I, edited by Fiero, Pfeffer, and Allain (120–31), and not given as a variant; the text in Florence, Bibl. Laurentiana, Plut. XLII 41, breaks off at vs 190 of the edition of Heyse (63–71).

4. This poem is unedited. The only transcription is in Stengel (40–49).

5. I use the words "jongleur" and "minstrel" interchangeably here to avoid repetitiousness, aware of the difficulties of defining the terms.

6. "Edited" in vol. 2 of Montaiglon and Raynaud's *Recueil général et complet des fabliaux* (242–56). The twenty-line prologue on p. 242 is entirely spurious, having

been composed in 1818 by Francis Palgrave, and taken over as gospel by every subsequent editor, including Francisque Michel, the Abbé de la Rue (both 1834), and Montaiglon-Raynaud, none of whom obviously consulted the manuscript. See Nolan 292–93, n. 9. More useful is the edition in Ulrich. The Thomas of Erceldoune piece has been edited most recently by Robbins (29).

    7. In her excellent article, Nolan also points out that "bourde" is frequently used to designate a fabliau (303).

    8. This version of *Urbain* remains unedited.

    9. I am unable to identify "Milanqe," who is obviously meant to be a romance hero. The reading may be corrupt as it appears in the first line of a column, where scribes typically make mistakes. Oxford, Bodl., Selden Supra 74 here reads "Ke unke ne fist vilainie," which may have become "Onque vilainie ne fist" and eventually misread as something like the line in Harley. See Parsons 411.

Works Cited

Aspin, Isabel S.T. *Anglo-Norman Political Songs*. Oxford: Blackwell, 1953.

Busby, Keith. "Conspicuous by its Absence: The English *Fabliau*." *Dutch Quarterly Review*, 12 (1982), 30–41.

———. *Codex and Context: Reading Old French Verse Narrative in its Manuscript Context*. 2 vols. Amsterdam: Rodopi, 2002.

Fein, Susanna. *Studies in the Harley Manuscript: The Scribes, Contents, and Social Contexts of British Library, MS Harley 2253*. Kalamazoo, MI: Medieval Institute Publications, 2000.

Fiero, Gloria K., Wendy Pfeffer, and Mathé Allain, eds. and trans. *Three Medieval Views of Women: La Contenance des Femmes, Le Bien des Femmes, and Le Blasme de Femmes*. New Haven: Yale University Press, 1989.

Heyse, Paul. *Romanische inedita auf italiänischen Bibliotheken*. Berlin: Wilhelm Hertz, 1856.

Jubinal, Achille. *Nouveau Recueil de contes, dits, fabliaux, et autres pieces inédites des XIIIe, XIVe et XVe siècles*. 2 vols. Paris: Challamel, 1842; vol. 2.

Ker, N.R. *Facsimile of British Museum, MS. Harley 2253*. London: Oxford University Press, 1965.

Miller, B.D.H. "The Early History of Bodleian MS. Digby 86." *Annuale Medievale*, 4 (1963), 23–56.

Montaiglon, Anatole, and Gaston Raynaud. *Recueil général et complet des fabliaux*. 6 vols. Paris: Librairie des Bibliophiles, 1877; vol. 2.

Murray, J., ed. *Le Château d'amour de Robert Grosseteste, Evèque de Lincoln*. Paris: Champion, 1918.

Nolan, Barbara. "Anthologizing Ribaldry: Five Anglo-Norman Fabliaux." In Fein, *Studies in the Harley Manuscript* 289–327.

Nykrog, Per. *Les Fabliaux: Etude d'histoire littéraire et de stylistique médiévale*. 1957; Geneva: Droz, 1973.

Parsons, H. Rosamond. "Anglo-Norman Books of Courtesy and Nurture." *PMLA*, 44 (1929), 383–455.

Revard, Carter. "Scribe and Provenance." In Fein, *Studies in the Harley Manuscript* 21–109.

Robbins, Rossell Hope. *Historical Poems of the XIVth and XVth Centuries.* New York: Columbia University Press, 1959.

Short, Ian, and Roy J. Pearcy. *Eighteen Anglo-Norman Fabliaux.* London: Anglo-Norman Text Society, 2000.

Stengel, Edmund. *Codicem manu scriptum Digby 86 in Bibliotheca Bodleiana asservatun descripsit, excerpsit, illustravit Dr. E. Stengel.* Halle: Niemeyer, 1871.

Tschann, Judith, and M.B. Parkes. *Facsimile of Oxford, Bodleian Library, MS Digby 86.* Oxford: Oxford University Press, 1996.

Ulrich, Jakob. "La Riote du monde." *Zeitschrift für romanische Philologie,* 8 (1884), 275–89.

Wilkins, Nigel. *Catalogue des manuscrits français de la Bibliothèque Parker (Parker Library), Corpus Christi College, Cambridge.* Cambridge: CCCC, ca. 1993.

Wright, Thomas. *The Latin Poems Commonly Attributed to Walter Mapes.* London: Nichols, 1841.

———. *Specimens of Lyric Poetry, Composed in England in the Reign of Edward the First.* London: Richards, 1842.

———, and James Orchard Halliwell. *Reliquiæ antiquæ. Scraps from Ancient Manuscripts Illustrating Chiefly Early English Literature and the English Language.* 2 vols. London: Pickering, 1841–43.

Marie de France in the Manuscripts: Lai, Fable, Fabliau

Rupert T. Pickens

One or more of Marie de France's lais are transmitted in five medieval manuscripts: London, BL, Harley 978, and Cotton, Vespasian B. XIV; Paris, BnF, fr. 2168, fr. 24432, and nouv. acq. fr. 1104.[1] Three of these also preserve in sets some or all of Marie's 102 fables: Harley 978, Vespasian B. XIV, and fr. 2168, which also transmits fabliaux.[2] The remaining two, which do not contain fables, intersperse lais and fabliaux or fabliau-like texts: fr. 24432, and especially nouv. acq. fr. 1104.[3] Meanwhile, six other manuscripts transmit some or all of Marie's fables in sets in context with one or more fabliaux, but not lais: BnF, fr. 1446, fr. 1593, fr. 2173, fr. 12603, fr. 19152, and fr. 25545. Not all of these manuscripts are of equal interest; however, as they illustrate, fabliaux, fables, and lais do not exist independently in isolation from other genres, but coexist in anthologies in a kind of symbiotic relationship (see Revard), often in context with still other forms. In this article I propose to explore some of the consequences of such generic "contamination" (Vitz 29–63) which is a matter of both the production and the reception of Marie's *Lais* and *Fables*.

One reason for a mutual attraction among lais, fables, and fabliaux is their common brevity. Fables, fabliaux, and "Breton lais," which may include those attributed to Marie de France as well as "anonymous" lais (Tobin; Micha), most of which are found in fr. 1104, and lais identified with other writers (Jean Renart's *Lai de l'ombre*), are relatively short narratives, by comparison with more substantial genres such as romances and chansons de geste, which in fact they sometimes imitate or parody. The longest of Marie's lais, *Eliduc*, counts fewer than 1200 lines, while the average length of all of her lais comes to much less than half that; meanwhile, the "anonymous lais" range from around 300 lines (*Doon*) to 700 or so (*Graelent, Desiré*). Marie's fables tend to be much shorter, from an exceptionally brief eight lines (no. 63) to 116 (no. 72). Fabliaux, which seldom have as few as eighteen lines (*Le Prestre et le mouton* [Noomen, VIII, 151–56]), rarely exceed 1000 lines (*Le Prestre comporté* [Noomen, IX, 1–66]). The average is around 300 lines.

Another bond between the fable and the fabliau in particular, in addition to the terms' common etymological roots in *fabula* [narrative discourse, falsehood], is a common didactic purpose. Explicit and implicit morals are a defining characteristic of the fable. By contrast, although some fabliaux, like fables, offer positive moral examples (*La Housse partie* [Noomen, III, 175–209]), many more of them, in their vulgarity, obscenity, and cynicism, function negatively in context with other, more conventional moralizing texts. Yet another affinity between the fabliau and the lai especially is that the fabliau often draws inspiration from the same world of wonder and chivalry that informs the Breton lai. Like Marie's Lanval and Graelent in their eponymous lais, the knight "who could make cunts (and asses) talk" (*Le Chevalier qui fist parler les cons* [Noomen, III, 45–173]) receives his gifts from fairies bathing in fountains whom he encounters by chance as he travels through a forest. Similarly, just as the lady in Marie's *Yonec* no sooner wishes for a mysterious lover (like Lanval's) than his shadow falls over her, the young woman in *La Demoisele qui sonjoit* (Noomen, IV, 45–55) dreams that a handsome knight is making love to her and awakens to find that he has wandered into her bed.

Finally, a not insignificant factor in the relationship among fabliau, fable, and lai is the porous nature of the generic boundaries that separate them. MS. fr. 1104, for example, includes among its "lais de Bretagne" texts that are generally considered to be fabliaux or fabliau-like: *Le Lecheor, Le Cort Mantel* (*Mantel mautaillé*), *Aristote*, and *Oiselet*. A Breton source is attributed to *Le Lecheor*, and *Cort Mantel* is Arthurian, but *Aristote* and *Oiselet* are not "Breton" in any way. Busby rightly concludes from these facts that by the end of the thirteenth century the term "lai breton" may have broadened to include many kinds of brief narrative (1: 470–71); he also observes (1: 467–68) that the fabliau-like *Nabaret* (Tobin 359–64) is self-identified as a Breton lai (vs. 1). The point to be emphasized here is the fact that fabliaux, whether "Breton" or not, are found among fables as well as texts designated as lais.

It is also well-known that the status of *fabliau* as a generic term is unstable, for many texts accepted as fabliaux in fact identify themselves as fables: notably the version of *La Vieille qui oint la palme au chevalier* in MS. B (Noomen, VI, 294–96), ("D'une uielle uos uoil conter / Une fable por deliter" [I want to tell you an amusing fable about an old woman; vss. 1–2]); *La Gageure* (Noomen, X, 1–10) is also a "fable" (vss. 1–4). Others, like *Le Prestre et Alison* (Noomen, VIII, 183–206), use the terms interchangeably: it is a "fable" (vs. 437) as well as a "fablel" (vs. 452), as is *La Demoiselle qui ne pooit oïr parler de foutre II* (Noomen, IV, 84–89) ("fable novele" [vs. 1], "fabliaus" [vs. 210]). Meanwhile, *La Vieille Truande* (Noomen, IV, 313–44) proposes an integral relationship between "fable" and "fabliau" as that between matter and finished product (or, to recall Marie de France's poetics, between the Ancients' lais and her own): "Fabliaux are made from fables, as new music is made from notes, songs from [other] matter, and stockings and leggings from cloth. And so I want to tell you a little fabliau drawn from a fable I heard" (vss. 1–7). Similarly, in *Trubert* (Noomen, X, 143–262), Douin de Lavesne also derives fabliaux from fables, but to different effect: "There must be fables in fabliaux…. It is called a fabliau because it is measured out in fables" (vss. 1–4; see Rossi 55). He thus suggests a correlation between concatenations of fables and his poem's episodic structure (Trubert as a Perceval-like Simpleton, as a Carpenter, as a Physician, as a Knight, as a Woman (1) taken into the duke's court and (2) wed to the king), in which the whole is greater than its parts as the hero's success spirals upward. Theoretically, the fabliau participates in the paradox of the Aesopic fable in the manner of Marie de France, a tissue of lies (talking animals, animals that converse with humans, fictitious plots and settings, etc.) from which the perceptive storyteller nevertheless draws truthful meaning. As for *Trubert*, it has no moral purpose, for it ends abruptly without commentary.[4]

The mutual attraction among the genres manifest in the manuscript tradition is in part a function of the works' reception throughout the thirteenth century and well into the fourteenth, but the manuscripts also bear witness to currents in evidence in the twelfth century as well. Many scholars agree with Bédier that the earliest fabliau preserved in writing is *Richeut*, which is dated ca. 1160.[5] *Richeut* was so popular that decades later a subtle allusion to it could be understood in a sermon preached in 1230 (Haddad 2). Other, more conventional fabliaux were also written in the twelfth century: internal evidence dates *La Plantez* 1192–93 (Noomen, VII, 205–06), and the fabliaux of Jean Bodel were certainly written between 1190 and 1202. Meanwhile, many fabliaux that meet Noomen's criteria for "early dating" (primarily respect for the two-declension system in the absence of internal evidence to the contrary) correspond to practices of the twelfth as well as the mid–thirteenth centuries (cf. Noomen, I, 3). In any event, Marie de France lived and wrote in a period when the fabliau was in full development and indeed was reaching maturity, and I am convinced that, as she worked with both her lais and especially her fables, she was engaged in the genre as a reader and as a writer.

Marie's *Fables* fall into two groups. The first forty in Harley 978 are translation-adaptations of fables in the medieval collection now called the *Romulus nilantinus*.[6] In stark contrast, the remaining sixty-two fables have no known source, a fact that has given rise to a great deal of speculation about influences. It is in the *Romulus*, however, that Marie came into contact, perhaps not for the first time, with a text — or with a textual tradition — that also surfaces in the fabliau: the matron of Ephesus motif. Marie's translation of *The Woman Who Dug up Her Dead Husband's Body and Hung it on a Cross* (Book 2, no. 13) (see Runte 1983 and 1992) appears in her collection as no. 25 (*La Femme qui fit pendre son mari*). This is Marie's only fable among the first forty with all human characters, which constitutes a nexus with the world of the fabliau. In her version, Marie modernizes her source and brings it in to the world of courtliness. In the *Romulus*, a soldier guards the body of a criminal executed on a cross, while nearby a lady weeps over her husband's grave. They strike up an acquaintance, and every day she gives him water. One day, after visiting her, he discovers that the body has been stolen. When he asks her what he can do to conceal his dereliction of duty, she suggests that they hang her husband's body on the cross. Later, the lady cleanses herself of her impious act.

In Marie's translation, the Roman cross becomes a medieval gallows, while the *miles* on guard duty, a simple soldier, turns into a knight, as *miles* is understood in the Middle Ages. She makes the crucified criminal the knight's kinsman, whom he cuts down for decent burial. When news spreads that the authorities will hang whoever stole the body, his mind turns to the lady who mourns her dead husband nearby. He speaks to her "cuintement" [with practiced courtesy; vs. 20] and abruptly asks her to become his lover. She too is experienced in courtly manners, for she joyfully accepts his offer. He explains his dilemma, and she offers her husband's body as a replacement for his "missing" kinsman: "Delivrer deit hum par le mort / le vif dunt l'em ad [tant] cunfort, " she observes ["The dead man must be used to free the living man, from which we'll have great comfort" vss. 35–36]. Meanwhile, Marie corrects the lady's cynical comment with her own moral: "One can understand in this fable how little the dead can trust in the living, so false and deceitful the world is" (vss. 37–40). In translating the fable, Marie has written her own fabliau, but one in which courtly language is not compromised and elicits not raucous laughter, but knowing smiles.[7] Significantly, in this light, Marie does not translate texts in Book 2 that might seem to provoke more vulgar fabliau registers: *The Man Who Gave Birth to a Mouse* (no. 5) or *The Whore and the Youth* (no. 14).

It is no accident that fr. 2173 and fr. 1593, which transmit *La Femme qui fit pendre son mari*, include among their fabliaux one that likewise embodies the Matron of Ephesus motif, *Cele qui se fist foutre sur la fosse de son mari* (Noomen, III, 375–403: see Lacy 1–17). The fabliau could have derived from Marie's immediate source or from another descending from Petronius's *Satyricon* (110.6–113.4) (Ernout). In any case, the fabliau version eliminates any reference to a crucified (or hanged) criminal and to a guard, but it does retain and exaggerate one element in Petronius that is only implicit in *Romulus* and in Marie's translation: the soldier's realization that the lady's excessive mourning for her husband stems from sexual frustration (111.8). In the fabliau, a knight and his squire pass by the cemetery and hear the lady bewailing her loss. The knight is struck by pity for her (vss. 47–51), but the squire, expressing the Petronian soldier's insight in the most cynical terms, bets his master that he will succeed in having her on the grave where she lies weeping (vss. 52–57). And so he does, as the astonished knight nearly faints from laughing. The misogynistic moral, at odds with Marie's, is that a man is a fool to have faith in inconstant women who will weep or smile at a trifle (vss. 108–24). In the context of the two exemplary manuscripts, the two fabliaux—Marie's within the corpus of her fables and the anonymous fabliau on the outside—offer a mutually-illuminating dialogue across generic borders.

If Marie is reticent in embracing the fabliau as she translates the *Romulus*, she is far more open to its possibilities in the second part of her *Fables*, where she is apparently relieved of the necessity to follow a Latin model.[8] Whereas *La Femme qui fit pendre son mari* is unique among her *Romulus* fables (2.5 percent), thereafter she produces eighteen texts with all human characters (30 percent), eight of which occur among the first nine. This first section of the second part is further divided by the insertion of an animal fable, no. 46 (*Les Oiseaux et leur roi*). I shall concentrate on the five fables preceding no. 46, for it is these that most resemble fabliaux. *Le Riche et les serfs* (no. 41) enacts a good joke: a landowner, riding through his fields, sees two of his serfs huddled together in whispered conversation like courtiers in a crowded hall, and, when he asks them why, since no one could possibly overhear them out in the open, they respond that they want to talk like experienced, clever men. Marie's moral comments on how ignorant people's affectations do them no good.

One of the untranslated *Romulus* texts finds resonance in the next two fables. In no. 42 (*Le Riche qu'on saigne*), a physician bleeds a man to diagnose his illness. The man's daughter takes the blood out of the room to care for it, but accidentally spills it, so she substitutes her own blood for her father's. When the doctor's diagnosis that her father is pregnant understandably upsets him, she confesses her deception. Marie's moral asserts that the deeds done by cheaters, criminals, and deceivers turn against them, and they are caught in their own devices. In no. 43 (*Le Paysan et l'escarbot*), a beetle crawls into the backside of a sleeping peasant who later suffers terrible pains. A physician tells him that he is pregnant, and people who hear about the monstrous occurrence fear that it portends evil events. When the beetle and not a child comes out "par la fenestre, / u il entra" [through the "window" where it had gone in; vss. 22–23], all realize that they have been deceived. Marie's moral points to the ignorant who are upset by "vanitez" (vs. 28) devoid of meaning.

Finally come a pair of fables devoted to a mainstay of the fabliau, the foolish husband and his deceitful wife. In no. 44, a peasant peeks through a hole in his door and sees another man in bed with his wife "taking his pleasure" (vs. 4). When he confronts his wife with what he saw, she answers that he was mad to believe what he could not have seen. "I believe what I saw with my own eyes," he insists (vs. 14). "Then you are crazy to believe everything you see" (vs. 15). She then fills a tub with water and asks him to look in and tell her what he sees. When he answers that he sees his own image, she points out that it cannot really be himself because, if he were in the tub, he would not be wearing clothes: "Don't put faith in your eyes, for they can lie" (vss. 27–28). He repents and affirms that a man must always believe his wife when his own eyes are so deceitful. This tale proves, Marie concludes, that intelligence and savoir-faire ("sen e quointise" [vs. 34]) are worth more than one's possessions or family connections. In the companion piece, no. 45, another peasant sees his wife go into a forest with her lover, so he chases after them and frightens the man away. As he berates his wife as they return home, she asks him why he is so harsh. When he tells her what he saw, she makes a show of fear and tells him that the same thing happened to a forebear of hers and to her own mother: someone saw them walking with a young man, and both were dead within a short time. His concern for his wife overrides his anger: "Mençunge fu quan que vi" ["Everything I saw was a lie" vs. 36], and he swears never again to reproach her if he sees her with man. This time Marie's moral targets deceitful women: "les vezïez et unverrable / unt un art plus ke li deable" [Those who are sly and untruthful are more clever than the devil; vss. 55–56].

Marie's moral in no. 44, where she cleverly adopts the wife's point of view, reverses that of Jean Bodel's *Le Vilain de Bailluel* (Noomen, V, 223–49): "...li fabliaus dist en la fin / C'on doit por fol tenir celui / Qui mieus croit sa fame que lui" [The fabliau tells us in the end that we should take for a fool a man who believes his wife better than himself; vss. 113–16], whereas the moral of no. 45 is misogynistic. More significantly, no. 44 reflects, and no. 45 offers a variation upon, a common fabliau paradigm: the husband unexpectedly returns home, he discovers his wife is in bed with another man, he confronts his wife (with the lover either gone or hiding in the same room), and the wife succeeds in convincing him that what he has seen is not real (see Schenck 34–70). The paradigm informs fabliaux such as *Les Tresces II* (Noomen, VI, 248–58), where the wife makes her husband believe that what he saw was a hallucination, and *Le Cheva-*

lier a la robe vermeille (Noomen, II, 241–308), where the wife, saying that she fears her husbands hallucinations are caused by devils, persuades him to go on a pilgrimage: "Qui li a fet de voir menchonge, / E tot li a torné a songe / Ce qu'il a veü a ses ieus" [She made him take a lie for the truth, and she made what he saw with his own eyes seem like a dream; vss. 304–06]. Meanwhile, *Le Clerc qui fu repus derriere l'escrin* (Noomen, X, 57–69) offers a variation when the husband, who discovers not one but two of his wife's lovers, avoids the confrontation when she tells him there is no need to argue about it: "Vrais wihos estoit ses maris" [Her husband was a true cuckold; vs. 141]; "Ele en sot si bien a chief traire," concludes the narrator, "Ke ja atant m'en vorrai taire!" [She knew so well how to put an end to things that I'll stop talking right now; vss. 147–48].

Turning to Marie's *Lais*, "Breton" themes such as encounters with fairies in the forest and otherworldly lovers who appear when summoned are subjected to parodic inversion in fabliaux, as we have seen, but for some time scholars have linked one lai in particular, *Equitan*, to the fabliau tradition. This text also serves as a nexus with the *Fables* thanks to its moral, "Tel purchase le mal d'autrui / Dunt tuz li mals revert sur lui" [If anyone seeks to bring harm to another, the harm will come back upon him; vss. 309–10], which recurs verbatim in fable no. 68 (*Le Lion et le renard*), vss. 55–56 (see Pickens 717–20), as well as paraphrastically in no. 42 (above). Hoepffner is undoubtedly the first to discuss *Equitan*'s connection with the fabliau, and the comparison is flattering neither to Marie's lai nor to the fabliau: *Equitan* is merely "un médiocre fait-divers sans grandeur qui fournirait plutôt matière à un fabliau ou à un conte drôlatique qu'à un de ces contes sentimentaux qui sont dans la manière de notre poétesse" (151; see also Mickel 34–36, etc.; and Ménard 28–30, 97–98, etc.). Scholars have not been meticulous in comparing *Equitan* with the fabliau or with particular fabliaux, but a few have drawn attention to the lai's outcome, which involves the plot to murder the lady's husband that leads to the lovers' doom (Burgess 13).

Like Marie's first fable about the husband and his unfaithful wife, and like other fabliaux reflected in her fable, the central episode in *Equitan*'s dénouement begins when the adulterous lovers enter the conjugal bed and the husband returns unexpectedly. A major difference is that another strand in the plot has previously been set into motion, for Marie has woven the conventional fabliau plot into a more complex narrative that begins with the inception of love, continues with the meeting of the lovers and their growing affection, and intensifies as the lady draws her lover into a scheme to murder her husband so that they may marry. For when the lovers get into bed, they are in the presence of what they intend to be the instrument of the seneschal's murder, a bath tub full of boiling water.

In the fabliau, the tub is well integrated into the plot of the returning husband (*Les Tresces II*, *Le Prestre comporté*, etc.), and it is eroticized when found in a bed chamber (*Le Cuvier* [Noomen, V, 135–44], *Le Maignien qui foti la dame* [Noomen, VI, 301–11], etc.). Marie is unambiguous when she stresses that Equitan and the seneschal's wife begin their fatal lovemaking in response to the lethal tub that has been brought into the bed chamber: "Sur le lit al seignur cuchierent / E deduistrent e enveisierent. / Ileoc unt ensemble geü / Pur la cuve, ki devant fu" [They lay down on the husband's bed and began playing and taking their pleasure. They lay together there because of the tub that stood before them; vss. 281–84]. And, as the fabliau plot requires, the husband comes home and discovers them. To cover his "shame" (*vilenie*, his uncourtliness; vs. 294), which refers to both his disloyal adultery and his genital display, Equitan jumps into the tub of scalding water and dies. The seneschal then thrusts his wife head first into the same tub.

Allusions to two more fabliaux, perhaps, or to others resembling these, also present themselves in this passage. In *Le Pescheor de Pont seur Saine* (Noomen, IV, 107–29), the fisherman finds the body of a drowned priest who will contribute his penis to settle an argument between the fisherman and his wife. The narrator insists on telling how the priest died: a jealous knight began spying on him until he found him in bed with his wife. The priest jumped to his feet and fell into the Seine, where he drowned without losing his erection (vss. 83–93). Exchange the river for the hot bath, and it could be the description of Equitan's death. Unfortunately, Noomen dates *Le Pescheor de Pont seur Saine* from the second half of the thirteenth century (IV, 110), but there could have been other texts. Finally, it is worthwhile turning to a horrendously graphic text, *Connebert* (Noomen, VII, 215–37), in order to understand legal implications in the seneschal's murder of his unfaithful wife. In this text a jealous smith catches his wife in bed with a priest, and he exacts an excruciating punishment when the priest, his scrotum nailed to the smith's anvil, must castrate himself in order to get free. Later he takes his tormentor to court, but the judgment goes against him: "God help them, the smith did well: if only all priests born of woman who turn the sacrament of marriage to shame and whoredom were equipped as he is!" (vss. 301–05). This text dates from the same period as *Le Pescheor de Pont seur Saine*, so its pertinence to Marie's lai must also remain speculative.

More certain is the relevance of yet another aspect of the lai-fabliau relationship in *Equitan*. In nouv. acq. fr. 1104, we recall, lais by Marie de France are interspersed with anonymous "Breton lais," on the one hand, and, on the other, "lais" that are generally accepted to be fabliaux or fabliau-like. The first fourteen texts are all "Breton lais," some by Marie, some anonymous. The fourteenth is *Le Freisne*, which is followed by *Le Lecheor* and *Equitan*, the last of Marie's lais in the manuscript. It is significant, I believe, that, of Marie's lais, the compiler of the manuscript "contaminated" only *Le Freisne* and *Equitan* with a fabliau. Despite its title, *Le Lecheor* is one of the most courtly of the fabliaux, and the quality of its register, before it is undermined, may be compared with that of *Le Chevalier a la robe vermeille* or *Le Chevalier qui recovra l'amor de sa dame* (Noomen, VII, 239–53; see Lacy 46–59):

> The Bretons tell us that the greatest nobles and most beautiful women of Brittany celebrated the feast of St. Pantaleon by holding court, jousting, and exchanging stories of love and adventure. All sorts of stories were told, retold, remembered, and written down. Every year they also composed one lai that bore the name of the one whose adventure it told, and it was recorded and spread abroad. One year eight ladies sat apart, listening to knights telling about all their adventures. They noticed that the knights never mentioned for whom or for what they exercised their talents and skills. Do they not achieve all their triumphs with but one thing in mind: cunt? Even the most beautiful woman in the world would not be sought after if she lost her cunt! So together they composed a new lai about cunt and set it to music. All others abandoned their lais in favor of the ladies,' which has been cherished down to this day. Many call it *The Rake's Lai*, but the narrator refuses to give its real name [Tobin 354–57].

Despite the poem's courtly register in other respects, the word *con*, repeated three times in quick succession (vss. 90, 93, 97), brands it as a fabliau. In context with *Le Freisne* and *Equitan*, the ladies' message may be construed to give insight into the motivations and the nature of the amorous conquests of both Equitan and Gurun in *Le Freisne*. Like Marie's *Chievrefueil*, which is also found in the corpus of "Breton lais," *Le Lecheor* relates the composition and dissemination of a lai that survives to the present day. In addition, its status as a fabliau casts light on generic implications in *Equitan*, while its high courtliness likewise guarantees that of *Equitan* especially as the coarseness of the word *con* finds no response in the textuality of Marie's lais. What is most prominent in *Le Lecheor*, however, is the status of the ladies in courtly society and especially their position as observers and judges of people and events and as poets working in concert to commemorate them. Moreover, the history of the lai as a genre portrayed in *Le Lecheor* reflects Marie's own poetics as she proclaims it in her commentaries that embrace each lai just as two of these embrace *Le Lecheor*. These last observations about Marie as poet bring up the question of her identity with the lais in nouv. acq. fr. 1104, where her name does not appear at all (missing in this manuscript are vss. 1–18 of *Guigemar*, where it is found in Harley 978 and, slightly garbled, in fr. 2168) and where the corpus of her lais is broken up, albeit into sporadic clusters (*Guigemar, Lanval ... Yonec ... Chievrefueil ... Les Deus Amanz ... Bisclavret, Milun, Freisne, Le Lecheor, Equitan*). The clusters suggest a modicum of authorial identity within the corpus, which, I would insist, is verified by the very fabliau that intrudes within it.

Analysis of the relevant manuscripts that transmit works by Marie de France reveals, more generally, the nature of the manuscripts that transmit the fabliaux themselves. There are no fabliau manuscripts per se. Rather, fabliaux exist in symbiosis with other kinds of texts that "contaminate" them as they "contaminate" works by Marie de France, who was herself engaged in the genre. Such studies as those by Busby and by Revard point the way to fresh approaches to the fabliau in light of their reception and their status in the manuscripts in which they are preserved.

Notes

1. For Marie's *Lais*, see Rychner. On Marie de France manuscripts, see Busby, 1: 463–84.

2. See Whalen; on fabliau manuscripts, see Busby, 1: 437–63. For Marie's *Fables*, see Brucker.

3. The status of the fabliaux, or fabliau-like texts, in fr. 1104 is disputed. Bédier admits *Lecheor, Cort Mantel*, and *Aristote* as fabliaux, but Nykrog reluctantly cuts the first two (15) and others (257) as twelfth-century precursors of the fabliau.

4. See Norris Lacy's article in the present volume.

5. Bédier (304–09, cf. 40–42): late 1150s; Dufournet (1): 1160; also Vernay and Haddad: last third of the century. Nykrog and Noomen reject *Richeut* as a fabliau. Muscatine restores *Richeut* and, despite Nykrog, *Trubert* (203–14).

6. *Romuli nilantii Fabulae*, in Hervieux (513–48), henceforth Romulus. On Marie's use of the collection, see Martin (18–24), and, following her, Brucker (3–11); also Pickens (716–17).

7. On certain of Marie's fables as fabliaux, see Nykrog (250–54); he accepts nos. 25, 41–42 (see below), 57, and 94 (311–24), as does Muscatine (203–14), but Noomen rejects them, as had Bédier.

8. As in the *Lais*, where she rejects the *matière de Rome* in favor of the *matière de Bretagne* (Prologue, vss. 28–32).

Works Cited

Bédier, Joseph. *Les Fabliaux: Etudes de littérature populaire et d'histoire littéraure du Moyen Age*. 1893; Paris: Champion, 1964.

Burgess, Glyn S. *The Lais of Marie de France: Text and Context*. Athens: University of Georgia Press, 1987.

Busby, Keith. *Codex and Context: Reading Old French Verse Narrative in Manuscript*. 2 vols. Amsterdam: Rodopi, 2002.

Dufournet, Jean. *Fabliaux du Moyen Age*. Paris: Flammarion, 1998.

Ernout, Alfred, ed. *Petronius Arbiter: Le Satiricon*. Paris: Belles Lettres, 1922.

Haddad, Gabriel. "*Richeut*: A Translation." *Comitatus*, 22 (1991), 1–29.

Hervieux, Léopold, ed. *Les Fabulistes latins depuis le siècle d'Auguste jusqu'à la fin du Moyen Age*. 5 vols. Paris: Firmin Didot; vol. 2, 1894.

Hoepffner, Ernest. *Les Lais de Marie de France*. 1935; Paris: Nizet, 1959.

Lacy, Norris J. *Reading Fabliaux*. 1993; Birmingham, AL: Summa, 1999.

Lazar, Moshé. *Amour courtois et fin'amors dans la littérature du XIIe siècle*. Paris: Klincksieck, 1964.

Marie de France. *Les Fables*, ed. Charles Brucker. Louvain: Peeters, 1998

Martin, Mary Lou, trans. *The Fables of Marie de France*. Birmingham, AL: Summa, 1984.

Ménard, Philippe. *Les Fabliaux: Contes à rire du Moyen Age*. Paris: Presses Universitaires de France, 1983.

Micha, Alexandre, ed. *Lais féeriques des XIIe et XIIIe siècles*. Paris: Flammarion, 1992.

Mickel, Emanuel J., Jr. *Marie de France*. New York: Twayne, 1974.

Muscatine, Charles, *The Old French Fabliaux*. New Haven: Yale University Press, 1986.

Nykrog, Per. *Les Fabliaux: Etude d'histoire littéraire et de stylistique médiévale*. 1957; Geneva: Droz, 1973.

Pickens, Rupert T. "Marie de France et la culture de la cour anglo-normande: Corrélations entre les *Lais* et les *Fables*." In Dominique Boutet et al., eds. *Plaist vos oïr bone cançon vallant? Mélanges de langue et de littérature médiévales offerts à François Suard*. 2 vols (Villeneuve d'Ascq: Université Charles-de-Gaulle — Lille 3, 1999). II, 713–22.

The Old French Fabliaux

Revard, Carter. "From French 'Fabliau manuscripts' and MS. Harley 2253 to the *Decameron* and the *Canterbury Tales*." *Medium Aevum*, 69 (2000), 261–78.
Rossi, Luciano, ed., with Richard Straub. *Fabliaux érotiques*. Paris: Livre de Poche, 1992.
Runte, Hans R. "'Alfred's Book,' Marie de France, and the Matron of Ephesus." *Romance Philology*, 36 (1983), 556–64.
———. "Marie de France dans ses Fables." In Chantal A. Maréchal, ed. *In Quest of Marie de France: A Twelfth-Century Poet*. Lewiston, NY: Edwin Mellen Press, 1992. 28–44.
Rychner, Jean, ed. *Les Lais de Marie de France*. Paris: Champion, 1966.
Schenck, Mary Jane Stearns. *The Fabliaux: Tales of Wit and Deception*. Amsterdam: John Benjamins, 1987.
Tobin, Prudence Mary O'Hara. *Les Lais anonymes des XIIe et XIIIe siècles*. Geneva: Droz, 1976.
Verney, Philippe, ed. *Richeut*. Bern: Franke, 1988.

About the Contributors

F.R.P. Akehurst is soon to retire from the University of Minnesota, where he has taught since 1968. His B.A. (1962) is from Oxford, his Ph.D. (1967) from Colorado, and his J.D. (1986) from Minnesota. He published with Judith M. Davis the *Handbook of the Troubadours* (1995), and translated from Old French the *Coutumes de Beauvaisis* of Philippe de Beaumanoir (1992) and the *Etablissements de Saint Louis* (1996). In collaboration with Peter T. Ricketts, he has completed the digitizing of all the texts of the Old Occitan troubadours (CD *COM1* 2001). A keen photographer, he also makes Adirondack chairs.

Kristin L. Burr is an associate professor of French at Saint Joseph's University in Philadelphia. Her research has focused largely on gender-related issues in thirteenth-century Old French literature and in verse romance in particular, with articles on *Le Roman de la Violette*, *Meraugis de Portlesguez*, and *Le Roman de Silence* among her publications. She is currently working on the representations of the arts in literature. Never one to let the opportunity for a good meal pass her by, she is also interested in the role that food plays in medieval texts.

Keith Busby is the Douglas Kelly Professor of Medieval French at the University of Wisconsin–Madison. He has held offices in the International Courtly Literature Society and the International Arthurian Society, whose *Bibliographical Bulletin* he edited from 1993 to 2002. He has been visiting professor at the Ecole Nationale des Chartes and museum scholar at the J. Paul Getty Museum. Among his publications are *Gauvain in Old French Literature*, a critical edition of Chrétien de Troyes's *Perceval*, *The Manuscripts of Chrétien de Troyes* (co-authored), and *Codex and Context*. His current major project deals with the relationship between text and

About the Contributors

image in manuscripts of French romance from England, Italy, and Burgundy.

Anne Cobby is librarian of the Faculty of Modern and Medieval Languages in the University of Cambridge, where she also teaches. She has published two books, *Ambivalent Conventions: Formula and Parody in Old French* and (with Glyn S. Burgess) *The Pilgrimage of Charlemagne, Aucassin and Nicolette*. Otherwise, most of her work is on the fabliaux, on which she has published several articles. She is currently working on a critical bibliography of the Old French fabliaux for the Research Bibliographies and Checklists series, and on an edition of the fabliau of *Le Prestre et le chevalier*.

Joan Tasker Grimbert is professor of French and chair of the Department of Modern Languages & Literatures at Catholic University of America. She has published largely on medieval French romance and lyric, and on Arthurian cinema. Her books include *"Yvain" dans le miroir* (1988), *Tristan and Isolde: A Casebook* (1995), *Songs of the Women Trouvères* (2001), *Philologies Old and New: Essays in Honor of Peter Florian Dembowski* (2001), and *A Companion to Chrétien de Troyes* (2005). Although she has a finely-honed sense of humor, her contribution to the present volume represents her first official foray into the delightful world of the fabliaux.

Caroline A. Jewers is an associate professor of French at the University of Kansas in Lawrence. Past president of the Société Guilhem IX, her research interests cover the lyric and narrative poetry of twelfth- and thirteenth-century France and Occitania, and medievalism on film. She has published numerous articles on the troubadours and courtly romance (from the *trobairitz* and the poetry of Guilhem IX to *Guillaume de Dole* and *Richars li biaus*), and a book, *Chivalric Fiction and the History of the Novel* (2000). Her current project assesses the nature and importance of medieval emotion theory and its impact on literature.

Jean E. Jost is professor of English at Bradley University, where she teaches Chaucer, Arthurian literature, and other medieval subjects. She has published *Ten Middle English Arthurian Romances: A Reference Guide* and edited a collection titled *Chaucer's Humor: Critical Essays*. Currently she is editing the Southern Recension of the *Pricke of Conscience*. Her articles have considered Chaucer's Performative Criseyde, masculinities in the

About the Contributors

Friar's and Summoner's Tales, various Middle English romances, the poetics of sexual desire in the *Merchant's Tale*, *The Un-Chaucerian Tale of Beryn*, and lately the configuration of space in *Sir Gawain and the Green Knight*. Her last NEH seminar on the Old French fabliaux has provided a new interest which she is pursuing.

Elizabeth Kinne is currently a Ph.D. candidate in medieval French literature and women's studies at Pennsylvania State University. She is living in France while completing her dissertation on the relationship between gender and politics in fourteenth- and fifteenth-century conduct literature in France and England. Her past research has also focused on the Old French fabliaux.

Norris J. Lacy is the Edwin Erle Sparks Professor of French and Medieval Studies at Pennsylvania State University. He is honorary president of the International Arthurian Society and holds the rank of officier in the French Ordre des Palmes Académiques. As author or editor he has published a number of books, primarily on Arthurian subjects; they include *The Craft of Chrétien de Troyes*, *The New Arthurian Encyclopedia*, and most recently *A History of Arthurian Scholarship*. On the subject of fabliaux, apart from co-editing the present volume, he has authored a monograph (*Reading Fabliaux*) and a series of articles.

John F. Moran is a clinical assistant professor at New York University, where he is also the director of language programs for the Department of French. His recent publications, focusing mainly on questions of language and identity, include an article on Patrick Chamoiseau's *Solibo Magnifique* as well as liner notes concerning medieval Picard for the New Orleans Musica da Camera's *Les Motés d'Arras: The Songs of Arras*. He has also recently begun a parallel career in residential education and now serves as a faculty fellow in residence.

Rupert T. Pickens is professor of French at the University of Kentucky, where he has taught for the past thirty-eight years. He has published books and articles on topics ranging from Chrétien de Troyes, the Grail, and troubadour lyrics to the French poems of Thomas Merton, and is currently preparing a book on Marie de France. He is now taking a "phased retirement," which allows him to remain in the classroom while

About the Contributors

beginning to enjoy extra time off for research, personal pursuits, and extended stays in France.

Elizabeth W. Poe is professor of French at Tulane University. She has published two books: *From Poetry to Prose in Old Provençal* (1984) and *Compilatio: Lyric Texts and Prose Commentaries in Troubadour Manuscript H* (2000). She has written articles on the alba, the vidas and razos, Marie de France, the salut d'amour, and the fabliau. She is presently engaged in a book-length project on verse love-letters that appear in Old French and Old Occitan narrative texts.

Adrian P. Tudor is lecturer in French at the University of Hull and secretary to the Editorial Board of the Brepols series Medieval Texts and Cultures of Northern Europe. He has given guest lectures at the Collège de France and Trinity College, Dublin, and was visiting fellow and Kennedy scholar at Harvard University. He has published a monograph and numerous articles on the first *Vie des Pères*, prepared a translation of *Le Lay de l'Ombre*, edited *The Medieval Comic Presence*, *Framing the Text*, and *Transgression in French Literature*, and published articles on the fabliaux, Virgin Miracles, performance, and text and image.

Logan E. Whalen is associate professor of French at the University of Oklahoma. He has served as president of the International Marie de France Society and as secretary-treasurer of the International Arthurian Society, North American Branch. He authored the book *Marie de France and the Poetics of Memory* (2007), and is organizing and editing *A Companion to Marie de France*. He has worked extensively with the medieval manuscripts that preserve Marie de France's texts, and his current research focuses on the co-presence of fabliaux and fables in some of these codices.

Index

Abelard, Peter 57
Aloul 7–8, 10–11, 12, 13–14, 15, 16
Amis et Amiloun 162
Amors tençon et bataille 140
Anel qui faisoit les vis grans et roides 48
animals, animal imagery 44–45, 50–52, 69–79, 80n8, 80n10–11, 83, 84, 88–89, 127, 129, 136, 143–44
Aristote 185n3
Auberee 154
Aucassin et Nicolette 82
auctoritas, authority 59–60, 62, 65, 67
Audigier 82

bacon, pork 7–18, 51
Bakhtin, Bakhtinianism 120–25, 131, 132n3
Barat et Haimet 7–10, 11, 13, 16, 17n6
bargain *see* contracts
Beaumanoir, Philippe de 43, 45–47
Bédier, Joseph 2, 56
Benchley Robert 3
Bernhard, Sandra 33
Bestournee 162
Biket, Robert 162
Bisclavret 184
blackmail 82, 84, 91n5, 93, 98–99, 115
Blasme des femmes 164, 168
Bloch, R. Howard 71, 127–28, 132n4
Bodel, Jean 40, 177, 180
Boivin de Provins 19–24, 28n7, 28n8, 37, 38; performance of 26–27
Borgoise d'Orliens 1, 5, 47, 91
Bouchier d'Abeville 12, 17n7, 39, 84, 90
Bourse pleine de sens 19, 20–21, 22–23; dramatic character of 25–26
Braies au cordelier 47
Braies le priestres 36
Brunain, la vache au prestre 44
Brut 162

Camille, Michael 76

Canterbury Tales 160
Capellanus, Andreas 145n9
carnival 120–131, 132n3; *see also* Bakhtin
Carson, Johnny 34
castration 49, 71, 121, 182
Cele qui fu foutue et desfoutue 34, 35–36, 161
Cele qui se fist foutre sur la fosse de son mari 1, 5, 148, 178–79
C'est de la dame 71
Champagne, fairs in 22, 23, 27, 27n2
Chanson de Roland 42
Chapelain 45, 52–53
Charlot le Juif 36
Chastiemusart 163, 164
Chastoiement 162
Château d'amour 166
Chaucer, Geoffrey 160
Chevalier a la corbeille 169
Chevalier a la robe vermeille 43, 121, 125, 180–81, 183
Chevalier au barisel 94
Chevalier et sa dame et un clerk 47–48
Chevalier qui fist parler les cons 1, 5, 42, 154–56, 169, 170
Chevalier qui recovra l'amor de sa dame 183
Chievrefueil 184
Cho, Margaret 40
Chrétien de Troyes 135–36, 137, 140, 145n11–14
class (social) 1, 31, 86, 91n5, 121; *see also* courtliness, vilain
Clerc qui fu repus derriere l'escrin 181
clergy 7, 10, 12, 14, 48, 52, 95–100, 109, 111, 113, 116182, 183
Cligés 137–39, 145n11, 145n14
clothing 86, 100, 122, 126; inadequacy of 127–29
Coille noire 49
Colbert, Stephen 3
Complainte de Jerusalem 162
Con qui fu fet a la besche 45

Index

Condamnation de Banquet 42
Connebert 49–50, 182
contracts 47–49, 116–117
Cooke, Thomas 36–37, 71–72
corpse: reappearing 10, 111–14; stolen 177–78
Cort Mantel 185n3
Couille noire 154
courtliness 51, 56, 61, 93–94, 101, 109, 135–39, 170, 177
Couvoiteus et l'envieus 33
cross-dressing 76, 82, 83, 87–88, 122
Crote 74
cuckoldry 1, 7, 10, 12, 14, 48, 52, 82, 83, 85, 111, 126, 128, 179–83
Cuvier 182

Dame escolliee 6
Damoisele qui ne pooit oïr parler de foutre 71, 72, 79n2, 80n7, 157, 176
Damoiselle qui sonjoit 44
De conjuge non ducenda 169
De la crote 148
De la dame qui aveine demandoit pour Morel sa provende avoir 79n2, 80n8
De un chivaler e de sa dame e de un clerk 161–62
"De un vallet qui soutint dames et dammaiseles" 162
DeGeneres, Ellen 33, 38
Desour l'Ave Maria 95
Deus Amanz 184
didacticism 104
Diller, Phyllis 31, 40
Disciplina Clericalis 161
disguise 9, 86–87, 92n8
disputatio 56–57, 60, 65–66
Du con qui fu fait a la besche 156–57

Eliduc 175
enjambment 107
Equitan 167, 181–83, 184
Esquiriel 69–79
Estormi 4, 17n7
Estula 12
euphemism 69, 73, 88
excrement 14, 85
exhibitionism 88, 89

"Fablel del gelous" 162
fables, relation to lais and fabliaux 174, 176
fabliaux: anonymity 136; conclusions 16; dates 5; definition 1–2, 32–33, 120; intention 2–3; length 103, 175; names in 136; normative nature 131, 133n8; number 2, 147; physical settings 34; rhyme 107–119, 131; subjects of 1, 4–5; transgressive action in 120–28; *see also individual titles*
Fabre-Vassas, Claudine 12–13, 15, 17n11
falcon 143
Farai un vers, pos mi sonelh 80n8
Farce de Maistre Pathelin 42, 53, 91n3, 144n8
faux-semblant 125
Femme qui fit pendre son mari 177–78, 179
Fevre de Creil 7
fidelity, test of 8, 22
flatulence 82, 85
food, feasting 7–12, 75, 84, 85
Foteor 49
Freisne 183–84
Frere Denise 105

Gageure 169, 176
Garin 150
Gautier de Coinci 94, 97–98, 101
Gawain 169
gender roles, reversal of 1, 75, 121–23, 126
genitalia 1, 7, 10, 12, 39, 44, 45, 48–49, 51, 55, 71–75, 78, 100, 151–57, 162–63, 182
genre, problems of 32–33, 134, 147, 174
gesture 26–27, 37, 94, 101
Gravdal, Kathryn 86
greed 13–14
Grosseteste, Robert 166
Gui de Warewic 162
Guigemar 184
Guilhem IX 80n8
Guillaume au faucon 134–46
Guillaume de Blois 76–77

Héron 71, 161
homosociality 128
Housse partie 43
Huon de Saint-Quentin 162
Hussein, Saddam 53

Ivins, Molly 3
Izzard, Eddy 33

Jean de Condé 93–96, 104–05
Jehan et Blonde 47–48
jeu parti 137
Jews, relation to animal imagery 15, 17n11
jokes 4, 139, 147–58
Jongleur d'Ely et le roi d'Angleterre 166–67, 170
Jugement des cons 67n2
jurisprudence 42–53, 127

192

Index

Kohler, Michelle 65–66

Lacy, Norris J. 33, 70–71, 94, 133
lai 135, 144, 174–86
Lai de l'ombre 135, 141, 145n14, 174
Lai du cor 162
language: ambiguity of 166; deceptiveness of 129–30; power of 51–52, 55, 64–65, 70, 71–74, 77, 78; subversive 123
Lanval 42, 184
law 42–53
Lecheor 183–84, 185n3
Leno, Jay 38
Lion et le renard 181–82
logic 59, 66

Maignien qui foti la dame 182
Male Honte 45
Man in the Moon 171–71
Man Who Gave Birth to a Mouse 178
manuscripts: Berlin, Staatsbibl., Hamilton 257 22, 160; Bern, Burgerbibl. 354 158n4, 160; Cambridge, Corpus Christi College 50 162; Clermont-Ferrand, Archives Départementales du Puy-de-Dôme F2 161; London, BL Cotton, Vespasian B. XIV 174; London, BL Harley 978 174, 177, 184; London, BL Harley 2253 160–61, 166, 168, 169, 170–71, 171n1, 171n3; Oxford, Bodl. Digby 86 158n4, 160–61, 163–66, 171n1; Paris, BnF, fr. 837 22, 152, 160; Paris, BnF fr. 1446 174; Paris, BnF fr. 1593 22, 174, 178; Paris, BnF fr 2168 174, 184; Paris, BnF fr. 2173 174, 178; Paris, BnF fr. 12603 107, 158n4, 174; Paris, BnF fr. 19152 134–35, 174; Paris, BnF fr. 24432 22; Paris, BnF fr. 25545 174; Paris, BnF nouv. acq. fr. 1104 174, 184; Pavia, Bibliotecca de l'Università, Aldini 21, 22
Marie de Champagne 145n9
Marie de France 42, 161, 167, 168, 174–86
Mary of Burgundy 80n11
Matron of Ephesus 177
Ménard, Philippe 71
merchants 19–27
Merchant's Tale 131
Meunier d'Arleux 17n7, 50–51
Milanqe 172n9
Milon d'Amiens 109–10, 111, 115, 118
Milun 184
Miracles de Nostre Dame 94–95
Miracles de Nostre Dame par Personnages 95
misogyny 45–46, 71–72, 73, 76–78, 79n4, 87, 136, 139, 147, 156–57, 163–64, 167–68, 179–80
mistaken identity 9, 10; *see also* disguise
money 19–21, 83, 118
morals 53, 103, 125, 103, 178–80
Moussaoui, Zacharias 53
murder 59, 87, 111, 121, 182
Muscatine, Charles 71
mutilation 87, 89

nature vs. nurture 67
Nonete 93–105
Noomen, Willem 22–23
Nykrog, Per 56

Oiseaux et leur roi 179
Ordre de bel ayse 169, 170

parody 61, 101, 105
pathelinage 91n3
Paysan et l'escarbot 179
Pearcy, Roy J. 59
Perceval 144n7
performance 25–27, 30–40, 42, 53, 55, 91n3, 93–105
Pescheor de Pont seur Saine 43–44, 182, 183
Pet du vilain 67n3
Petronius 178
Petrus Alfonsus 161
Philippe de Remy 47–48
pigs, relation to greed 13–14, 16
Plantez 50, 177
Pliçon 95
Porcelet 17n7, 71, 79n2, 80n8
pregnancy 88, 92; erroneous diagnosis of 179
Prestre comporté 35, 44, 107–08, 111–15, 118, 182
Prestre et Alison 176
Prestre et le chevalier 48–49, 107–11, 115–18, 119n4, 119n6
Prestre et le mouton 175
Prestre et les deus ribaus 43
Prière Nostre Dame 162
priests *see* clergy
Proverbs of Hendyng 171
Pucelle qui vouloit voler 71
puns 4, 116, 134, 135, 143–44, 145n17, 166
purse as metonym of testicles or scrotum 20, 28n5, 92n7, 99

Quatre Filles de Dieu 162
Quatre souhais Saint Martin 151–53, 154, 162–64, 165–66

Index

Rabelais, François 169
register (style) 61–62, 78, 90, 121, 134
Renart, Jean 135, 141, 144n6, 145n14, 174
revenge 48, 84, 90
Riche et les serfs 179
Riche qu'on saigne 179
Richeut 177
Roberson, Jeffery 39
role reversal 121–23
Roman de la rose 71
Roman de Renart 42, 90, 164
Romulus nilantinus 177, 179
Rutebeuf 105

Sacristain 7–8, 11–12, 14, 15, 16, 154
Saineresse 121–23, 124
St. Martin 98
Satyricon 178
Schenck, Mary Jane Stearns 133
scholastic tradition 55–57
seduction 1, 4, 69–79, 79n5, 88, 165, 178
Segretain Moine see *Sacristain*
Seinfeld, Jerry 33, 38
sexual intercourse 12, 19–20, 83; connection with food 7, 14; *see also* seduction
Sohait des vez 38
Sot Chevalier 36
speech: primacy of 63, 64; *see also* language
stereotypical characters 124
storytelling 21–22

tavern scenes 113
Testament de l'asne 50, 51
theft 8–9, 11, 42
Thibaut d'Amiens 162
Thomas of Erceldoune 171
Togeby, Knud 56
Trailbaston 170

Treces 33, 180, 182
trials 49–51
Trois Dames qui trouverent l'anel 39
Trois Dames qui troverent un vit 51, 167
Trois Mechines 39
troubadour lyric 138–40
Trubert 82–92, 119, 176
"*trubertage*" 84, 87, 91
truth claims in 35, 59, 96, 100

Urbain le courtois 168, 169

Vallet aus douze fames 44–45
Vescie a prestre 43
Vie de vn vallet amerous 165
Vieille qui oint la palme au chevalier 176
Vieille Truande 176
vilain 67n1
Vilain Asnier 1, 5, 151
Vilain de Bailluel 180
Vilain qui conquist paradis par plait 51–52, 55–67
violence, physical 4, 6n6, 45–47, 52, 84, 85–90
Virgin Miracles 94, 97, 98, 99, 101, 103–04
voyeurism 179

Wace 162
White, E.B. 3
Whore and the Youth 178
Woman Who Dug Up Her Dead Husband's Body and Hung It on a Cross 177–78
women: sexual appetites of 17n7, 19, 70

Yonec 167, 184
Ysopet 161
Yvain 145n12–13

www.ingramcontent.com/pod-product-compliance
Ingram Content Group UK Ltd.
Pitfield, Milton Keynes, MK11 3LW, UK
UKHW042011140426
5217IPUK00015B/1102